MASCULINE MIGRATIONS:
READING THE POSTCOLONIAL MALE IN
'NEW CANADIAN' NARRATIVES

This book examines the representation of masculinities in the fictions and autobiographies of some of Canada's most exciting writers, including Austin Clarke, Dany Laferrière, Neil Bissoondath, Michael Ondaatje, Ven Begamudré, and Rohinton Mistry, to show how cross-cultural migration disrupts assumed codes for masculine behaviour and practice. It is the first book-length study of masculinities in Canadian literature and also the first to discuss these prominent postcolonial writers in relation to one another.

Coleman founds his study on the belief that literary endeavour is socially productive, reflecting but also participating in the production of social practices and identities, and therefore it is a work of cultural commentary as well as literary criticism. The book contends that we can produce alternative masculinities by reading masculinities that challenge our current assumptions and that are themselves composed of contradictory segments rather than monolithic wholes, and by reading alternatively to elaborate a variety of masculinities. By including fragments of his own autobiography in the text, Coleman also dispenses with the illusion of the all-knowing, unbiased author/critic/reader.

Masculine Migrations is cutting-edge scholarship and an eminently readable book, which will challenge, provoke discussion, and encourage cross-disciplinary dialogue.

(Theory/Culture)

DANIEL COLEMAN is an assistant professor in the Department of English at McMaster University.

THEORY/CULTURE

General editors:
Linda Hutcheon, Gary Leonard, Jill Matus,
Janet Paterson, and Paul Perron

DANIEL COLEMAN

Masculine Migrations: Reading the Postcolonial Male in 'New Canadian' Narratives

UNIVERSITY OF TORONTO PRESS
Toronto Buffalo London

© University of Toronto Press Incorporated 1998
Toronto Buffalo London
Printed in Canada

ISBN 0-8020-4264-3 (cloth)
ISBN 0-8020-8102-9 (paper)

∞

Printed on acid-free paper

PR
9188.2
.M44
C65
1998

Canadian Cataloguing in Publication Data

Coleman, Dan, 1961–
   Masculine migrations : reading the postcolonial male in 'new Canadian'
   narratives

   (Theory/culture)
   Includes index.
   ISBN 0-8020-4264-3 (bound) ISBN 0-8020-8102-9 (pbk.)

   1. Canadian fiction (English) – 20th century – History and criticism.
   2. Canadian fiction (English) – Minority authors – History and criticism.*
   3. Canadian fiction (English) – Men authors – History and criticism.*
   4. Masculinity (Psychology) in literature.   5. Sex role in literature.
   6. Immigrants' writings, Canadian.   I. Title.   II. Series.

   PS8191.I5C65 1998   C813'.5409'353   C97-932225-1
   PR9192.6.I5C65 1998

This book has been published with the help of a grant from the Humanities
and Social Sciences Federation of Canada, using funds provided by the
Social Sciences and Humanities Research Council of Canada.

University of Toronto Press acknowledges the financial assistance to its
publishing program of the Canada Council for the Arts and the Ontario
Arts Council.

Conditional

'If ...
[19 premises]
... you'll be a Man.'

– Rudyard Kipling in the age of Empire

Contents

Preface

To the extent that writing is the product of a writer's perceptions and experiences, it is always autobiographical. However, to the extent that a writer's perceptions and experiences are shaped by his or her social environment, that writing is also always the product, not simply of the individual, but of the way he or she is 'written' by the social milieu. This is as true of works of literary criticism as it is of novels, poems, or magazine articles. *Masculine Migrations* is no exception.

The energy to write this book rises out of my need to work through some of the major issues of my own social and intellectual milieu. These include my desires, first, to begin to chart for myself, as a straight man, ways to participate in contemporary movements towards egalitarian sexual relations; second, to bring into meaningful relation my present life as a Canadian literary scholar with my cross-cultural upbringing as the child of missionary parents who worked in East Africa; third, to try to understand some of the complex negotiations involved in the Canadian multicultural society that is my adult home; and, fourth, to try to bring concerns of social justice into my scholarly work.

A seminar class in feminist theory and criticism I attended while doing my Master's degree first alerted me to the possibility that literary studies could involve something more than purely intellectual and aesthetic analysis. That class charged me with a strange mixture of excitement and embarrassment. The excitement came from a profound experience of revelation. I was being introduced to a whole new avenue of perceptions, an entire range of concerns of which I had been previously ignorant. Unlike opening a door into a new world, it was like getting a new set of glasses or having cataracts removed. I was being given a new view of the world I had assumed I already knew. I had never before wondered why our canons contain no literary 'sister' to Shakespeare, why the plot of a Jane Austen novel always ends in the young woman's marriage, why I had never heard of the spy and novelist Aphra Behn until graduate school. I had never questioned the systematic ways women are disenfranchised in economic, political, and domestic spheres. My embarrassment came when I noticed that none of the women – there were about ten women and two men in the seminar class – seemed to be having a similar experience of awakening. They seemed to have known about these concerns all along. What was a startling paradigm shift for me was old news to them. They seemed to have encountered in life the issues that I was belatedly discovering in literary study. Such was my first experience of theory and criticism that made direct links between public justice and literary study.

I responded with a leap onto the bandwagon: feminist critique was a matter of social equality and, as a conscientious man, I signed myself up to right what social wrongs I could. I read feminist theory, taught classes informed by this reading, and wrote essays which called attention to the suppression of women's voices in English literature. I described how William Wordsworth borrowed whole phrases for his famous daffodil poem straight out of his sister Dorothy's journal. I won a prize for an essay on how Thomas Hardy's male narrator consistently keeps Sue Bridehead from being able to explain her own motives in *Jude the Obscure*. 'See?' I was saying through my work; 'I'm not a pillar of the patriarchy. I'm one of the enlightened.' But something was ringing hollow, and the realization slowly began to form within me that I was becoming a kind of 'voyeur of feminism' who took pleasure from an unselfinvolving fascination with feminism's dynamic energy. All of my attention was focused on how dominant gender codes affected the lives of women. Was there not something dishonest about sighting down the scope at women's issues and concerns but not letting the light of feminist analysis fall on my own gender constitution? If one feminist activity involves educating people to the ways in which current gender orders shape and constrain our social interactions, should not that education encourage men to become more aware of their own participation within these orders? Should not my studies of gender relations make me more aware of how these codes shape my life too?

These questions led me to the problem of how to integrate what I was learning from feminist thought with both literary studies and my own masculine gender. Feminist critics have pointed out that male-centred thinking has constructed an ingenious system for avoiding an awareness of men's privileged position in relation to women by valuing a kind of scientific rationalism which turns attention away from the subjectivity of the scholar and focuses solely on the object of knowledge. Thus, through the pose of disinterested objectivity, the (male) scholar disappears in the scene of inquiry, where only the objects of knowledge come under scrutiny. In the Humanities, this means that 'others' – women, children, people of other ethnic or racial groups, those considered 'abnormal' – become the objects of analysis, while the 'subject' who performs these analyses remains unexamined.

Having been alerted to the limitations of this tradition of masculine inquiry, I felt two principles would need to shape my methodology. First, I would deliberately put men under the microscope. As a literary critic, I would start analysing the kinds of men depicted in literary texts and try to formulate from these analyses the kinds of masculine ideology conveyed in literature. Where my introduction to feminist criticism had taught me to pay attention to representations of women in a given text, I would now pay similar attention to representations of men. But it occurred to me right away that, unless the masculinities under scrutiny related in some way to my own life and history, the exercise would remain too cold-blooded. My work would fall back too easily into the kind of objective rationalism I wished to avoid. It might be an interesting intellectual exercise to examine the men in Hemingway or Mailer or Lawrence, but these American and British masculinities said little to my own cultural and personal history. I needed to work with masculinities that related to my own construction as a male.

Two books, Michael Ondaatje's *Running in the Family* and Kristjana Gunnars's *The Prowler*, introduced me to the rich tradition in Canadian literature of immigrant writing. Both of these books express, in both form and content, the fragmentations of a cross-cultural life. I found myself resonating with the questions that haunt both of these undefinable texts (are they novels? autobiographies? poems? pastiches?): Is there a meaningful relationship between the 'past over there' and the 'present over here'? What has been lost in the transfer from one culture to another? What has been gained? How do the two (or more) worlds of a migrant's history fit together into one life? Most important for a study of gender, what happens to a person's assumptions of various cultural formulations when he or she moves from one culture to another? I recalled my own adjustments on arriving in Canada at age nineteen, my confusion over the subtle codes of male behaviour that were similar to but also different from the ones I had learned in boarding-school.

These migration narratives excited me. I had found an area of study that would allow me to reflect upon masculine gender codes in a way that I hoped would allow me to try to understand some of my own formation within and between these codes. My own history of disjuncture had begun to inform my scholarly pursuits. Indeed, the confusions I had encountered at nineteen gave me my central hypothesis for *Masculine Migrations*: since the experience of migration involves a process in which the immigrant brings one set of cultural codes and assumptions into a setting where another set predominates, the immigrant is likely to have to negotiate between the two. In other words, values and beliefs that may be unconsciously assumed at home are disrupted in migration, and the immigrant usually goes through a process of re-evaluation and adjustment. This means that often transparent codes such as those of gender – the same would be true of the codes about family, religion, class, ethnicity, and so on – are likely to be made visible in narratives by or about immigrants.

The migrant narrative therefore becomes an ideal site in which to explore gender in moments when it is unstable and in crisis. This instability is extremely valuable to a study of masculinity for several reasons: first, because it contradicts the illusion of masculine permanence and uniformity that founds male dominance; second, because it is born of the concussion of two or more cultural codes for masculinity – it rises out of conflict among a plurality of masculinities; and, third, because it reminds us that gender is in continual process as various social interests maintain, redefine, regulate, or resist its codes. Masculinities in migration emphasize the dynamic process in which varieties of men negotiate and practise a diverse range of male ideologies.

While I was delighted to have found such a fruitful and personally invigorating way to study masculinities, I soon realized that I was facing a new set of issues. In current debates within Canadian multiculturalism, concerns have been raised by members of various ethnic groups over the ethics of white, Anglo-Saxon writers appropriating other racial and ethnic groups' cultural materials. First Nations people, particularly, have objected to white writers, artists, and critics using Native legends, images, or other cultural materials in their own productions that are then consumed and circulated in mainstream cultural marketplaces that have little respect for or understanding of those aboriginal cultures. Members of other racial and ethnic groups have joined these Native critics in seeing a direct link between the conquests of colonialism and these latter-day cultural invasions and appropriations.

The debate is far from simple. A strict enforcement of a 'hands-off' policy could easily produce a kind of cultural apartheid, where each cultural group circulates its traditions and materials only within its own small community. Other writers and artists of ethnic-minority backgrounds have argued that only when various groups' cultural products are understood and appreciated by surrounding communities can the nation as a whole hope to achieve the unity-in-diversity ideals of a multicultural society. But, then again, there is no guarantee that an 'outsider' critic's commentary upon a minority artist's work will produce accurate understanding or appreciation. It is far too easy for a reader's misunderstanding to become a critic's misinformation.

For me, the debate raises a further question: since I am a white Canadian who spent the first half of his life in Ethiopia, what culture do I claim as my own? I was raised neither in Ethiopian nor in Canadian culture, but in a kind of United Nations compromise, among the missionaries' and diplomats' children who populated the boarding-schools I attended in Ethiopia and Kenya. My situation is not utterly unique. Canadian Métis, francophones on the prairies, immigrant families, city Indians from the reserve, and other Canadians who have moved from rural to urban locations have all faced similar experiences of cultural hybridity. For many people the categories of cultural affiliation are not watertight. Perhaps, then, for those of us whose history has placed us between cultural identities, rather than firmly in one or another, our contribution to the debate may constitute the attempt to articulate that 'betweenness,' to speak from and about cultural hybridity.

Such an articulation requires a fine-tuned sensitivity to distinctions. For example, while my own experience of moving from Ethiopia to Canada makes me feel a certain amount of identification with the immigrant figures in this study, I need to state clearly that this makes me no 'expert' on immigration. Despite being born overseas, I came to Canada with a Canadian passport, a pink skin, English as my first language, a private-school education, and a whole network of relatives and family friends who could help me adjust to Canadian life. My experience was very different from the stories of immigration from the Caribbean or South Asia that I focus on in *Masculine Migrations*.

So I must balance two potentially conflicting commitments in the following pages: to break the male tradition of disinterested objectivity, I must deploy a self-reflexive critical mode that brings 'me' into the critical purview, but in so doing I must be careful to keep my own interests from engulfing and obscuring the very real differences between the narratives of migration I read and my own migrant story. The attempt to honour both commitments has resulted in what I hope is a productive dialogue: I have alternated passages of critical analysis with fragments of autobiographical narrative in the pages that follow in the hope that the autobiographical passages will serve to distinguish 'me' – and my cultural, ethnic history – from the migrant figures I examine. By describing my own cultural location, I wish to clarify my relation to and difference from the cultural locations of the various masculinities studied here. In this way, I intend to dispense with the pose of unimpaired autonomy and authority inherited from the tradition of male scholarship and instead give my readers a way to trace the investments which inevitably shape and delimit my critical vision.

Acknowledgments

The research and writing of *Masculine Migrations* have challenged my thoughts and perceptions in ways which I could not have foreseen and which have given me much wonder and delight. I am fortunate to have lived and worked in a community of people who are passionate about literary and cultural life and who are ready and eager to share generously from their own research and reflections. For stimulating discussions and thoughtful critique during various phases of this work, I must thank Diana Brydon, Paul Hjartarson, Shirley Neuman, Nasrin Rahimieh, Daphne Read, and Stephen Slemon.

I also celebrate the inspiration and support of the members of several discussion groups at the University of Alberta: the Postcolonial Studies group including Romita Choudhury, Kwaku Larbi Korang, Catherine Nelson-McDermot, Linda Warley, and K. Jane Watt; the Masculinity and Literature group including Chris Bullock, Glenn Burger, Paul Hjartarson, Andrew Mactavish, and Don Randall; and the Canadian Literature group including Dale Blake, Kathryn Carter, Michele Gunderson, Tim Heath, Lisa Laframboise, Allan Richards, Linda Warley, and Doris Wolf. In addition, several correspondents have commented on various segments of this work: Michael Bucknor, John C. Ball, and Pamela Banting.

Fellowships from the Social Sciences and Humanities Research Council of Canada, the Alberta Heritage Scholarship Fund, and the Secretary of State (Multiculturalism), in addition to PhD scholarships from the Government of Alberta and the University of Alberta, made this project possible. I am thankful to the editors of *Studies in Canadian Literature* for permission to reprint sections of my article 'Masculinity's Severed Self: Gender and Orientalism in *Out of Egypt* and *Running in the Family*,' in chapter 4 of this study. I am thankful to Austin Clarke, David Homel,

Michael Ondaatje, and Ven Begamudré for generous permission to quote from their works. Emily Andrew provided helpful guidance and encouragement as editor for University of Toronto Press. Linda Hutcheon met my initial proposals for this book with a ready welcome.

I wish to thank my friends Cam Yates and Dave Gray for their company on the long road. Erica Grimm-Vance, too, has been good company over the years, and I am thankful for her permission to reproduce her painting *Surface and Sinew* on the cover of this book. Wendy Coleman, more than any other, has provided wisdom, criticism, and encouragement. Finally, I gratefully acknowledge Grandma Tulloch's armchair, whose steady support bore me up under weighty thoughts.

Sources and Permissions

MASCULINE MIGRATIONS

Introduction:
Reading Masculine Migrations

This book is about masculinities in migration: when men emigrate, they take a familiar, though not necessarily unified, set of masculine practices with them; when they immigrate, they encounter a second, less-familiar set of masculine practices. Migration thus involves a process of *cross-cultural refraction*. Just as the transition between elements makes the straight drinking-straw appear to bend in the glass of water, so, too, the transition from one culture to another produces distortions. Any movement between distinct social communities will involve such perspectival shifts; a move between rural and urban environments, for example, or between different linguistic or ethnic enclaves, occasions an encounter with a different set of social codes, including those of masculinity. The greater the combined geographical, cultural, and political difference between origin and destination, the greater the index of refraction between the migrant male's two sets of masculine practices. For this reason, I have focused on narratives of men's international, intercultural, interracial migration from geopolitical and cultural locations far removed from Canada's WASP cultural mainstream. *Masculine Migrations* hypothesizes that the migrant male's narrative of refraction offers a unique opportunity to examine masculinities in moments when their usually assumed ideologies and structures become exposed to conscious reconsideration in the encounter with a new cultural environment or medium. My primary purpose is to describe the tensions between forces of masculine innovation and constraint as they are revealed in contemporary Canadian men's narratives of migration, for it is my hope that such an analysis will contribute to the gradual, tentative process of masculine re-evaluation and reinvention that has begun in the last decade.

An exemplary moment of masculine cross-cultural refraction occurs in

Neil Bissoondath's novel *The Innocence of Age*. It is Christmas Eve in Toronto, and two lonely men are having a beer together. Pasco, a widowed owner of a greasy-spoon, is listening to Montgomery, a black Guyanese letter-carrier, complain about his Canadian-born daughter's rebellious ways. 'Where I come from,' Montgomery exclaims,

'it ain't hard to know what a man is. A man is this –' He patted the bulge of his wallet in his back pocket. 'A man is food and a house. And a man' – he grasped his crotch in an uncharacteristically indecent gesture – 'is chil'ren. Chil'ren' – his voice took on a hard edge – 'who know their place ... I believe in good ol' fashion discipline, Pasco. Beat the shit out o' them if you have to ... But the girl – Man, lay a hand on that one and she screamin' 'bout rights. What rights a harden sixteen-year-ol' girl have, eh, Pasco? You could tell me? You should hear her. Is the law, is the law!' (212)

Montgomery's complaint identifies migrant refraction as the cause of his masculine uncertainty. Somewhere between a certainty he posits 'back home' and his present distress, it has become hard for him to know what his manhood is.

Significantly, the contrast he sets up between Guyana and Canada is a false opposition. His own racial history as a descendent of African slaves reminds us that masculine subjectivity has had little opportunity to enjoy an illusion of unimpaired authority in Guyana, and the patriarchal images of masculinity he identifies – the male as provider of food and shelter, as controller of family finances, as inseminator of women, and as (violent) law-enforcer – are as familiar to Canadians as they are to Guyanese. This familiarity shows that the immigrant does not represent 'pure' difference, does not figure as racial and cultural Other to WASP Canadian society. The opposition between cultures of origin and destination is not absolute.

But if Montgomery's complaint does not come from pure opposition, where does it come from? His certitude has been undermined by the disruptions of cross-cultural refraction. His move from Guyana to Canada has brought him into a new cultural medium, a whole new constellation of civil codes, cultural regulations, social norms, and even legislated laws that challenge and displace his preconceptions. His status as recent non-white immigrant marginalizes him from positions of authority not only in the public streets, but also in his own apartment and with his own family. In their article 'Cross-Cultural Uses of Research on Fathering,' Rivka Eisikovits and Martin Wolins observe that, along with prolonged unemployment, migration generates the greatest upheavals in family relations. The father, they suggest, 'is often the member of the family who is hardest hit. This is so because he derives status in the family from his occupational and social role in the larger community' and migration usually means forfeiting these authorizing roles (239). This stress upon the father need not produce family collapse, however; it can also force him and the family to adapt to the new circumstances. In opposition to a widespread belief that the loss of status as an immigrant often causes the father to desert the family, Eisikovits and Wolins cite a pair of studies, one of Indian and Pakistani immigrants in Canada and the other of Italian immigrants in Australia, showing that, in fact, fathers often become more active parents (Siddique; Phillips). Cut off from the support of their extended families back home, these families have to become self-reliant, a process requiring a more egalitarian division of labour between the parents (241).

In Montgomery's case, the Canadian legal code reflects a different set of beliefs about appropriate fatherly behaviour, family discipline, and the rights of children than the laws he grew up with in Guyana. Here, the state can and will intervene in family and neighbourly disputes that he believes to be under his own jurisdiction as the 'man of the house.' There is a continuity between the patriarchal codes of masculinity in Canada and Guyana, just as the drinking-straw is in fact straight above and below the water-line. What changes is that Montgomery's entry into the new cultural medium has put him in a different relation to those patriarchal codes, and the change makes him become aware of those codes in a new way. He becomes aware of their unreliability – or at least of the ways in which cultural disruption can lever him out of a comfortable reliance upon them. Cross-cultural refraction thus involves a change, not just in social *conditions*, but also in the way one *perceives* one's relation to social conditions.

Sadly, Montgomery's inability to adapt to Canadian laws, and to his new position in relation to social and masculine authority, ultimately destroys him. Drunk from worry and anger at his daughter's flight from the family home, he starts a fight with a neighbour. The police are called in to settle the dispute, and a trigger-nervous white constable, frightened by his own stereotype of a black man's rage, fatally wounds Montgomery in the apartment-building hallway. Immediately, media uproar ensues: activists decry the killing as one more instance of police brutality against Toronto's African community; the police claim Montgomery rushed them with a knife and they had to shoot in self-defence. Pasco, watching the news on TV, is horrified: Montgomery, his friend who loved a wayward daughter, has become a shifting referent in a war of representations. Suddenly, it seems, everyone knows what this man was, and no two of them agree. The image of the immigrant male becomes the locus of intense political, racial, and cultural conflict.

Masculine Migrations

Montgomery's story demonstrates not only how an immigrant's movement between cultures places him in a troubled relationship to conflicting codes for masculine behaviour, but also how ideologies of masculinity themselves are contested in cultural conflicts such as those he encounters. His story shows that, while some understandings of masculinity do range widely across cultural boundaries, the male subject's performance of those codes is constrained by his local and specific cultural situation. Sidonie Smith and Julia Watson observe in their introduction to *De/Colonizing the Subject: The Politics of Gender in Women's Autobiography* that 'just as there are various colonialisms or systems of domination operative historically, there are various patriarchies operative historically, not one universal "patriarchy." There are various positions of men to patriarchy, not just an equivalence among them' (xv). In naming these two systems of global domination – colonialism and patriarchy – and in asserting the need for a diversified understanding of them, Smith and Watson identify a contemporary tension in both feminist and postcolonial theories between the recognition of the international, transhistorical structures of patriarchy and colonialism and the need for analysis of the ways in which these far-reaching structures are inhabited and contested in specific, local contexts. 'While attention to specific colonial regimes,' they write, 'helps us resist certain totalizing tendencies in our theories, thinking broadly of the constitutive nature of subjectivity and precisely of the differential deployments of gendered subjectivity helps us tease out complex and entangled strands of oppression and domination' (xvi). This tension is nicely schematized by the metaphor of refraction. If a sound wave passes from cold into warm air, its frequency changes, and therefore so does its pitch. The wave has an integrity that can be traced back to its source, but what we hear, the very nature of the sound, depends upon its contextual medium. In the same way, masculine structures such as patriarchy and phallocentrism maintain continuities across many different cultures, but this does not make them historically transcendent and immutable. Instead they are subject, like all other social identities, to the flex and pull, the crises and abrasions (to borrow David Rosen's term), of social history and cultural context. Masculine ideologies – the same is true of other ideologies as well – are refracted when they encounter the medium of a new cultural context. This observation does not deny the fact that, in cultures around the world, masculinities have proved themselves remarkably proficient at adapting diverse institutions of patriarchal privilege to new social conditions; for the model of cross-cultural refraction recognizes both continuity and disruption.

Often, masculine ideologies maintain male privilege through a strategy of diffusion by which specifically masculine modes and behaviours are generalized as universal social norms and assumptions, leaving their particular masculine inflections unexamined as they become the standards which arbitrate the protocols, regulations, and differentiations of all social identities. In his discussion of how the ideal of disinterested rationality operates as a strategy of diffusion, British philosopher Victor Seidler argues: 'This makes masculinity as power invisible, for the rule of men is simply taken as an expression of reason and "normality." This constitutes, at the same time, a source of women's subordination, and a loss of quality in the lived experience of men. So it is that men become strangely invisible to themselves' (4).

I have chosen to focus attention on men's narratives of migration because international migration, as Montgomery's story suggests, troubles the immigrant's relation to cultural norms, and in the disjuncture, in the re-evaluation and reassessment that the migrant male undergoes as a result of cross-cultural refraction, many of the masculine ideologies that so often remain assumed become objects of conscious attention. They are revealed as masculine rather than universal. But the migrant narrative does more than this. It also situates the ideologies of a given masculinity in what we might call, after Foucault, a specific discursive and historical genealogy. Because the migrant man moves physically from one geocultural location to another, his narrative emphasizes in spatial and temporal, as well as social and political, terms the uneven history of his masculine subjectivity. His story delineates the continuous, though distorted, trajectory of a specific practice of manhood. Montgomery's gesture towards a secure Guyanese past includes the historical irony that causes a man of African descent to think of a post-slavery, post-plantation society as 'home.' It places his present conflict with Canadian codes for manhood in relation to a long genealogy of colonial and postcolonial conflict over African manhood.

The works of three gender theorists, Judith Butler, Robert Connell, and

Teresa de Lauretis, have convinced me of the importance of cultural-genealogical analysis of masculinities, and it might be useful for me to outline briefly their contributions to current debates on gender and how they inform my own discussion of migrant masculinities. Two influential theories tend to predominate in contemporary discussions of masculinity: the first, an essentialist and often Jungian-influenced theory of the universal 'deep structures' of men's psyches and behaviours; and, the second, a social-constructionist theory of human subjectivity that attends to the ways in which social circumstances and structures determine personhood. My readings of migrant men's narratives such as Montgomery's have persuaded me to align my thinking with the latter theory. While I have benefited enormously from the growing social-constructionist literature on men and masculinities, and refer to many of its authors in the pages that follow, I am indebted, like most of its male practitioners, to feminist scholars and critics, who have produced the most far-reaching and sophisticated analyses of the social constructions of sexuality and gender.

In fact, the three theorists I have mentioned above have produced theories of gender that are not focused particularly on masculinities. In all three cases, what has proved useful to me is the way in which these theorists set their discussions of gender in the general context of the cultural formation of human self-identification to expand the ways in which gendered subjectivities are named and described. Though their theories emerge from very different institutional and personal investments – de Lauretis is an American lesbian-feminist critic of film and literature, Connell a male Australian sociologist, and Butler an American philosopher and Queer theorist – they all insist that gender is constructed by representational acts or practices which elaborate and regulate the behaviours of sexed people, and these acts or practices are not only constrained by, but also reproduce (and sometimes misproduce), the conventions of a given society's sex-gender system. De Lauretis, for example, defines the experience of gender as 'the meaning effects and self-representations produced in the subject by the sociocultural practices, discourses, and institutions devoted to the production of men and women' (*Technologies* 19). Connell uses the Marxist-oriented term 'practice' to describe the method by which the human subject internalizes or conforms to socially regulated structures of gendered behaviour: '"Gender" means practice organized in terms of, or in relation to, the reproductive division of people into male and female' (140). Butler employs the concept of 'performance': 'Gender is the repeated stylization of the body, a set of repeated acts within a highly rigid regulatory frame that congeal over time to produce the appearance of substance, of a natural sort of being' (*Gender* 33). Gender reproduces its codes through a circular pattern by which the individual's repetition of socially recognized gender practices and performances reproduces gender's regulatory laws. In this way, Butler says, gender manufactures the illusion of its own original, natural essence (*Gender* 138, 140).

What I find helpful in all three theorists' formulations is their insistence upon both the power of social forces to constrain individuals' conceptions of their own gender and the power of individuals' actions, within those social constraints, to affect the social institutions and discourses under which they live. 'Practice,' writes Connell,

is always responding to a *situation*. Practice is the transformation of that situation in a particular direction. To describe structure is to specify what it is in the situation that constrains the play of practice ... [P]ractice can be turned against what constrains it; so structure can be deliberately the object of practice. But practice cannot escape structure, cannot float free from its circumstances. (95)

This understanding of human subjectivity as dialogic, as *produced by* but simultaneously *producing* the surrounding social structures, is flexible enough to describe the tension between structural constraint and innovative practice that I detect in the refracted masculinities that appear in the migrant narratives I examine in this study. Butler insists that, because one is always already 'inside' the social structures that regulate one's actions, 'it is only *within* the practices of repetitive signifying that a subversion of identity becomes possible' (*Gender* 145). This reworking of the relationship between determining social structures and the human subject enables these theorists to take into account Louis Althusser's influential formulations about the ways in which dominant ideology interpellates individuals as willing subjects, but also to envision the possibilities of the subject's political agency. De Lauretis observes that a theory which asserts a mutual interaction between the subject and the social gender codes under which the subject lives opens the possibility of agency at the 'subjective and even individual level of micropolitical and everyday practices which Althusser himself would clearly disclaim. I, nevertheless,' de Lauretis declares, 'will claim that possibility' (*Technologies* 9).

All three theorists, then, are committed to a liberatory sexual politics by which they wish to envision alternatives to the oppressive sex-gender systems imposed by capitalism, heterosexism, and patriarchy. To describe these alternatives, they call attention to the unevenness in any given society's constellation of ideologies: they insist that dominant ideology is not as seamless and uniform as widespread use of such theories as Althusser's often assumes. Rather, it is composed of a heterogeneous mixture of values, assumptions, and investments. And the subjects of a given society themselves have various relationships to the dominant systems under which they live.

In an article entitled 'Eccentric Subjects,' de Lauretis argues that a growing awareness of 'a diversified field of power relations,' which she attributes to a kind of postcolonial consciousness introduced to American feminism by women of colour and lesbians, has brought feminist theory beyond mere critique of male domination and into its own:[1]

By this I mean it came into its own with the understanding of the interrelatedness of discourses and social practices, and of the multiplicity of positionalities concurrently available in the social field seen as a field of forces: not a single system of power dominating the powerless. ('Eccentric' 131)

The important result of this recognition of diversity, she continues, is a conception of subjectivity as

a locus of multiple and variable positions, which are made available in the social field by historical process ... [I]t is neither unified nor singly divided between positions of masculinity and femininity but multiply organized across positions on several axes of difference. (137)

A striking example of the multiple axes of differentiation that can intersect in a single masculine narrative occurs in the first-time novelist Shyam Selvadurai's *Funny Boy* (1994). In this collection of linked stories that together compose a gay *Bildungsroman*, Arjie Chelvaratnam negotiates his emerging manhood between the overlapping and contradictory codes of Tamil ethnic identity, postcolonial Sri Lankan politics, and class conflict in Colombo, as well as his own nascent sexuality. This complex negotiation comes to a crisis when Arjie's father, concerned about his son's effeminate tendencies, sends him to the exclusive Queen Victoria Academy for boys, which, he tells his son, 'will force you to become a man' (210).

Ironically, it is at the academy that Arjie meets his first lover, Shehan, and is given a way to channel his hitherto unfocused desires. But Shehan is Sinhalese, and the school is caught up in a political battle between the older, liberal principal, who insists the school remain multi-ethnic, and the younger, government-appointed vice-principal, who wishes to replace the British ethos of the school with an anti-colonial nationalism which privileges Sinhalese and excludes Tamils. The principal, true to his colonial education, dispenses canings and detentions regularly in an effort to produce future national leaders of discipline and virtue. He picks on Shehan repeatedly. When the principal entrusts Arjie with the honour of reciting a visiting government minister's favourite poems at the annual prize-giving ceremony, Arjie deliberately garbles his recita- tion and destroys the principal's last hope for attracting political patronage from the Sinhalese-dominated government. By destroying the principal's political future, Arjie frees Shehan from his daily punishments.

There are many ways to assess Arjie's subversive act. It can be read as the rebellion of a postcolonial boy against the brutal discipline of a tottering colonial school system. In so far as it constitutes a dramatic affirmation of his love for Shehan, it can also be read as a coming-out gay narrative. In trading off the pro-Tamil principal for his Sinhalese lover, Arjie rejects the ethnic fundamentalism that has fuelled a quarter-century of civil war in Sri Lanka. And finally, in deliberately messing up his performance, he rebuffs the class ambitions of his parents. To choose any of these interpretations to the exclusion of the others is to misrepresent the complexity of Arjie's action. His is not a single choice between gay and straight, Tamil and Sinhalese, upward and downward mobility, or colonial subject and postcolonial agent. It is an action that impinges on all these axes of difference at once.

My readings of masculinities as they are represented and performed in texts by immigrant male writers attempt to elaborate the several axes of difference across which masculine subjectivities such as Arjie's are organized. Although Arjie's gay identification sensationalizes the refraction of masculinities in Selvadurai's narrative, *Masculine Migrations* shows how equally profound refractions occur in straight masculinities as well. By examining the discourses – by which I mean the discursive systems, the ideologically invested social narratives – that constrain the migrant's masculine practices, I want to show how the categories of class, race, and ethnicity situated within the inherited histories of capitalism, slavery, colonialism, indentured labour, and post-independence politics expand and diversify our perceptions of the field of gender relations. By tracing the ways in which these 'eccentric' masculinities manifest what Connell calls the 'lumpy' history of gender (149), I want to outline a few specific examples of a 'political genealogy of gender ontologies,' which, Butler suggests, works to 'deconstruct the substantive appearance of gender into its constitutive acts and locate and account for those acts within the compulsory frames set by the various forces that police the social appearances of gender' (*Gender* 33). In tracing the constellation of social conditions and the genealogies of specific masculinities in this study, I wish to align my efforts with the kind of sexual politics identified at the opening of Antony Easthope's *What a Man's Gotta Do*: 'In trying to define masculinity this book has a political aim. If masculinity can be shown to have its own *particular* identity and structure then it can't any longer claim to be universal' (1). This study of various migrant masculinities contributes significantly to Easthope's aim by pluralizing his terms.

Postcolonial Male and 'New Canadian' Narratives

The subtitle of this book states that *Masculine Migrations* consists of readings of 'the postcolonial male' in 'new Canadian' narratives. But who or what do I mean by 'the postcolonial male'? And what are 'new Canadian' narratives? I use the term 'new Canadian' because it signals a lumpy, chequered genealogy. On the simplest level, all the narratives I examine are new; Austin Clarke is the oldest of the writers I consider, and his first publications appeared in the 1960s. All of the primary texts I read are from the 1980s and 1990s. So they are new, and they participate in the recent groundswell of publications by writers of diverse cultural and ethnic backgrounds whose emergence has coincided with the establishment of Canada's policy of official multiculturalism. But while they may be new, these texts serve as the latest challenge to the old conundrum about what constitutes Canadian literature – and, by implication, Canadian national identity. Several of the narratives I examine in this study are set entirely in the author's country of origin and hardly mention Canada at all. Yet they were written in Canada, often with financial support from federal or provincial government arts agencies.[2] And their authors are Canadian citizens whose works are printed by Canadian publishers and sold mainly to Canadian consumers. So these narratives are 'new Canadian' in so far as the very conditions of their production reflect the most recent tensions and contradictions in Canadian cultural and literary identifications.

Nevertheless, as Donna Bennett suggests in her article 'English Canada's Postcolonial Complexities,' the stories of post-1960s immigrants may 'be seen as having continuity in a cultural fabric begun by early English settlers, who had come to Canada because they lacked money; and the Scots, who had been thrown off their lands; and the Irish, forced to find another country or starve; and the Chinese, indentured by necessity to a life in another country' (189–90). Susanna Moodie and Catharine Parr Traill were once considered new Canadians, as was each successive wave of immigrants arriving in Canada over the past three centuries of European exploration and settlement. Indeed, 'newness' constitutes a recurring problem in Canadian consciousness: to the early explorers everything was new; they had come, after all, to the 'new' world. And, to some extent, they were right in a way they could not have anticipated, if current geological theories of plate tectonics and the glacial epoch are accurate. But, of course, the perception of newness that gripped them and their settler successors eclipsed the ancient continuities of the cultures and ecosystems they were displacing. Newness can be blinding, and from Fort Michilimackinac to Batoche to James Bay, we witness the continuing fallout from that blindness. To attend to the new in Canada, therefore, is to follow an old and troubling path.

In the context of immigration, the term 'new Canadian' functions as a euphemism for 'immigrant' or 'refugee,' often standing in for more blatant ethnic or racial designations. For veterans during and after the First World War, for example, new Canadians were often those Slavic or Ukrainian or Baltic people who occupied the jobs to which the returning soldiers felt entitled when they came home from defending the colonial motherland. Accented English, strange garb, a love of garlic, or reverence for the Pope were among the signs of newness which could mark such interlopers off as strangers, foreigners, or even enemy aliens. 'New Canadian' wore a veneer of politeness even as it carried the distancing power of these more irascible epithets. The phrase conveys to this day the same equivocality. 'I reject all these terms such as "immigrant," "New Canadian," a "hyphenated-Canadian,"' says Neil Bissoondath. 'They all imply that you don't belong yet, that you are not Canadian' ('Possibility' 18). M. Nourbese Philip, who finds much to disagree with in Bissoondath's writing, agrees on this point. 'Africans be long here now,' she writes, signalling the long history of slavery and enforced exile through her use of Tobagan Creole dialect. 'Sometimes it appears we be too long here, but there *is* nowhere else to go' (23). One of the dangers of a project such as mine is that, in designating a group of writers as 'immigrants' or 'new Canadians,' one can participate in the very ghettoizing gestures which the overall project wishes to avoid.

None the less, these writers do present a new perspective upon, a new approach to, questions of Canadian consciousness and identification. In other words, 'new Canadian' can refer to a group of Canadians whose experiences are shaped under new conditions that distinguish their perspectives from those of previous generations of Canadian immigrants. Consider, by way of contrast, the narrative Northrop Frye derived from pre-1960s literary accounts of European immigration to Canada in his famous 'Conclusion' to *The Literary History of Canada*:

The traveller from Europe edges into [the Atlantic seaboard] like a tiny Jonah entering an inconceivably large whale, slipping past the Straits of Belle Isle into the Gulf of St. Lawrence, where five Canadian provinces surround him, for the most part invisible. Then he goes up the St. Lawrence and the inhabited country comes into view, mainly a French-speaking country, with its own cultural traditions ...

It is an unforgettable and intimidating experience to enter Canada in this way. But the experience initiates one into that gigantic east-to-west thrust which ... historians regard as the axis of Canadian development ... This drive to the west has attracted to itself nearly everything that is heroic and romantic in the Canadian tradition. (336)

Frye penned this passage only thirty years ago, yet within that short interval the narrative to which he traces so much of Canadian mythology has changed dramatically. None of the authors of my study arrived in Canada by ship. None of them steamed from Halifax up the legendary river to the Canadian heartland. None of them boarded the Canadian Pacific Railway to participate in the mythical journey through Winnipeg to the opportunities of the future-oriented West. Instead, the scene of arrival that appears in their narratives takes place in a metropolitan airport, whose plastic waiting-lounge chairs are indistinguishable from those of any other airport in the Western world. In this terminus which serves as their beginning, disoriented travellers answer suspicious questions about the curious contents of their foreign-looking luggage; they stand in long lines while immigration officials check their documentation for any evidence of a criminal record; they follow pictograph signs out into the streets of Vancouver or Toronto or Montreal, and many of them never see any more of the legendary Canadian landscape than they saw through the portal on the jet's fuselage when they were landing.

In many ways, then, the writers I am considering here are members of a distinct wave of Canadian immigrants. We might call this particular subgroup 'postcolonial,' because they came to Canada during and after the widespread independence of many colonial countries around the middle of this century. In this sense they are participants in a general global migration from the ex-colonial hinterlands to the imperial metropolises of Europe and America. They follow a pattern Raymond Williams identified in *The Country and the City*:

unemployment in the colonies prompted a reverse migration, and following an ancient pattern the displaced from the 'country' areas came, following the wealth and the stories of wealth, to the 'metropolitan' centre, where they were at once pushed in, overcrowded, among the indigenous poor, as had happened throughout in the development of the cities. (283)

'Thus,' he explains, 'one of the last models of "city and country" is the system we now know as imperialism' (279). Williams uses 'imperialism,' the term available to him in 1973, to refer to the vast complex of social forces that increasing numbers of contemporary critics would identify as 'postcolonial.' What distinguishes the generation of critics who call themselves postcolonial from previous 'Commonwealth' scholars is that, rather than working within the parameters of national literatures, they are products of and participants in the migratory pattern identified by Williams. Edward Said, Gayatri Spivak, and Homi Bhabha, to name three of the most prominent postcolonial theorists, all migrated from ex-colonial locations to live and work in European or American metropolitan centres. The historical and social forces that shaped their theories are similar to those that shaped the narratives I am studying here. From their own experiences of intercultural movement, these theorists have produced the analyses of colonial discourse, of the operations of cultural and racial stereotypes, and of cultural hybridity and marginality that provide the general groundwork for *Masculine Migrations*.

The term 'postcolonial' is important to my study for another reason as well. For the 'post-' in postcolonial points towards as much trouble as the 'new' in new Canadian. It is another term that signifies a bumpy genealogy of continuity and disruption. 'We use the term "post-colonial,"' write Bill Ashcroft, Gareth Griffiths, and Helen Tiffin in the introduction to *The Post-Colonial Studies Reader*, 'to represent the continuing process of imperial suppressions and exchanges throughout this diverse range of societies, in their institutions and their discursive practices' (3). Thus, the 'post-' prefix signifies simultaneously the prefixes 'ex-' and 'neo-' in relation to colonialism. At the same time that it refers to the historical period following a given ex-colonial nation's achievement of independence from European governance, it also calls attention to the neo-colonial (or neo-imperial) relations between the new nation and its erstwhile governors, not just in economic and political terms, but also in cultural and aesthetic ones. Postcolonial studies, then, like the concept of cross-cultural refraction, recognize both difference and continuity.

The term signals other bumps as well. Ashcroft, Griffiths, and Tiffin are Australians, and we might well ask whether their settler-colony heritage makes their concept of postcoloniality different from those of Said, Spivak, and Bhabha. The contrast between Australian colonial history and the histories of colony-to-metropolis migration is only one instance of the diversity that can easily be homogenized under the rubric of the postcolonial (see Arun Mukherjee, 'Exclusions'). Of course, a Canadian's inheritances of colonial history will be markedly different from a Trinidadian's or an Algerian's. And a woman's postcolonial experience in any of these locations will be different from a man's, as will a low-caste man's from an upper-caste woman's. Within Canada, for example, those who are the descendants of English or French settlers have their own particular complex colonial inheritance, positioned as they are between the European imperialist powers who exploited their labour and resources and the Native peoples whose lands and resources they themselves exploited (see Alan Lawson; Slemon, 'Unsettling'). In regard to First Nations peoples, one can hardly trust the illusion of completion implied by the 'post-' (or 'ex-') in postcolonial (see King). Clearly, the postcolonial experiences of Canadian settler populations are markedly different from those of the colonized peoples of Africa and Asia who were dispossessed of their lands and self-governance. The migrant whose ancestors were transported from Africa or India to the Caribbean and who later travelled from the islands to Canada brings one set of postcolonial complexities into contact with another when he or she settles among the Canadian descendants of European white settlers. This migration brings about a confrontation between different colonial histories, constitutes a dialogue between postcolonial subjectivities.

This understanding of the postcolonial perspective as an approach to diversity and contestation in contemporary cross-cultural relations is clearly articulated in Bhabha's discussion of the term:

Postcolonial criticism bears witness to the unequal and uneven forces of cultural representation involved in the contest for political and social authority within the modern world order. Postcolonial perspectives emerge from the colonial testimony of Third World countries and the discourses of 'minorities' within the geopolitical divisions of east and west, north and south. They intervene in those ideological discourses of modernity that attempt to give a hegemonic 'normality' to the uneven development and the differential, often disadvantaged, histories of nations, races, communities, people. ('Postcolonial' 437)

I have used the term 'postcolonial' not just to call attention to the 'colonial testimony' borne in the male migrant narratives I examine in the chapters that follow. Nor do I use it merely to signal the 'minority' register of these stories. Primarily, I use the term to emphasize the way in which the uneven genealogies of postcolonial migration intervene in discourses of hegemonic 'normality' that erase or occlude a diverse and uneven range of Canadian masculinities. I wish to focus attention on how narratives of postcolonial migration refract hegemonic discourses of masculinity.

Vijay Mishra and Bob Hodge, in their discussion of the role that *The Empire Writes Back* has played in the emergence of the postcolonial field of inquiry, observe that beneath that book is the dialogism of Mikhail Bakhtin, which in turn depends upon the might of the novel form (280). While Mishra and Hodge intend their comment as a critique of the ways in which postcolonial criticism can occlude native, non-Western languages and literary genres, their fingering of Bakhtin and the novel identifies some foundational premises of my study. If the novel is, as Bakhtin claims in *The Dialogic Imagination*, fundamentally a site of dialogism, of polyphony in contest, then it stands to reason that the dialogue between competing ideologies of gender and culture of the nature I have described above will be readily discernible in narratives by migrant writers. And, to paraphrase Bakhtin again, if the novel emerged as the literary form in which the low-born, common folk contested and destabilized previous aristocratic forms, then, in its most recent evolution, the colonized and marginalized, strangers and sojourners, have deployed that 'novelization' to effect their own destabilizing contestations. But, as Bakhtin points out, narrative does more than dismantle and deconstruct. It also constructs. To use de Lauretis's phrase (from *Technologies*), it is a very powerful 'technology of gender'; that is, narrative representations of various gender practices participate in the process of gender's reproduction, maintenance, and reinvention. I propose in the following chapters to delineate some of the many forces – both liberatory and constraining – that compete within the processes of masculine reproduction, maintenance, and reinvention as they are played out in these postcolonial immigrant men's narratives.

Chapter 1 opens my study with an analysis of two short stories by Austin Clarke in which a black West Indian man improvises the kind of upper-middle-class masculinity that signifies male power and success on Toronto's Bay Street. By successfully enacting the role of corporate lawyer despite his lack of an actual position with a firm, this character's performance mimics the 'law' of white metropolitan capitalism to reap its benefits, but because the performance is inflected by the character's incorporation of Caribbean and African-American traditions of male performativity, it turns into a parody which exposes many of the contradictions inherent in that law.

In chapter 2, I argue that Dany Laferrière's controversial novel, *How to Make Love to a Negro*, addresses quite directly the discursive codes that determine black men's sexuality. I examine Laferrière's parody of the discourse of racialized sexuality which has been used repeatedly throughout colonial and postcolonial history to demonize men of African descent as supersexual savages, and therefore justify their political and economic oppression. The chapter evaluates the success of Laferrière's parodic subversion in light of the tenacity with which the discourse of racialized sexuality continues to constrain public representations of black men.

Chapter 3 explores a different kind of masculinity. Neil Bissoondath's novel *A Casual Brutality* represents a retiring or 'passive' male who distances himself from images of aggressive masculinity. In declining various modes of masculine dominance, he raises important questions about the possibilities of men's passive resistance to male hegemony. This character's passivity can be traced to his particular inheritance of 'historical trauma,' and I suggest that his disidentification with ideologies of unimpeded masculinity presents the image of a man learning to live with lack.

In chapters 4 and 5, I try to articulate more directly the kind of refractions cross-cultural and postcolonial narratives cause in established Euro-American understandings of sex-gender identification and of masculinity. By delineating in chapter 4 the ways in which the social and political discourse of Orientalism works as a 'family system' within Michael Ondaatje's *Running in the Family*, a system that severs him from his father and his place of birth, I mean to demonstrate that such public discourses cooperate with a psychic structure such as that described in the Oedipal narrative. In chapter 5, I turn my attention to the father–son relations in Rohinton Mistry's *Such a Long Journey* and Ven Begamudré's *Van de Graaff Days* to observe the ways in which the father's identity depends upon the love and obedience of the son. By placing the father–son relations of the nuclear family in their larger social and political contexts, these two novels demonstrate how such considerations as ethnic identity, post-independence political intrigue, the inevitable process of ageing, the betrayal of friends, marital breakdown, and the disruptions of emigration undermine the father's authority. An accurate genealogy of masculine ideologies, then, must take into account these multiple and often contradictory forces.

My hope is that in describing the disruptions encountered by masculinities in migration, in delineating the tensions between social constraints and innovative practices, *Masculine Migrations* contributes to a more kinetic understanding of masculinities. This kinetic understanding dismantles the phallocentric illusion of masculine self-sufficiency and fixity and enables us to envision masculinities in process, in struggle and contention. Such an understanding can contribute not only to a theorization, but also to a politics of masculine change.

Reading Male: An Erotics of Reading

In the preface to *Masculine Migrations*, I sketched a personal narrative indicating how I arrived at the topic and methodology for this book. At this point, I should supply some of the theoretical meditations that link my reading strategies to that sketchy personal narrative. Born and raised in Ethiopia as the son of white Canadian missionary parents, I have often been asked since moving to Canada in my late teens, 'Do you ever want to go back there to live?' The question has always raised in me a profound unease about my relation to my own boyhood, about growing up relatively wealthy in a country beleaguered by poverty, and about being the child of Protestant missionary parents who distrusted and were distrusted by the devotees of the ancient Ethiopian Orthodox faith. Mostly, the question makes me aware of an embarrassment which I cannot shake. A combination of circumstances worked together to sever me from a deep and intimate connection with Ethiopian life and culture. I was sent, like my brother and sisters, to a boarding-school for missionaries' children in Addis Ababa at age six. The curriculum was American, and we neither studied the Amharic language nor read Ethiopian history or culture. I read my first African novel when I was living in Canada in my twenties.

More significantly, though, the revolutionary government that emerged after Emperor Haile Selassie was deposed in 1974 was very suspicious of all foreigners, particularly those from NATO-pact countries. Now, suspicion of outsiders has a long history in Ethiopia and is one among many reasons why Haile Selassie's nineteenth-century predecessor, Menelik II, was able to resist European overtures during the colonial scramble for Africa. This new suspicion was so intense, however, that our friendship became dangerous to Ethiopians. A person who associated with us could be accused of undermining the revolution, or even of collaborating with the CIA. As a result, during my teenage years in the 1970s, I was effectively severed from the few close Ethiopian companions I did have. By the time I finished high school and left for Canada, my circle of acquaintances was confined to the other missionaries' and diplomats' children who attended the schools I did. The embarrassment, then, has to do with the sense that I am from a place about which I am very ignorant, that I lived in a place whose relation to my present life is not immediately obvious.

It was this sense of tension about a past geographically and culturally distant from my present life, along with a sense that my feelings of severance had as much to do with my own political and social history as with any psychoanalytic model of severance, that motivated me to produce the readings of masculine migration in this study. So the readings which follow arise out of my own investments, some conscious, and many, I am sure, unconscious. On the conscious level, I desire to read towards a clearer understanding of the imbricated social structures of capitalism, colonialism, sexism, homophobia, and racism that combine to form the prevalent ideologies of masculine self-sufficiency and privilege. By definition, the unconscious levels are less available to me, but I do believe my desire to deal with my own implication within the very structures I have identified above indicates generally the direction these unconscious impulses take. These desires are likely to produce in my critical procedure elements of confession and self-exoneration, self-accusation and denial. And they are likely to operate through projection and identification, misrecognition and understanding.

I do not apologize for these personal investments, for I believe they are unavoidable. There is no such thing as a neutral reading. 'Literature has no outside,' writes Shoshana Felman in her influential essay 'Turning the Screw of Interpretation': 'there is no safe spot assuredly outside ... from which one might demystify and judge it, locate it in the Other without oneself participating in it' (200). She goes on to assert, in language that anticipates Connell's and Butler's, that, when a reader engages with a text, he or she recites the text, rehearses it, enacts it. In this way the text produces, calls forth, the reader's performance. Felman makes an analogy between reading and dreaming, claiming that 'just as a dream is a transference of energy between the "day's residue" and the unconscious wish, so does the act of reading invest the conscious, daylight signifiers with an unconscious energy' (137). In other words, when we read, signification results when our unconscious attaches its knowledge and desire to the text. There, in the text, we 'see' our unconscious knowledge for the first time, misrecognize it as the text's meaning; whereas in reality, the text has caused us, been the occasion for us, to perform our own knowledge or desire.

Felman's engagement with psychoanalytic theory is deliberate, for she wants her discussion of the reading process to 'write back' to Freud's founding formulation of the unconscious. 'The discovery of the unconscious,' she claims, is 'Freud's discovery, within the discourse of the other [the analysand], of what was actively reading within himself: his discovery, in other words, or his reading, of what was reading – in what was being read' (118). Reading, then, calls forth the unconscious, constrains it, not to express an essential inner core, but to perform or recite its attachments or desires within the inscriptions of the text. And, as with dreaming, one can attend, or not, to the momentary and partial revelations these performances offer. One can trace the 'erotics' of one's own reading.

For me, the process of reading narratives by recent immigrants to Canada produced the trip I had never wanted to make: a journey back to Ethiopia. The feelings of ambivalence I described above had left me unwilling even to visit. Having moved to Canada at the age of nineteen, I wanted to forget the place my parents referred to as the 'field' and get on with life in the country they had always called 'home.' Not until years later, when I began this project on masculine narratives of migration, did I feel the first glimmerings of a desire to revisit the place where I was born. The pervasive sense in so many migrant stories of a disjunction between a past that was 'there' and a present that is 'here,' and the disconcerting awareness that, despite its increasing unreality, the distant past still informs the present, awoke in me a curiosity, a desire to reconnect with my past. So, in the summer of 1993, knowing that my parents were soon to retire and return to Canada, I went to visit them in south-central Ethiopia. And I learned what I had known before I went: at the same time that you cannot escape your past, you can also never return to it. It is always relevant and always out of reach.

During that trip I did some reading. I wanted to remedy my embarrassing ignorance of the history and culture of the nation where I had spent the first half of my life. As I was reading Richard Pankhurst's *A Social History of Ethiopia*, the following passage discussing a nineteenth-century Amharic phrase for Orthodox Christian devotion leapt from the page:

On entering a church people would likewise 'always bow and kiss the corners of the doorway,' as well as any religious pictures shown to them.

Such customs were so deeply ingrained that people would use the expression, 'I go to kiss the church of such a saint,' or 'I go to kiss St. Mikael, St. George, etc.' Religious persons might indeed kiss several churches in succession, and 'to convey the idea that a man was truly pious,' Gobat says, it might be said of him, approvingly, that he was a 'kisser of churches.' (187)

Adolescence. I'm learning exciting things from Vanessa, a girl who's a grade ahead of me at Good Shepherd School, a private academy on the outskirts of Addis Ababa. She's an American army kid and knows how to do things that I've never done before. Between classes, on recesses and lunch hours, we go out behind the buildings near the fence and 'make out.' Her tongue twines around mine; the tip of my tongue traces the smooth surfaces of her teeth. Her breath is warm and moist, her mouth sweet and musky. Her hands inside my shirt set my skin ablaze where she clutches my back. My heart hammers in my ears. We are addicted. At nights, after track meets and soccer games; during breaks in our rehearsals for the school operetta; mornings, before chapel; afternoons, before the buses arrive to take us separate ways; we meet behind the classroom buildings to make out.

I'm fascinated by the illicitness, the danger, the mutual vulnerability, the sense of fusion with a person so different from me. It seems strange that people show love or veneration for something by pressing it with their mouth. I've known kissing my whole life long. My parents have kissed me throughout my childhood with that closed-lipped, smacking kind of kiss that is at once loving and respectful of my – and their own – privacy. I am used to the pecks on both cheeks that are part of the ritual of greetings in rural Ethiopia between people regardless of their sex. But Vanessa's kind of kissing (she calls it 'French' kissing) is completely different. The whole thing of being close-close, face to face, and tasting her lips and accepting her tongue into my own mouth, cooks up a steam I've never experienced before. It feels 'deep' somehow – emotional, spiritual. It is mutual acceptance and openness: I share my body, my health, my hygiene, my very inner stuff with her, and allow her into my private places, where nobody goes except those I really trust.

I'm also sure that this pleasure must be wrong. We go out behind the

*buildings to do it. We don't want others to catch us. I, at least, do not think I
could survive my parents' knowing what Vanessa and I do out behind the
classrooms.*

So the phrase 'kisser of churches' catches my eye. And it does so for all
the wrong reasons. The nineteenth-century Ethiopian who kissed churches
did so in a cultural context that used that public kind of kiss widely and
commonly in the most ordinary greetings. Even during the 1993 trip,
when my parents introduced me to their friends at Hosa'ina, without
exception my shoulders were grasped and I was drawn forward to
exchange three or four loud, smacking kisses on each cheek, alternating
sides. When a devout Orthodox Ethiopian meets a priest, it is expected
that he or she will kneel and kiss the cross or the priest's ring, or even his
hand. 'Kissing the church' is part of a whole system of significations in
the culture of Coptic Christianity which was itself brought to Ethiopia
centuries ago by Syrian missionaries of the Orthodox church.

But when I read the phrase, my inappropriate cultural background,
refracted through the peculiarly North American, back-seat-of-the-Chevy
developmental phase of adolescence with all its sexual overdeterminations
and neuroses, puts that kiss into an intensified, even illicit context. It
makes the phrase register in a way that is troubling and spicy, makes it
jump off the page, even though I know it is a misreading. I know what is
meant – at least, I can imagine what it was intended to mean – but I also
know the distance between my culture and the nineteenth-century Ethiopian's even while I recognize a range of shared common understandings
and meanings. Within the official system of signs, there is the subtle and
powerful nuancing of meanings that is the product of my own experience, my readerly archive. So I read the phrase 'kisser of churches' and it
resonates with certain aspects of my own formation. My Calvinist upbringing, which taught me respect for the Church but also fear of the
bodily and the sexual, attaches a delightful complexity, a charged eroticism, to the phrase. There is something about making the *inappropriate*
connection that opens 'me' up, that brings forgotten or ignored elements
of my own historical and social formation into visibility.

I believe that, to some degree, this kind of inappropriate reading –
what we might call an 'erotics of reading' – is inevitable in cross-cultural
communication. I do not say this to exonerate misreadings of other
cultures, nor to excuse wholesale appropriations of the texts of other
cultures into one's own. Rather, I believe that attending to the cathexes
and intensities that emerge in cross-cultural reading can alert us to the

circumstances that structure our own readings. Just as the contrast between the certitudes of Guyana and the perplexities of Canada is a
product of Montgomery's experience of cross-cultural refraction, and just
as the ethos of Canadian gay and lesbian politics necessarily influences
our interpretation of Arjie's life in Colombo, so we must remain aware
that we are reading in a cultural medium different from those in which
these migrant narratives have their origin. We need to remember that our
readings participate in and reproduce the paradigm of cross-cultural
refraction.

An awareness of the cultural medium in which we produce our own
interpretations can help us to distinguish between authorial intention
and readerly desire. None of the straight-male narratives I examine in
this study declares an overt intention to disrupt traditional modes of
masculinity. None is a narrative of open rebellion against patriarchal
stereotypes or phallocentric institutions. Even gay narratives such as
Selvadurai's *Funny Boy* or H. Nigel Thomas's *Spirits in the Dark* (a novel I
discuss in the afterword to this book), which obviously do rebel against
compulsory heterosexuality, do not put forward settled commitments on
questions such as postcolonial resistance, Canadian multiculturalism, or
equitable gender relations. Generally, the political commitments in these
male narratives are ambivalent at best. For all that has been written in
Canada about the divided loyalties experienced by the immigrant, about
the fundamental ambivalence that structures migrant consciousness (see
Kroetsch; Loriggio; Blodgett; Godard, 'Discourse of the Other'; and
Hutcheon, 'Introduction'), no critic seems to have noticed that this ambivalence seldom characterizes writings by women of colour in Canada.
The narratives of Dionne Brand, M. Nourbese Philip, Norma de Haarte,
Claire Harris, Joy Kogawa, Makeda Silvera, Himani Bannerji, and Suniti
Namjoshi bear a kind of political certitude about them that none of the
male writers I examine here can muster. On the whole, the writings of the
male immigrant authors are much less politically clear: they are ambigu-
ous, noncommittal, shifty, sometimes even reactionary. My guess is that
the ambivalent position of the straight male Canadian writers of colour –
privileged on the axis of sexuality and gender, marginalized on that of
race – undermines the kind of certitude the women writers develop in the
face of disenfranchisement on all sides: gender, race, ethnicity, and class.
(Bharati Mukherjee's exception indicates that privilege on the axis of
class can undermine a woman's political certitude as readily as men's
privilege on the axis of gender.)

The masculine struggles and dislocations I discuss in this study, then, are not the focus of authorial intention. Instead, they are the products of an inappropriate interpretive process, a reading that operates through cross-cultural refraction. The personal experiences I outlined in the preface led me to formulate the hypothesis that narratives of migration would emphasize masculinities in moments of crisis and re-evaluation. I then applied this hypothesis to my readings of migrant narratives. While the testing of a guiding hypothesis is hardly an innovation in literary criticism, the application of this method in a postcolonial, cross-cultural context raises certain dangers. For, as Edward Said has pointed out in the context of Middle Eastern colonial and postcolonial relations, it is out of the desire of the West that the imperial knowledge of Orientalism is produced. The imperial image of Europe's others that mainstream Canadian cultures imbibed through our French and English umbilical cords follows the pattern by which the Occident projected its own fantasies and fears onto the Orient. The danger in a study like mine lies in the possibility that my invested readings – whatever the virtue of my intentions – will reproduce a knowledge similar to that of Orientalism, occluding the subjectivity of the other with my own authorial representations. My hope, however, is that, by attending to the orientations of my own readerly desire itself, through a reflexive erotics of reading, these readings will produce 'dis-oriented' knowledge. For, if 'to orient' means to face *east*, then readings that face *west*, readings that attempt to reverse the projective paradigm, that attempt to read the desire that projects itself, make disorientation.

'For a European or American studying the Orient there can be no disclaiming the main circumstances of *his* actuality,' writes Said; 'to be a European or an American in such a situation is by no means an inert fact' (11). In an attempt to avoid the reproduction of the Orientalist paradigm, I have interrupted my critical interpretations regularly with references to the by-no-means inert fact of my own specific readerly position. I mean these intrusions to disturb the illusion of objective, scholarly disinterest which, as I observed in the preface, marks the post-Enlightenment transcendent persona of the male literary critic. Seidler argues that men must learn to speak honestly about themselves, 'rather than constantly falling back into speaking for others in the supposedly neutral and impartial language of reason ... It has been the historical identification of masculinity with reason and progress that has led men so readily to speaking for others, creating a blindness around the particular experience of heterosexual men' (3). I also mean these intrusions to disqualify me specifically from any claim to special authority about the texts I read. While I myself moved from Ethiopia to Canada, my experience gives me only a superficial sense of what an Asian or African or West Indian immigrant goes through. I was moving 'home' with the benefit of a Canadian passport, pink skin, English as my first language, a Western education and upbringing, and a whole support system of family members and relatives already in place. Rather than establishing my authority, then, the autobiographical references dramatize my readings in a refractive mode; they indicate not only my routes of approach to these immigrant narratives, but also the distortions or limitations inherent in these routes. Iain Chambers, writing of his similarly self-referential critical method, suggests that in breaking into his own body of critical writing and in

opening up the gaps and listening to the silences in my own inheritance, I perhaps learn to tread lightly along the limits of where I am speaking from. I begin to comprehend that where there are limits there also exist other voices, bodies, worlds, on the other side, beyond my particular boundaries. In the pursuit of my desires across such frontiers I am paradoxically forced to face my confines, together with that excess that seeks to sustain the dialogues across them. (5)

This constitutes a reach for experience, not in the tradition of the Cartesian *cogito ergo sum* which would found the authority of one's perceptions, but rather within a framework that understands experience as, in de Lauretis's words, 'a *process* by which, for all social beings, subjectivity is constructed' (*Alice Doesn't*, 159). In other words, a person's experience is the product of that person's ongoing interaction with the various social formations he or she passes through during the course of life. 'It is not individuals who have experience,' writes the historian Joan Scott, 'but subjects who are constituted through experience' (25–6). African-American critic Michael Awkward argues convincingly, in his survey of white critics' discussions of black texts in the United States, that self-reflexivity is no guarantee that a white scholar's writings will avoid systems of representation that are antithetical to black interests (60, 84). Similarly, my self-reflexive writing does not rule out the possibility of my own unconscious reproduction of stereotypical representations. But they do at least give my readers a way to trace a cultural genealogy for the representations I do produce out of what I call 'my own experience.' An attention to experience, then, becomes one way to detail the determining influences and constraints one's cultural medium has upon his or her life and perceptions. To return to Chambers's phrase, an attention to experience becomes a way for the critic to face not only his or her desire for dialogue, but also his or her confines within that dialogue.

Consistently, the privileged category in various binaries of human identification remains transparent and unmarked. Women are marked as subjects of gender; black and brown people are marked as subjects of race; non-Anglo, non-Protestant people are marked as subjects of ethnicity. Such elaborations of difference occlude the specific behaviours, confines, and investments of the privileged category. My deployment of segments from my personal history constitutes my attempt to bring the biases and constraints of my own gender, sexuality, race, and ethnicity out of that occlusion and into dialogue with the texts I read. Through what is, I hope, a 'scrupulous declaration of self-interest,' I want to avoid the sentimental illusion which often haunts postcolonial and transcultural critical writing that through one's 'privileged speech, one is helping to save the wretched of the earth' (Chow 117, 119).

But any writing of one's own experience necessarily produces fiction. The selection and arrangement of various memories and sensations, the very process of composition, imposes meaning and causality upon them. This, as theorists of autobiography have shown, is the way in which narration makes pattern and order out of the random events of one's life.[3] There is a sense, then, in which my self-referential writings are themselves fictions. So how can my autobiographical reflections produce anything but a palimpsest of fictions, a layering of my fictions onto the fictions I am reading? Chambers addresses this issue when he writes:

our sense of our selves is also a labour of imagination, a fiction, a particular story that makes sense ... [W]e imagine ourselves to be the author, rather than the object, of the narratives that constitute our lives. It is this imaginary closure that permits us to act. Still, I would suggest, we are now beginning to learn to act in the subjunctive mode, 'as if we had' a full identity, while recognising that such a fullness is a fiction, an inevitable failure. It is this recognition that permits us to acknowledge the limits of our selves, and with it the possibility of dialoguing across the subsequent differences – the boundary, or horizon. (25–6)

To turn Chambers's phrase to my own account, I am attempting here to read and write in the subjunctive mode, to read – as Felman says Freud did – in dialogue with the other what is actively reading in myself. Perhaps this dialogic kind of writing will enact what Stephen Slemon, in his article 'Post-Colonial Writing: A Critique of Pure Reading,' has called a 'knowledge in *suspension*' (52), a knowledge which minds its p's and q's – the provisos and qualifications inherent in its own production. I hope to produce in the following literary examinations of postcolonial masculinities a critical disorientation, a reflexivity in the desirous gaze, a writing that participates in, while it remains aware of, the unsettling process of cross-cultural refraction.

1

'Playin' 'mas,' Hustling Respect: Multicultural Masculinities in Two Stories by Austin Clarke

Austin Clarke has published fifteen volumes of fiction and autobiography since 1964, making him one of the most prolific writers living in Canada today. Yet, despite the Barbadian-born writer's considerable Canadian success, most of the responses to Clarke's work to date have come from critics who share his Caribbean background. Lloyd W. Brown's *El Dorado and Paradise: Canada and the Caribbean in Austin Clarke's Fiction* (1989); the 1994 biography by Stella Algoo-Baksh; articles by Victor Ramraj, Horace Goddard, Frank Birbalsingh, Anthony Boxill, and Keith S. Henry – all make use of that background to delineate the complex genealogy of Caribbean migration in Clarke's works. Their analyses focus on the important issues of immigrant dislocation, the residual effects of colonial history, West Indian family structures, the migrant character's ambivalent relations to places of origin and destination, and conflicts in Canada over employment or racial prejudice.

I wish to focus, in the following reading of two short stories from Clarke's Penguin Short Fiction collection *Nine Men Who Laughed* (1986), on the ways in which the male West Indian migrant's experience of cross-cultural refraction produces disruptive parody when he takes on certain urban Canadian norms for masculinity. Such a focus involves a reading strategy that is, as I said in the introduction, 'inappropriate': first, where Clarke and his critics in general emphasize issues of race over those of gender, I have tipped the balance in the other direction; and, second, I have linked three discussions of gendered performativity that were formulated in completely different disciplinary paradigms. The first is Judith Butler's influential theory, articulated in philosophical and post-structuralist terms, of gender as a socially prescribed performance; the second is the folklorist Roger Abraham's description, based on ethnographic research and methodology, of the performative tradition of what he calls the 'man-of-words' in Caribbean Creole culture; and the third is the identification by sociologists such as Julius Hudson of a common African-American urban form of masculine performance called the 'hustler.' I hope that this inappropriate linkage will produce a mutually informative dialogue among these diverse methods of analysis.

Clarke's two stories about Joshua Miller-Corbaine, 'A Man' and 'How He Does It,' are excellent sites for an analysis of masculinity in multicultural transition. At the same time that the two stories demonstrate how gender is in fact something we 'do,' how masculinities are practised or performed, they also show how these performances can become troubled and troubling when they negotiate the displacements of cross-cultural refraction. The two stories about a Caribbean man in Toronto address not only the social codes for masculinity that he encounters in the Canadian metropolis, but also the ways the masculine codes he brings from the island and from contact with African-American urban culture displace and challenge these metropolitan ones.

Every morning, when all the men on his street are leaving for work, Joshua Miller-Corbaine, this 'tall and black and majestic' man (123), emerges from his three-storey suburban Toronto house dressed in a dark, pinstripe suit spanned by the gold chain of his pocket watch, a snow-white shirt with a soft silk tie, and black Bally shoes. He carries a black leather attaché case engraved with his initials. The case is stuffed with law books and sheaves of jurisprudence. He eases himself carefully onto the leather seat of his silver-grey Cadillac Eldorado, and, having loaded in his wife and son, slides the car noiselessly out of the circular driveway in the direction of Yonge and York Mills, where he will drop off his son, Winchester, at Upper Canada College and his wife, Mary, at the high school where she teaches. He then wheels the automobile around and heads towards the part of the city called the Annex, where he spends part of his working day.

Joshua has carefully gathered around himself all the accessories of the man of taste, the man of wealth. He is very conscious of his image – of the way clothing, possessions, diction, gestures, posture, even gait, 'make the man.' 'He hunched his shoulders when he walked,' we are told in 'A Man.' 'He felt it gave him a determined, academic and serious look. He felt it was the look of someone burdened by intellectual problems, the look of someone who spent most of the day and most of the night pouring over academic and legalistic matters which ordinary men could not grasp' (123–4). He has cultivated a nervous tic, which he soothes regularly by shrugging his shoulders to adjust the fit of his jacket and the straightness of his tie. This mannerism, the narrator informs us, 'was born of his admiration for an Englishman who taught literature in private school back in Barbados' (124). This comment suggests that one of the major influences on Joshua's performance comes from the class structure of the colonial West Indies; there he learned to admire the cut of suits made in London, which, we are told, was where 'his heart, his standards of fast living and his first love remained' (119).

With some adaptation to the social protocols of Toronto, Joshua's upper-class performance has garnered him the success he dreamed about back in Bridgetown. He has married the wealth of a mining-company president's daughter; his son attends Canada's most prestigious private school; he has three mistresses, two of whom are also extremely wealthy; he lives in luxury and is the envy of his male West Indian friends. His house, his clothes, and his money, like his car, constitute the Eldorado of the immigrant's dream.[1]

But it is all a masquerade. In Creole terms, Joshua is 'playin' 'mas' to good effect in Toronto. For, despite appearances, he is not a Bay Street corporate lawyer. He is not a bachelor. He is not the independent man of means he has claimed to be for the past thirty years. Instead, he is a kept man. He spends his days visiting the women who sponsor his front. His house, his car, his attaché case and gold watch, even his suits – all the accoutrements of his impressive image – are gifts from his wife and lovers. Completely dependent upon the white women to whom he is a refined gigolo, Joshua must carefully craft every action to contribute to the masquerade upon which, not only he, but also his various audiences – the women, his neighbours, and his West Indian male friends – depend. And the performance is taking its toll. He has a stomach ulcer, and his temper is getting short. One wonders how long he can keep it up.

I'm putting on my favourite blue shirt this morning and find my fingers fumbling with the buttons. Oh yeah. This is the shirt Wendy's mom bought me because it's just my colour of blue. And it is. I get regular compliments when I wear it. Brings out the blue in my eyes. But she found it in Ladies' Wear. Hey, it's the right colour, so who cares what section of Eaton's she bought it in? I'm fumbling with the buttons. Who sat around in the back room of what clothing-design shop, deciding that women's belts and buttons should do up this way, and men's that? And how did my fingers come to believe that is a more natural way to do it than this? Makes me think of the leotards. Blue leotards.

I must have been around three or four years old. Our family was going to

Addis Ababa from Woliso. An early-morning trip – on the road at dawn, mist in the chilly air. What I remember is riding in the back of the Jeep in utter mortification. To make sure I was warm, Mom had put me in leotards. Leotards! I'd seen my sister wearing leotards. Boys do not wear leotards. 'Nobody will see.' Mom jabbed my shirt-tail into the waistband. 'They'll look just like socks. Your pants cover the rest. And they'll keep you warm. Stop fussing.' This is no comfort. It's not a matter of seeing; it's a state of being. I am in leotards. And I'm gonna meet other kids in Addis, kids I don't know, and there will be this inner hidden defect, this debilitation, just when I need to feel my strongest, my most confident. I'll be negotiating the toys, the games, the sandbox, the leader–follower stuff in leotards. This is impossible. Unthinkable.

The rest I don't remember. Did Mom relent as the day grew warmer and relieve me of the navy blue tights? Or was I exposed before the other tots as a sham, a fake, an oddity? It's one of my earliest memories of indignation.

Joshua is a prime example of the kind of heightened performativity that is a striking feature of so many of the male characters, not just of Austin Clarke's fifteen published volumes, but also of other male Caribbean authors such as Earl Lovelace, Dany Laferrière, Samuel Selvon, Harold Sonny Ladoo, and George Lamming. These characters are very conscious about *acting male*, about using all the techniques of drama, from gestures to costumes to props and sets, even to dialogue from a script. While we can usefully examine this striking performativity with reference to Butler's gender theory, her formulations need to be balanced by the specific cultural analysis of Abrahams's research in African-Caribbean traditions of male performativity. For her abstract theory assumes a more universal, coherent social order than the folklorist would allow.

Butler writes that 'gender is always a doing' (*Gender* 25). Gender is the product, she insists, of a person's enactment of socially imposed scripts for sexed behaviour. The impeccably attired Joshua illustrates nicely her assertion that 'gender is the repeated stylization of the body, a set of repeated acts within a highly rigid regulatory frame that congeal over time to produce the appearance of substance, of a natural sort of being' (33). Joshua's posture, the practised shrug of his shoulders, the cut of his suits, the upper-middle-class Trinidadian-mixed-with-English accent[2] constitute this 'repeated stylization' of his body that produces him as man of wealth and influence. Each of these elements of his performance plays to specific social scripts, not just of gender, but also of ethnicity, race, and class.

Now, it would be easy at this point to misunderstand Butler's performance theory by concluding that a person puts on a gender in the morning like choosing which suit or dress to wear today. 'Performativity,' Butler cautions in her second book, *Bodies That Matter*, is 'not a singular "act,"' (12). A human being becomes gendered, she insists, by a repeated process of citation, by re-citation, where the 'norm' of sex is cited in each person's daily practices. Connell makes much the same point when he suggests that a person's physical sense of gender 'grows through a personal history of social practice, a life-history-in-society' (84). Gender, therefore, is not a matter of spontaneous deciding; rather, it is the accumulation of performances or recitations of the social scripts by which we live. Society imposes and enforces such scripts, but Butler's troubling (and potentially liberating) point is that *people play them out*. And, in the inevitable uniqueness of each performer's own history, experience, and aptitude, there exists the potential for various interpretations, diverse recitations, even modifications of the socially regulated script.

This potential excites a gender-troubler like Butler, because it leads her to speculate about how to produce intentionally these variations on the social script. It leads her to the central question of *Gender Trouble*: 'If repetition is bound to persist as the mechanism of the cultural reproduction of identities, then ... [w]hat kind of subversive repetition might call into question the regulatory practice of identity itself?' (32). We need to look, she suggests, for 'self-consciously denaturalized position[s]' (110) – de Lauretis calls them 'eccentric' subject positions – from which we can observe how the naturalness of gender is constituted. Given the metropolitan, 'First World' purview of her work, Butler turns to drag parodies, and to gay and lesbian adaptations of heterosexual gender codes for this denaturalization, believing that the potential for gender transformation is to be found in the 'possibility of a failure to repeat, a de-formity, or a parodic repetition' (141). But there are many places to look for denaturalized or eccentric positions – some of them completely unselfconscious.

Joshua's performance of the man of means is flawless in its rendering of the social codes of class and gender, but it is 'denaturalized' by the inflections he brings to that performance from African-Caribbean culture. In *The Man-of-Words in the West Indies: Performance and the Emergence of Creole Culture* (1983), Roger Abrahams uses research he carried out on the islands of Nevis, St Vincent, Tobago, and Trinidad in the 1960s to describe the complex codes that inform men's social performances in the Caribbean.[3] After some years observing the patterns of verbal performance that distinguish African male behaviours in American cities – playing the dozens, jiving, rapping, etc. – Abrahams went to the Caribbean to see what relations he could find between African-American and African-Caribbean cultural performances. While he found remarkable continuities between the two (e.g., 'rhyming' is the Creole equivalent of 'playing the dozens'), he found in the West Indies a remarkably defined tradition of verbal and social performances, a tradition that was consciously and deliberately taught to young people as they were growing up.

Two distinct but related sets of values shape the performative tradition of what Abrahams calls the 'man-of-words.' On the one hand, there is the tradition of 'sweet talk' whose arena is the private, orderly world of house, yard, and church. The sweet-talker operates in the mode of the preacher or speech-maker whose polished and sophisticated rhetoric is called for at serious community events such as weddings, funerals, political gatherings, or 'thanksgivings' after a sickness or some other adversity. Sweet talk emphasizes being sensible, Abrahams notes; it has as its primary aim the achievement of respectability. The tradition of 'broad talk,' on the other hand, is the mode of the "mas' player or carnival performer whose arena occupies the public, male-dominated rum-shops and crossroads. The broad or 'bad' talker delights in nonsense and rudeness couched in colloquial diction and biting invective. He aggressively competes with other men-of-words by 'makin' mock' and 'givin' fatigue,' distinguishing his position in the group through wit and notoriety. Whereas sweet talk values respectability above all else, broad talk values reputation (151–2).

The two values of respectability and reputation reflect the hybrid inheritances of Creole culture, for respectability is often formulated in reference to the 'high' culture of colonial Britain, whereas reputation is formulated in terms of the African tradition of the Anansi or trickster figure whose rebellious disregard of the very idea of high culture itself affirms the 'low' and disempowered. Thus, for instance, the sweet-talker demonstrates his sophistication through allusions to Shakespeare and the Bible and employs as many Latinate phrases as possible, while the broad-talker uses Creole invective, elaborate curses and mockery, and delights in non sequiturs and puns. Sweet talk affirms the social order and its traditions; broad talk ridicules them. The sweet-talker wishes to solidify his status in a superior class, while the broad-talker wants to deflate the pretentious and (paradoxically) distinguish himself as the champion of lower-class solidarity.

We must keep in mind, however, that despite this distinction between sweet talk and broad talk, the truly effective man-of-words is the one who can adapt either expressive mode to a given situation. Abrahams insists that a man-of-words is worth nothing unless he can, on the one hand, stitch together a startling piece of oratorical rhetoric, and, on the other, capture the attention, the allegiance, and the admiration of the audience through his fluency, his strength of voice, and his social maneuverability and psychological resilience ... West Indian creativity, and indeed, Afro-American creativity are built upon this competitive and highly contrastive superimposition of voices, ones that speak in different codes and cadences. (xxx)

The ability to improvise, then, is key to the success of the man-of-words. Out of the repertoire of performances that stretch between the two poles of the 'sweet' and the 'broad,' he must produce one appropriate to the occasion before him. What happens, then, in Joshua's case? What happens when the man-of-words moves to another culture? How does the performative tradition he imbibed in his West Indian childhood shape his masculine practices in metropolitan Toronto?

Austin Clarke's two stories about Joshua describe a man who innovates; he brings the twin goals of respectability and reputation to the metropolitan context and tries to find ways to achieve them in his new situation. The division of values symbolized by the domestic yard and the public crossroads in island culture, however, needs reorientation in Toronto. Here respectability finds its primary expressions in public symbols such as high-status employment, an expensive car, a home in a wealthy neighbourhood, and other material possessions; a reputation for dramatic flair continues to need validation from a homosocial network of male relationships, but immigration means that Joshua's network is now limited to the circle of other West Indian men who can appreciate the performance, so it occurs in a much more circumscribed arena than it did back in the islands. Rather than establishing respectability in the yard at home, Joshua must seek it in the public arenas of corporate business and conspicuous consumption, and instead of establishing a reputation for wit and notoriety at the crossroads, he works on that reputation in the living-rooms and bachelor suites of his West Indian friends. So Toronto requires him to improvise his performances for a new symbolic landscape.

One sign of respectability does appear to transfer directly from the island to the Canadian city, and that is the deference commanded by the man in fine clothes. Throughout the two stories, the reader's attention is repeatedly drawn to the upper-middle-class elegance of Joshua's clothes. (A similar concern with the class register of clothing preoccupies the characters Boysie Cumberbatch, Henry White, and John Moore from Clarke's novels, as well as many of the male protagonists in his five collections of short stories.) This concern with fine suits and tailored shirts constitutes a kind of cross-dressing on the level of class. In *Vested Interests*, a far-ranging study of how cross-dressing produces cultural anxiety, Marjorie Garber asserts that 'class, gender, sexuality, and even race and ethnicity ... are themselves brought to crisis in dress codes and sumptuary regulation' (28). Joshua's clothes enable him to improvise a role for himself within the exclusive circles of upper-middle-class masculinity in Toronto. Along with his other accoutrements, they are meant to gain him respect. Why? Because Canadian corporate culture says you wear a business suit, glance at a gold watch, drive a Cadillac, carry an attaché case, have a son in Upper Canada College, regularly prove your virility in several women's beds, and practise corporate law to show you are a real successful man. With enough industry, talent, and capital, anybody can do it. But it assumes all along that you are white, too.

This quietly maintained racial barrier highlights the reason why, in migrating to a North American metropolis, Joshua encounters another performative tradition, a second set of codes for African men's behaviour. Where the tradition in the West Indies incorporated a contest between the African trickster and British 'high' culture, the North American one juxtaposes that trickster with American-style capitalism. Whereas the plantation paradigm in the islands maintained the inferiority of Africans by blocking their access to education, and thus to the civility of the 'gentleman,' capitalist metropolitan culture maintains their oppression by blocking their access to upper-echelon employment. The figure of the inner-city hustler represents an African-American performative tradition that has evolved in response to this consistent discrimination against African Americans in capitalist culture.

As long ago as the 1952 publication of *Black Skin, White Masks*, Frantz Fanon pointed out that economic exclusion was the primary cause of black men's feelings of inferiority (13). Robert Staples applies Fanon's analysis to the American urban scene: 'black male sexuality ... is a secondary symbol of manhood in a society that denies him the primary signs of masculinity, such as high status jobs' (14). Caught between expectations that a man prove his worth by achieving socio-economic success and the racism that disqualifies him from the marketplace, black masculinity, according to black British critics Kobena Mercer and Isaac Julien, 'is a highly contradictory formation as it is a *subordinated* masculinity' (112). In the Canadian context, Clarke's biographer Stella Algoo-Baksh claims that 'Canada often perpetuates the emasculation of the black male by denying him the resources he needs to discharge his conventional manly

duties to his family' (101). She quotes Clarke himself, who declares, on
the basis of his own early experiences trying to find work in Toronto, 'that
the "invisible but solid hand of prejudice" would always confront the
black man with barriers to respectable employment in Canada' (47–8).
Just as the tradition of the West Indian man-of-words combined the
aspiration for British-style respectability with a carnivalesque mockery
of high-culture proprieties, so also the tradition of the metropolitan
hustler combines an aspiration for capitalist success with a licentious
disregard for the social protocols for attaining that success. In both
traditions, the performer ascribes to and rebels against the codes and
practices of the status quo.

Thus, Joshua's masquerade as lawyer-about-town is inflected by both
island and metropolitan traditions, and, like them, it conveys both es-
pousal of and dissatisfaction with metropolitan codes for masculine
success. This duality allows Clarke to produce simultaneously a pathe-
tic portrait of the man who ascribes to codes that are hostile to him and
a critique of the racist logic that operates within those codes. It lets Clarke
show both how males benefit in the short-term by perpetrating a
phallocentric system[4] and how they suffer from that very participation.
For, to the extent that Joshua's charade succeeds, it shows how thin
the 'proofs' of mainstream masculine 'authenticity' really are, while, to
the extent that it fails, it reveals the violence these codes inflict on their
actors.

*It was the first time I'd seen a man carry a purse (that is, besides those little
brown leather bags they toss to underlings in Shakespeare plays). He was an
African American from Detroit, as were many of the regulars at the store, and
he was dressed in black from neck to toe – black leather jacket, black polo-
necked sweater, black slacks, slim black shoes, black purse – except for the
scarlet beret that leapt like a flame from the top of his closely groomed hair.*

*The handbag was definitely a purse. It wasn't a belly pouch and it wasn't a
briefcase. It was a dainty, soft-leather, shiny, black purse with a spaghetti strap
that marked a fine line from his shoulder across his chest to his hip. He
unzipped the purse, took out a thin billfold, counted out the money for his
purchase, and tucked the change neatly back inside.*

*But there were lots of things I'd never seen before I worked in Omstead
Fisheries' retail store.*

*It was my first year on my own in Canada. I'd been in the country of my
citizenship for short visits before, but now I was here permanently. I'd finished
high school, grown up, and left my childhood in Ethiopia. I was living with my*

aunt about forty miles southeast of Windsor, Ontario, in a small town called Wheatley. Two of us, Joani and I, worked in the tiny shop that clung to the great wall of the fishery like a barnacle. We sold Omstead products: mainly fresh fish trawled in daily from Lake Erie, but also Omstead onion rings, battered mushrooms, and frozen vegetables. We sold perch fillets, butterfly smelts, whole bass, and the occasional catfish or Coho salmon that came in with the nets. Once there was a sturgeon, a parody of a shark with a rubber eraser for a nose. Most of our customers were African Americans (another variety of 'Yankee' to us) from Detroit on an excursion 'up' to Canada, even though we were actually south of Detroit.

The relations between Canadians and Americans were new to me – the petty resentment of the local Wheatley residents towards the rich Yanks who came across the river from Michigan, thronging the campgrounds and provincial parks; the sense of being a smaller, weaker brother; the self-righteousness over lower crime rates and cleaner streets.

African-American urban culture was new to me too. I'd lived all my childhood conscious of my pink skin in Ethiopia, whose people were coloured from creamed coffee to red copper to ebony black. So the colour of these American customers was not new. What was new was their clothes and their cars. I had, still have, a stereotyped image of black urban life in DE-troit (that's how our customers pronounced it). I got it from the couple of times I'd got lost looking with friends for Joe Louis Arena, and we'd found ourselves wandering up and down newspaper-blown streets between run-down tenement houses and hoping anxiously that nobody would notice our obviously pink skin. I got it from the television news that came to us by cable from Detroit nightly, offering images of crack houses, drug murders, undernourished schoolchildren in dingy classrooms.

What I couldn't figure out was our customers' clothes and cars. How did people from those ghettos get these glamorous clothes, these luxury cars? Why did they get them? Wouldn't it be wiser to fix up the places in which they lived? To spend their money on lawns and flowers and brightly lit kitchens? School lunch programs? This guy with the purse, for instance, was ten years ahead of any fashion I knew. He looked like he'd stepped out of the pages of Ebony or GQ.

Basically, Joshua fuses the performative flair of the West Indian man-of-words with the metropolitan figure of the street hustler. The hustler emerged in the African-American ghettos of the early half of this century in response to the American Dream. This figure aspires to the *goals* of that dream, but, because of his race and class, he is disqualified from achieving the *means* to realize them. So he innovates. Hustling, as African-American sociologist Julius Hudson describes it, is 'a way of "making it" without killing oneself on whitey's jobs' (413). The hustler short-circuits his way to masculine success – that is, in socio-economic terms. The members of this subculture are conspicuous consumers, and the symbols they acquire are the clothes, jewellery, and automobiles that together compose an image of sexual and economic male potency.

The attire of the hustler represents one of the most significant aspects of his 'front' or *modus operandi* ... [O]ne's wardrobe is a factor in the determination of the hustler's peer-established prestige ranking ... [T]he Cadillac ... is the most popular car in this subculture ... Moreover, a special model Eldorado, renamed El Cavalaro ... is currently the ultimate in hustlers' automobile selection ... In addition to clothes and automobiles, hustlers spend a great deal of money on jewelry. They usually adorn themselves with gold-diamond rings and watches. (Hudson 413–14)

Their motto is: Dress for success. You will attract money if you look like you already have some. Jingle the keys to the Eldorado in your pants pocket.

Of the many kinds of 'hustles' or 'games' that Hudson describes – which include pool-hall speculating, drug-dealing, and petty larceny – the one that fits Joshua's scheme best is a kind of pimping game, not the kind that derives an income from prostitution or from professional female shoplifters, but one in which the hustler gets rich from functioning as a gigolo to women who already have money:

The pimp in this case is usually a good-looking, well-dressed, and well-built guy, but the most important characteristic in this type of pimping is the ability to sexually satisfy a female. Thus this pimp is the gigolo type. Once he establishes his superiority in this area, he encounters virtually no obstacles to the attainment of the female's money ... Often such pimps get their broads to buy them expensive automobiles and other desired goods. (420)

What I find fascinating about this figure is the way he simultaneously affirms and undermines the dominant culture's socio-economic codes of masculine success. What I find disturbing is the way he confirms the racist stereotype of the black stud in the process. In the next chapter, I examine Dany Laferrière's troubling parody of the black stud in *How to Make Love to a Negro*, and I ask whether Laferrière's parody subverts or subvents the racist stereotype.

Capitalist phallocentrism avers that a real man is rich and controls women. Joshua proves his authenticity on both counts, by controlling his women and making himself rich; but in doing so he undermines those codes by revealing how his hard-won masculinity – in both economic and sexual terms – *depends* upon the women it seeks to control. Here is a great paradox of phallocentric masculinity: that the supposedly autonomous male depends upon 'his' women. On the one hand, Joshua seems the paragon of male independence. He needs nothing outside himself – not his family, not his West Indian friends, not a university degree, not even the social system of employment or a position in the institution of the law – to succeed. But, on the other hand, he is absolutely a kept man. His wife has provided the house and car; his mistresses, the money for his expensive suits and jewellery. Collectively, they give him what he *does* each day. In this sense, his masculinity is something these women have made. They sponsor his performance.

But the conflict between the social script which urges him to assert independence and Joshua's real dependence chafes him until it erupts in hatred of the very women on whom he depends. He hates his wife (128); he hates the rich woman who lives in the Annex and buys his suits (131); and he is beginning to hate Rachel, the young mistress he likes most (145). He feels trapped by them, by the life they have made for him, and he lashes out in violent response. 'He had been beating her off and on for ten years,' says the narrator of Joshua's connection with the woman in the Annex. 'Whenever she cornered him about his work ... or about his wife ... he beat her' (131). But the entrapment is a mutual one. For, when she confronts him about his philandering, we are told that her strange love for him is based on her acknowledgment of what she calls his 'independence' (131). So she endures his beatings, even admires him, for the very fiction of his independence that she herself has created. 'In his sexual and social themes,' writes Brown,

Clarke emphasizes the reciprocal nature of roles and perceptions. Joshua succeeds in his schemes ... because in their own way the women need his illusions as much as he does ... Their female dependency complements his dependency on them for economic support and as props for his overweening ego. In fact, Joshua's women really duplicate his blend of dependency and manipulative power. (*El Dorado* 143–4)

Both trapped in the performance of their respective roles, Joshua and his mistress feed off of each other's need, perpetuating the recitation of their co-dependency.

By successfully hustling upper-middle-class status, and by maintaining the surface illusion of his self-sufficiency, Clarke's character demonstrates how metropolitan masculinity *is* in fact that surface, that performance. Joshua fakes the lawyer's life – mimics the law, as it were – to grab the golden apple of social prestige. He reaches the capitalist ideal's *ends* by short-cutting the *means*, and, in the process, reveals that the presumed codes of propriety (the Protestant work ethic,[5] the I'm-a-contributing-member-of-society ethic) are really in pursuit of that same golden apple with just as ruthless and 'lawless' a heart. His performance exposes one of the capitalist social script's most essential features – the hustle for respectability.

Joshua's cross-cultural refraction triggers this exposure. His performance of the corporate script for socio-economically based male success is inflected by the complex combination of West Indian and urban black performative traditions he has inherited through cultural and racial history. That inflection causes his performance to veer into a parody that exposes the corporate code's own superficiality. The two stories about Joshua are striking examples of the way the cultural disruption of the migrant narrative can bring to light repressed contradictions within what Kaja Silverman, in *Male Subjectivity at the Margins*, has called masculinity's 'dominant fiction' (15ff.). Like the other narratives of masculine migration that I examine in the chapters that follow, Joshua's story reveals much about how the masculinities conscripted in Bridgetown or Port-au-Prince or Bombay or Columbo are troubled by and bring trouble to the conscriptions of maleness in Toronto or Vancouver or Montreal. Joshua's refracted performance is unsettling, not because it constitutes a direct challenge to Canadian masculine ideologies, but because it elaborates a discomfort rarely acknowledged but widely felt by urban Canadian men: that Western capitalism is structured by men's aggressive overcompensation for inner self-doubt.

To assess the unsettling effects of Joshua's story, I will now focus on the very different narrative voices of the two stories 'A Man' and 'How He Does It.' My aim here is to attend to something Judith Butler says little about, and that is the question of audience. Who watches the identity performances she describes? She says 'society' invigilates gender performances, but who constitutes that society? Who interprets the performer's self-styling drama? How does the audience's gaze influence the performance? What roles do pre-existing performative traditions assign the audience? And what effect does the interaction between performance and audience have on the social script itself?

Abrahams, in contrast to Butler, emphasizes the determining presence of the audience in West Indian performative tradition. Not only does the man-of-words compete with other performers for the attention and approval of the audience, he says, but also the audience themselves often become competitors to the performer as they take on the broad-talker's role of hecklers who make some 'mock' and 'boderation' of their own. By placing the two versions of Joshua's story in two very different narrative voices, Clarke highlights the importance of audience to an understanding of the performative paradigm.

A couple of scenes in 'A Man' indicate the concerns of one section of Joshua's audience, the 'respectable' people up high, left and right of the stage, in the private boxes. In the first scene, Joshua is in his car, fleeing from his rich lover's accusations about his philandering. He is also fleeing his own violent response to her accusation, his slugging her in the eye. 'He had never driven so fast in the city,' the narrator tells us.

He had just gone through the second red light when he pressed the brakes. The Cadillac came to a standstill beside a yellow police cruiser. The officer looked at him. He glared at the policeman, his glare turned to terror and he lowered his eyes ... The police officer ignored him. The fear rose and he continued at a slower rate, limp as a dishrag. (134)

The policeman pairs logically with another watcher. In this second scene, Joshua is not alone in the car. Knowing that his wife will be away for the weekend, he has invited his mistress Rachel over to his place for a 'dirty weekend.' They pull up, and Rachel gets out, exclaiming loudly her delight at his lovely home. Joshua 'flashed his eyes across the lawn,' reports the narrator. 'Standing erect and sombre as a judge, which he was, was his neighbour ... [Joshua's] stomach dropped. He had no stomach now. And he was weak' (146). The policeman and the judge are watching. The law.

But it is not Joshua who tells us about them. Nor do they offer any comments themselves. It is the narrator who draws our attention to their silent, threatening presence. And it makes sense that he should do so, because that is where he himself belongs – in the box reserved for judges and policemen, arbiters of the law. The narrator of 'A Man' – with his third-person omniscience, his privileged access to Joshua's thoughts, his dignified prose and supposed objectivity, his security in the voyeur's unreflexive gaze – aligns himself with the law that judges. He intrudes, comments, analyses, and, in so doing, he appeals to, defines, a readership of social regulators and moral commentators. His concern for order and propriety connects him with that current in West Indian performative tradition whose prime concern is respectability, but, since the story takes place in Toronto, he is linked with institutions which arbiter respectability in Canada: the courts and the police. It is no coincidence that these institutions are the ones that most often express public disapproval of the newly arrived immigrant.

Right from the opening sentence, this narrator condemns Joshua's masquerade. Throughout the story, he reminds us of Joshua's stomach ulcer, the bodily sign of his hypocrisy. He tells us both about Joshua's abusive violence and about his consequent guilt. It is the narrator who breaks from the usual focalization upon Joshua to inform us that the rich mistress is not taken in by Joshua's performance: 'she thought he looked like a man who did not have schedules and appointments; seeing also beneath his handsome build the tension in his walk, which his well-tailored clothes that she admired and had bought, could not conceal' (125). Repeatedly, the narrator reveals Joshua as nothing more than a chimera created by Hugo Boss and Giorgio Armani. This is the message the narrator conveys when Joshua careens desperately around his house, trying to convert the family home into a bachelor pad in preparation for Rachel's visit. After grabbing pictures off the walls, dresses from closets, sanitary pads from the bathroom, nylons from the bedroom floor, he collapses exhausted in a chair. 'He noted with some disappointment,' the narrator informs us,

that nothing in this house in which he had spent so much time had his stamp on it. No one could guess that he lived here.

Here he was, for the last two hours, trying to remove all trace of his wife's presence in the house, and what did he discover? He had come face to face with the cold fact that no smell, no idiosyncrasy, no photograph, no snap-shot, no cigarette box used even for paper clips and for discarded calling cards, nothing of his stamp was on his own home. (140)

He has left nothing of his own stamp upon the house, the narrator implies, because he does not have a stamp of his own in the first place. Underneath the finery, there is only hot air. Through his assumption of moral superiority over Joshua, the narrator invites readers to enter into an ironic contract, a conspiracy of superiors between readers and narrator that Wayne Booth would call the 'Snotty Sublime' (211). Joshua thinks he is succeeding in his masquerade, but we know better. He has no idea how easily we can see through him. It is the irony of drama which lets characters make fools of themselves on stage, while we the audience chuckle knowingly, smug in the (authorized) perspicacity of our private booth.

In the ironic contract that operates between us and the narrator in 'A Man,' Clarke plays upon a pleasurable anxiety that structures many a masculine psyche: the male compulsion to prove over and over again – with *prima facie* evidence, as Joshua puts it – that 'I really am a man.' Really. Our anxious pleasure focuses on whether or not Joshua's performance will be exposed as a sham. How will he get past this challenge? and the next one? and the next? The titillating anxiety, though, is false suspense. And we know it is false. The narrator has told us all along that Joshua is a fake. But the suspense still operates through a kind of dramatic irony: when will the character learn about himself what we already know? He has been exposed to us right from the start; it is just a matter of time until he realizes it himself.

Here Clarke leads us to a fundamental critique of upwardly ambitious masculinity: a subjectivity that remains ignorant of what it knows, that refuses to know what it knows. That knows the artificiality of its performance and yet believes in that performance. This is a subjectivity structured by multiple layers of irony: the dramatic irony of the performer who does not know what his audience knows about him; the self-protecting irony that acts as if it did not know what it knows; the situational irony of the compulsion to enact an ideal that is itself bogus. The dominant fiction insists that 'male' is the standard, the substantial plenitude against which 'otherness' is measured; but the male performer (and often his audience, too) is plagued by the nagging feeling that the masquerade is wearing thin. He has too much invested, though, in the act to throw it all off. At the same time that he exposes to our censure the vacuum at Joshua's core, Clarke's narrator entices us onwards through the story with the prospect of an ultimate exposure – with which he duly gratifies us at the end. Joshua's wife comes home unexpectedly and finds Joshua with Rachel, naked in the living-room. The conclusion is a strange mixture of anticlimax and satisfaction: anticlimactic because the exposure does not tell us anything we did not already know; satisfying because the tension of whether or not the act will 'pass' is relieved – we are assured that it will not.

But the question remains: what does the irony accomplish? Presumably, ironic writing operates what Freud called a 'tendentious' project upon its reader. It wants to have a critical impact (*Jokes* 90–116). So what effect does the ironic contract in the story have on the gender performances of the audience? Does the pact of the 'Snotty Sublime' between us and the narrator invite any kind of self-knowledge? Or does it assure us that we are all immensely superior to such obvious foibles, and, therefore blind us to our own performative incoherencies? Certainly, it critiques the object of ridicule, but does this critique trouble or does it placate the audience? Does it do both?

I looked very plain in my very best suit at Edmonton's annual Black Heritage Gospel Choir performance last February. My friend Brenda, whose childhood in Bahamian church culture bred a love for gospel music into her very bones, had warned me that it would be wise to dress up, since, as she put it – tactfully? politely? – 'the West Indian community will be there. And you know how we like to dress up!' But I hadn't really realized what she meant until we paraded into Jubilee Hall.

I felt downright dowdy in my pure worsted virgin wool suit with the silk-lined pants by Alexander Julian (London), my slim Italian shoes by Filo Grana, my crisp Leo Chevalier dress shirt (Paris–London–Rome), my liquid silk Graham Ashley tie (Bond St, London), and my supple Pierre Cardin belt. I looked around me at the people in stunning silk suits, gold lamé caftans, satin tuxedos, velvet turbans. The diamond-pinned cravats, jewelled fingers, gilded necklines, pearled earlobes. And the choir gowns! Choir gowns like I'd never seen; the robes of royalty and the hats of Ascot.

But there was another sector of the crowd that made me feel not quite so out-of-place. After all, this was Edmonton, and there were the down-dressed white people, the sweaters-and-jeans people, the Birkenstock crowd. The have-suits-in-the-closet-at-home-but-prefer-to-go-to-these-public-events-in-rec-room-clothes crowd. The ones who can get what they want in this society without having to power dress.

Made me think of Wendy saying that she always dresses carefully when she wants to shop at ladies' fashion stores. If you don't, the sales woman looks you up and down, takes in your lack of a bank account, and leaves you to fend for yourself.

By deploying a very different narrator in the second version of the story, 'How He Does It,' Clarke gives us an alternative perspective on these questions. He ushers us to seats in a very different part of the theatre. In contrast to the disapproving narrator of 'A Man' – whose formal, 'standardized' Queen's English aligns him with the whole long line of 'respectable' narrators inherited by the colonies from Britain – this new narrator is not omniscient, not objective, not given access to Joshua's or anybody else's thoughts. He does not speak Oxonian, or even U-of-Torontonian, English, nor does he enjoy the voyeur's privilege of detachment. He does not know about – or, at least, fails to mention – the beating or the policeman or the stomach ulcer. A member of the group of Joshua's 'Wessindian' male friends, this narrator invites us to join the 'in' group who have blown their week's savings on the front seats in the house, right down on the main floor, centre stage. This new group is still very much involved in evaluating Joshua's performance, but they judge him by the codes of a very different tradition.

In place of the moralizing respectability of the earlier official-sounding narrator, this narrator is a member of the homosocial brotherhood who have a keen taste for Joshua's saga of male prowess. These men admire and envy their lawyer-friend's reputation-enhancing performance. Rather than ending his story with Joshua's final humiliation, he delightedly shows us how Joshua invents a way to survive a confrontation between his wife and his mistress: how he beats the system. In his story, Joshua 'play 'mas' so convincingly that Rachel more readily believes his improvised explanation ('She's my maid') than the wife's true story. But even in this much more convivial atmosphere, there still roves the watchful eye. 'He came from Trinidad in 1952,' our new narrator explains,

to go to University and this is now the year 1986, and all the boys who went to university with him, who know him, who come and gone and some who stay, and see him around the place, none o' these boys, not one, don't know yet if really and truly this fellow have a job, and what the job is. Or if, in all them years, he ever had a job!

Arguments have rage from 1952 till the present day, and still nobody can't come to a conclusion, stating that the fellow is a lawyer, a semi-lawyer, a community lawyer or no lawyer at all. And not one of his colleagues have the nerve or the gall to tell him to his face, 'Man, you only *playing* you is a lawyer!'

But behind his back they does-laugh and say, 'He *playing* he's a lawyer!' And some does-say after they laugh, 'But if he was a lawyer, he would be the best goddamn lawyer outta all the boys!', meaning all the Wessindian boys. (208)

Even in this friendlier narrative context, then, there remains an atmosphere of distrust, or at least of ironic distance. 'The boys' set a series of tests to try Joshua's credibility, and he passes them all. One of them follows him downtown and sees him emerge from the High Courts on Queen Street in the company of men dressed in lawyers' black robes (211). Another asks for a $500 loan, to see if he carries around the kind of money they expect of his status, and he pulls out a monogrammed wallet and skins off five brand-new hundred-dollar bills. 'After that ... we decide the boy is a hero. He got to be good! And he have class' (214). He passes the wine test, bringing to their next party, not some cheap hooch, but six bottles of Dom Perignon (215). He passes the virility test by possessing an expensive mistress. Upon meeting Rachel, the narrator reveals in his outburst of admiration how inseparably connected are the sexual and the commercial in his concept of respectable masculinity. This woman, 'full in the breasts, full in the hips, *solid as the best securities in the stock market down Bay Street*,' fits exactly his idea of the successful male's companion. 'This was woman. A lawyer's woman!' (217; emphasis added).

Lastly, Joshua passes the language test that the narrator sets for him on one of the days when he drops by to get the narrator to fill in some of the blanks on a legal form: 'I was so intrigue by the legalistic document and still trying to trap-he and see if he know these terms only by learning them by heart or from hearing a real lawyer use them, that I type-in '*Plainclothes*' instead o' *Plaintiff*. He spot it quick quick. And I decide that he is a real brilliant lawyer' (210). What interests me most here is not so much what we learn about Joshua, but what we learn about one audience he plays to, what we learn about the currency in which 'the boys' measure successful masculinity: high social circles, money, expensive tastes in wine and women, and sophisticated language.

It is particularly in the realm of language, though, that the irony I traced in the earlier story emerges again in this very different narrative structure. Where the first narrator claimed superiority over Joshua, this second one professes inferiority. And he does it on the level of language. On one of the afternoons when Joshua drops by with a form that needs filling out, the narrator says the

big big document ... begin with '*Whereas*', and have in '*aforemention*' and '*In the Metropolitan Court of the County of York, in the Judicial District of.*' I see these important-looking legalistical terms, and my brain stop working ... I try reading the thing, but it didn't mek no sense to me, 'cause my brain can't take '*Whereases*' and '*Wherefores.*' (209; emphasis in original)

He claims to be convinced of Joshua's verity by his own inability to comprehend the lawyer's polysyllabic sophistication, but then he goes on to pepper his speech with accurate and witty uses of the very terminology his brain supposedly cannot take in:

So we stop worrying ourselves concerning the *status quo* of the fellow aforemention, and conclude that it was a *prima facie* case that nobody, from 1952 till 1986, could walk-'bout Toronto dress like a lawyer, walk like a lawyer, talk like a lawyer, married to a woman, have a child from the woman and for fifteen years living with the same woman, having parties, living in a' exclusive street, as a matter o' fact *next door to a judge* ... unless the judge wasn't no *real* judge! ... and be brave enough to pretend that he was a more *bona fides* honourable gentleman than the honourable gentleman next door! And that his own *bona fides* could be questioned and that it was not a case o' *quid pro quo*. (211; emphasis and ellipses in original)

In mixing the Latin legal phrases with the contractions and enjambments of rhythmic patois, the Wessindian narrator combines sweet and broad talk to great effect. He demonstrates a casual mastery of Joshua's supposedly exclusive discourse and, by doing so, questions the respectability of the discourse itself. The judgmental irony that had been neatly channelled towards Joshua alone in the first story shoots now in a number of directions. If anybody can manipulate the highfalutin legalese, then might not the judge be a fake too? What is the 'good faith' – the *bona fides* – of being an 'honourable gentleman'? If social subjectivities are a series of performances, is any good faith possible? What about the narrator himself who plays naïve, but isn't?

The multidirectional irony (Hutcheon, *Splitting* 60–1; Ball) takes in not only the governing system represented by the judge, but also the homosocial system represented by the 'boys' who are so eagerly hoodwinked by Joshua's act and the educational system one product of which is a woman who has two PhDs, in Social Studies and Ethnic Cultures, and is absolutely in the dark about her own marriage. Does this general eruption of ironies produce anything except negative ground, a hermeneutic crater? How can the reader sort through the multidirectionality of this irony?

Risking the intentional fallacies of a bygone era of critical theory, and leaping over the many deaths of the author in a more recent one, I will appeal to the producer of Joshua's two performances for help. What are Clarke's purposes in these stories – at least as much as we can infer about them from the stories themselves and from their publication along with the other seven in the collection *Nine Men*? 'These stories were written,' writes Clarke in his bitter introduction to the collection, 'to destroy the definitions that *others* have used to portray so-called immigrants, black people' (6). Rather than letting others define this cultural community, he wants to discover a 'black aesthetic' (6). But, he hastens to add, 'I eschew my own term "black aesthetic" if it suggests that *Nine Men Who Laughed* is a literature about black men' (6–7). Well, we have seen how Joshua's performance disorients definitions, not only undermining white stereotypes of under-class immigrant men, but also exposing the contradictions in capitalist culture's own self-definitions. And we have seen how this parodic subversion and exposure is produced when an immigrant man's performances of metropolitan masculinity are inflected by two pre-existent African traditions of male performativity – the West Indian tradition of the man-of-words and the American tradition of the inner-city hustler. Thus, as Clarke claims, the stories 'A Man' and 'How He Does It' do indeed constitute more than a literature about black men. Among other things, they constitute a literature about how the multicultural genealogy of a black man in white-dominated capitalist culture can bring trouble to that culture's founding values even as that man tries to adapt himself to them.

Albert was another memorable customer at the fish store. He'd just bought eighty pounds of whole white bass. He told me that when he got back to DEtroit, he'd sell them for a profit out of the trunk of his Cadillac.

'*Can I carry these boxes to your car?' I ask.*

'*Sho'.'*

Tableau: Fifties-ish African-American man in sport jacket and flannel slacks walks out to the car, groping in his pocket for keys. Behind him a nineteen-year-old pink Canadian boy follows, lugging two forty-pound boxes of fish.

'*Jes dump 'em in,' says Albert swinging open the trunk.*

'*Straight in?' I'm bewildered. It's a brand-new Eldorado. Plush velour upholstery inside. He wants me to dump these slippery, dead fish straight into the trunk of his car.*

'*Do you want 'em still in the bags?' I ask hopefully.*

'*Nope. Jes dump 'em right in.'*

The customer is always right.

I dump them in. He pays me and drives off, sticky threads of fish slime running down like saliva from underneath his brand-new Cadillac.

El Cavalaro. The rich can do whatever they want, I guess.

Or, maybe this way those fish don't look like product he bought in Canada?

Maybe, loose in the trunk, they look like he just had real good fishing and that gets him by the Customs officials at the border? Or, maybe he hates the person whose car he's borrowed?

I don't know. I stare at the runners of fish slime shining on the tarmac and wonder what that Eldorado will smell like tomorrow.

As I pointed out earlier, the two traditions of the man-of-words and the hustler each incorporate a tension between complicity with and rebellion against the status quo. Accordingly, Clarke does not claim heroic resistance for the African-descended characters in *Nine Men*. Instead, his attitude towards them comprises a tension between censure and sympathy that produces the 'finely balanced ironies' that Brown says characterize the whole of Clarke's writings (*El Dorado* 7). On the one hand, Clarke provides this critique:

When a character says, 'This fucking system' or 'This system makes me laugh' (out of frustration or, more realistically, because he has become lazy, too lazy to think clearly), he is not trying to reduce either the seriousness of the hurt inflicted upon him by the system or to make the system's racism less abrasive: he is confessing to his own inadequacy to take a strict moral position and destroy the system. All nine men laugh because they are, perhaps, already morally dead. (5)

This is heavy censure indeed, blaming the disenfranchised for not having the inner resources to rise up in protest, for not having the power to defeat the system that marginalizes them. On the other hand, Clarke speaks admiringly about his characters' abilities to develop performances that resist the dominant system. 'Improvisation,' he writes, 'is the single most essential quality [these West Indian men] would have used in the islands to ensure victory over a formerly oppressive system or to prevent their lives from being shortened by that system. Improvisation made sure that they did not accede to complete human degradation' (7). The ability to improvise, he suggests, will enable them to resist degradation in Canada too. In the end, Clarke's attitude towards his characters remains a mixture of criticism and muted hope.

Clarke's assertion in this second passage returns us to Judith Butler's speculations about the value of performative subversions. In the ability to *improvise*, to 'read' a new scene and produce a performance, the actor demonstrates the ability to exert a kind of agency *within* the set of social circumstances, the cultural scripts, that he or she is given. For, as Butler reminds us, we do not choose whether or not to repeat the gender roles our circumstances assign us. 'The task,' she asserts, 'is not whether to repeat, but how to repeat or, indeed, to repeat and, through a radical proliferation of gender, *to displace* the very gender norms that enable the repetition itself' (*Gender* 148). Clarke's two stories about Joshua demonstrate how the narrative of cross-cultural migration, which involves refraction between diverse codes and traditions for gendered behaviour, can produce the proliferation and displacement Butler proposes. For when Joshua 'does' his version of metropolitan capitalist masculinity in Toronto, he brings elements of West Indian male performativity alloyed with elements of African-American urban male performativity into his new performance, and these 'imported' elements cause his improvisation of metropolitan codes to bend into parody that exposes the incoherent partialities and provisionalities within those codes. This exposure occurs whatever Joshua's – and perhaps even Clarke's – intentions might have been, for it is the result of the way the migrant narrative's mixture of diverse cultural genealogies and traditions pits ideological elements within these codes against each other.

Joshua does not function as a guide to a new masculinity. Simultaneously a producer and a product of capitalist phallocentrism, he perpetuates the system of misogyny that founds his very livelihood. Austin Clarke's achievement, however, is to have shown, through Joshua's multiculturally refracted performance, through these two stories of cultural disruption in a migrant male's narrative, how seamed with contradictions the category of manhood is in the first place.

2

How to Make Love to a
Discursive Genealogy:
Dany Laferrière's Metaparody of
Racialized Sexuality

Dany Laferrière, like Austin Clarke, takes up the scenario of the black male trickster who uses sexual relations with white women to gain social and economic advantages. Just as Joshua is a master of the improvising strategies of the West Indian man-of-words, so, too, is Vieux, the protagonist-narrator in Laferrière's 1985 novel *Comment faire l'amour avec un Négre sans se fatiguer* (translated by David Homel with the title *How to Make Love to a Negro*, 1987).[1] Vieux's tricky improvisations, like Joshua's, produce a parody that exposes and destabilizes often hidden ideologies of masculinity. But Laferrière addresses explicitly what remains implicit in Clarke. While Clarke's stories are mimetic-realist accounts of an African-descended male's struggle to establish himself in metropolitan Canadian society, Laferrière's novel is postmodern in that it addresses directly the discursive construction of the black male protagonist's sexual and racial subjectivity. Both Joshua and Vieux 'work' the performative codes of social identification (e.g., clothes, body movements and gestures, social networks, the accoutrements of class) to their own advantage, but, whereas Joshua's performance is oriented primarily towards the black man's representation in the 'theatre of the street' (Connell 134), Vieux's is oriented primarily towards the black man's representation in literature and history, and the shape those discourses give to the popular imagination.

Because *How to Make Love to a Negro* takes on, overtly and reflexively, the discourses that shape widespread images of black masculinity in popular culture, it is a good place to evaluate contemporary claims for the liberating power of parodic or counter-discursive practices – I am thinking here not only of Butler's claims as I outlined them in the previous chapter, but also of parallel claims by postcolonial theorists such as

Helen Tiffin, which I discuss below. By tracing Joshua's inheritance of diverse masculine performative traditions in chapter 1, we have seen how those traditions inflect his performance of Canadian metropolitan masculinity in such a way that contradictions and conflicts within that set of metropolitan codes are exposed and questioned. In so far as this second chapter shows how it is in the very counter-discursive nature of parody to produce such exposures, it affirms parody's liberatory potential.

But when one turns from general theory to Laferrière's specific text, troubling questions emerge. A close examination of the circulation of Laferrière's parody, for example, cannot avoid a growing apprehension of the very real constraints under which such parodies operate. What happens after the exposure? What happens when the targets of parody either do not recognize themselves as targets or cynically enjoy the exposure without confronting the need for change? Furthermore, is it not possible that the parodist's momentary inhabitation of a demeaning discourse and its stereotypes will reconfirm their power and fascination for the audience? Questions such as these do not rule out parody as a liberatory practice, but they do draw our attention to the structures that constrain certain liberatory impulses, and thus give us a more realistic way of assessing the possibilities of counter-discursive parody as a mode of social resistance and change.

In this chapter I argue that *How to Make Love to a Negro* is a metaparody that sets itself in and against the discursive genealogy of racialized sexuality. I will define my terms momentarily, but want to emphasize here that what makes Laferrière's novel so controversial and unsettling is that the mode of metaparody highlights a tension between *innovative improvisation* (i.e., a subversive or liberatory impulse) and *discursive constraint* (i.e., the determinations and limits of inherited discourses) in the overdetermined site of African male subjectivity. Because this tension settles neither into clearly postcolonial counter-discursive subversion nor into neo-colonial submission, the book remains troublingly ambivalent: at one and the same time, it exposes and ridicules the discursive system that produces the racist stereotypes which degrade men of African ancestry, and it recycles and recommodifies those very stereotypes in the process.

Vieux is a prime example of the broad-talking man-of-words described by Roger Abrahams. He employs all the rudeness, licence, gregariousness, and super-phallicism Abrahams associates with the tricky broad-talker (151–2), but he wants to be more than a man-of-words at the village crossroads. He wants to be a man-of-letters in metropolitan America; he aspires to literary stardom. Vieux's effusions about his writing process; his dreams for the instant success of the novel he is working on, *Black Cruiser's Paradise*; and his imagined interviews with the media upon its publication all operate as a kind of metafictional commentary on Laferrière's novel, of which he is the pugnaciously self-deprecating protagonist. 'What's it about?' asks Bouba, his room-mate.

'It's a novel.'
'No kidding ... A novel? A real novel?'
'Well ... a short novel. Not a real novel – more like fantasies.'
'Knock it off, man. Leave that number to the disabused, used-up critics who don't have any more juice. A novel's a novel. Short or long. Tell me about it.'
'There's nothing to it. It's about a guy, a black, who lives with a friend who spends all day lying on a couch meditating, reading the Koran, listening to jazz and screwing when it comes along.'
'Does it come along?'
'I suppose it does.'
'Hey, man, I like that, I really do. I like the idea of the guy who doesn't do fuck-all.'
'Of course you do. You're my model.'
'Writers! You can't trust them, they're all bastards!'
Bouba lets loose a big jazz laugh.
'Then what happens?'
'Nothing in particular.' (47)

On the level of narrative sequence, Vieux's disclaimer is accurate: nothing much does happen. *How to Make Love to a Negro* does not deploy plot as its main structuring device. Instead, it focuses on the structuring power of those fantasies that Vieux disparages, but that Bouba reclaims from critical hair-splitting. On the level of narration, the telescoping narrative layers – the African-descended Laferrière's Montreal novel about two men of the African diaspora in Montreal, one of whom is writing a novel about two African men in Montreal – creates a bewildering series of possible reflexivities that are constantly suggested throughout *How to Make Love to a Negro* but never directly affirmed. Through the slippage that results between Vieux and Laferrière, and through their shifty inhabitations of the fantasies that Vieux alludes to above, the novel produces what I am calling, after Gary Saul Morson, 'metaparody.'

Since metaparody is a subtype of parody, let us begin with a discussion of parody in the more general sense. In 'Parody, History, and Metaparody,' Morson outlines three criteria a text or utterance must satisfy in order to qualify as parody: '(1) It must evoke or indicate another utterance ...; (2) it must be, in some respect, antithetical to its target; and (3) the fact that it is intended by its author to have higher semantic authority than the original must be clear' (67). In her study of parody in music, visual art, and architecture, as well as language, Linda Hutcheon names 'trans-contextualization' as the method by which a parody registers its critical distance from the original utterance or work ('Modern' 91). By placing the reference to the original in a different or inappropriate context, parody refracts the original. By reciting it in an unfamiliar setting, it exposes presumptions or investments that might before have remained hidden. I will signal this defamiliarized recitation with the coinage 're-sitation.'

The general pattern of Laferrière's parodic mode is introduced in the second chapter, entitled 'The Great Mandala of the Western World,' where Vieux 're-sites' a serio-farcical history of North American race relations in the trivialized context of sexual experimentation in college co-ed dormitories. Back in the 1970s, he claims, 'America got off on Red.' The dormitories rang with the cries of white women being inseminated by Hurons, Iroquois, and Cheyenne. This situation ended when the Indian men came down with syphilis, and the Establishment, concerned for its own survival, halted the massacre. 'WASP girls received drastic doses of penicillin, and the Indian students were sent back to their respective reservations to finish the genocide begun with the discovery of the Americas' (18). The target discourse here has to do with the taboo of miscegenation and its infraction by liberal 'radicals' during the anti-Establishment movements of the 1960s and 1970s. Its parodic antithesis (and the narrator's intent) is signalled by the sobering reference to racial genocide and colonial expansion. What the radicals thought was the revolution turned out to be sexual tourism among the oppressed.

With the excitement dissipated, Vieux continues, the white women were about to succumb to the boredom of pallid Ivy League boys when 'the violent, potent, incendiary Black Panthers burst upon the campus scene.' The white girls, having almost resigned themselves to 'the medicine-dropper sex of conventional unions,' were liberated to sample the exotic sexuality of black men:

And America loves to fuck exotic. Put black vengeance and white guilt together in the same bed and you had a night to remember! Those blond-haired, pink-cheeked girls practically had to be dragged out of the black dormitories. The Big Nigger from Harlem fucked the stuffing out of the girlfriend of the Razor Blade

King, the whitest, most arrogant racist on campus. The Big Nigger from Harlem's head spun at the prospect of sodomizing the daughter of the slumlord of 125th Street, fucking her for all the repairs her bastard father never made, fornicating for the horrible winter last year when his younger brother died of TB. The Young White Girl gets off too. It's the first time anyone's manifested such high-quality hatred towards her ... If you want to know what nuclear war is all about, put a black man and a white woman in the same bed. (18–19)

It is not the taboo of miscegenation alone that is ridiculed here; nor is it solely the masochistic rebellion of the white liberal female; rather the parody targets a whole discursive system that operates along the border of black and white relations. The parody takes in not only the racist Razor Blade King, not only the Young White Girl, but also the Big Nigger from Harlem who sees the white female's rebellious lust as an opportunity to avenge his family's racial oppression. In other words, the parody inhabits and resituates the larger discursive system of representations that produces these typological figures.

I don't know what age I was. Old enough to recognize the sexual subtext of Dad's euphemisms. Old enough to know that it was the unspeakable that fuelled our conversation. Someone I didn't know had crossed a line, and Dad, with customary delicacy, was telling me about it.

'It was when we first moved to Woliso mission station. You were a baby then, Dan, a toddler. I was station head. The only man on staff. The nurse and teacher had been there some time before your mother and I arrived from mission HQ in Addis Ababa. You wouldn't know either of the two women – teacher and nurse. They both had been placed elsewhere when you were quite young.'

Why was he telling me this story? Had I asked about it? Had something come up in family conversation that required an explanatory story? Why can't I remember the context for this telling? All I have are the bits of story that cling like cobwebs in the corners of memory. I don't even know if the words I'm putting in Dad's mouth are anything like the ones he actually used. But I suppose what matters is what I've retained. The charge, the forbiddenness, the taboo that shot like neon through the grey tube of his words.

One of the two ladies in Dad's story was youngish, I have no idea whether nurse or teacher. Missionsville is populated with a great many single women. As an adolescent, I delighted in their company; they were sparky, lively. It wasn't until I was in my twenties that I began to think back to them and wonder how they dealt with the loneliness. What attracted them to mission work in the first place? Religious conviction? But they could work in church-related jobs in the States or Canada. So why leave home and family to work for the Lord in Africa? Did the restriction of women to supportive roles in North American Evangelicalism make the responsibility and teamwork of the 'foreign field' a much more vital and engaging vocation? What double standard disqualifies women from pulpit and leadership at 'home,' but happily commissions them to these same ministries abroad?

This young woman had formed an 'attachment' with an Ethiopian man in Addis. The possibility of such a romance, apparently, was unthinkable to the men on mission council, so they had posted her down-country to Woliso. Maybe absence would, this time, make the mind grow stronger, and she would see the precipice she had been drawn to. But such was not the case. Somehow a letter arranging a tryst in a hotel in Addis fell into Dad's hands.

It is significant that Vieux's parody re-sites a history. 'Parody is the etiology of utterance,' writes Morson. By targeting a pre-existing discourse and resituating it in a subsequent context, parody's double voice contains (a version of) a discourse's genealogy. In so doing, parody often identifies not only those human subjects involved in the original discourse, but also those who have since been influenced by or responded to it. Morson goes on to explain: 'Parodies are usually described and identified as being of (or 'after') a particular *author* or *work*, but the parodist's principal target may, in fact, be a particular *audience* or *class of readers*. The etiology of utterance includes the pathology of reception' (72). Vieux's parodic history includes both the 'original' prohibition of miscegenation and later subversions (e.g., the white woman's rebellion) of and confrontations (e.g., the Harlem Black Panther figure) with that prohibition. It includes the continuing pathology of the original discourse's reception. Parody's discursive etiology – and the trace of that discourse's effects on its producers, inheritors, and reproducers – makes it a rich site for my study of masculine practices of innovation and their social constraints. In the present instance, Vieux's parodic narrative enables me to trace the discursive history, the constraining genealogy of a predominant stereotype of new-world African masculinity: the black stud. I call the 'original' discourse at the root of this genealogy the 'discourse of racialized sexuality,' a term coined by Abdul JanMohammed.

In his article 'Sexuality on/of the Racial Border,' JanMohammed critiques Foucault's *History of Sexuality* for focusing exclusively on European bourgeois sexuality. 'Whereas bourgeois sexuality is a product of an empiricist, analytic, and proliferating discursivity,' JanMohammed writes, 'racialized sexuality is a product of stereotypic, symbolizing, and condensing discursivity: the former is driven by a will to knowledge, the latter by both a will to conceal its mechanisms and its own will to power' (105–6). To unpack JanMohammed's terms, we need to review briefly the pathological interrelations of discourses of sex and race in colonial and slave histories.

'What is often called the black soul is a white man's artifact,' wrote the Martiniquean psychoanalyst Frantz Fanon in 1952 (16). His book, *Black Skin, White Masks*, initiated a projection/internalization theory that has proved powerfully influential in late twentieth-century discussions of racial, colonial, and sexual politics. Fanon considered racism a process whereby white Europeans projected their own 'darkest' fantasies and fears onto the dark-skinned others whom they encountered in their colonial and imperial quests. The African wore fewer clothes than the European explorer, so it was assumed that the African was closer to nature, less impeded by the constraints of civilization. Logically, then, the African must also be sexually unrestrained. Those impulses of the white person's unconscious which were unacceptable in 'civilized' society were projected onto the black other, who became the bearer of this psychic excrement. Fanon insists that the tragedy of black subjectivity consists in black men's and women's internalization of the degraded representation of themselves proffered by white European culture. They grow up in a world-culture dominated by images of white supremacy – studying history, reading comic books, viewing films filled with white heroes and black beasts (see Paul Hoch's *White Hero Black Beast*). Europeans' projection and Africans' internalization of this mythology, according to Fanon, constitutes the psychopathology of racist colonialism.

Laferrière's metaparody is very aware of the global reach of the pathological discourse of racialized sexuality, and this explains why this novel addresses an international, mass-culture audience rather than limiting its frame of reference to a more localized constituency such as Haitians or francophones, or even African Canadians. Of course, each of these local audiences will find familiar references in the St Denis setting or the Canadian urban milieu of the novel, but Laferrière deliberately generalizes the novel's context. Vieux, for example, never identifies his country of birth and he refers more often to artistic and literary figures from the general African diaspora – from Ella Fitzgerald to the Nation of Islam to James Baldwin – than he does to Haitian or Canadian figures. Indeed, Laferrière likely had the issue of global address in mind when he told his translator not to worry about making the English version. 'It's already in

English,' he assured Homel. 'Just the words are in French' (Homel, 'How to Make Love with the Reader' 10).[2] Clearly, Laferrière's parody is aimed at the larger ideological system of racialized sexuality that finds expression in the various European languages spread through the colonies during the colonial era. Thus, Vieux refers indiscriminately to Caribbean and American slave history, the figures of the Harlem Renaissance, the Koran, American jazz musicians, the lynching of blacks in the United States, and *National Geographic* depictions of Africans. His archive of references includes all cultures influenced by the dispersion of Africans through Europe and America.[3]

In *Black Macho and the Myth of the Superwoman*, African-American critic Michele Wallace explains that the evolution from colonial farm to slave-driven plantation had a significant impact on the emerging discourse of racialized sexuality. Whereas the small-time colonist farmer had needed a partner in labour, the emerging patriarch of the large plantation needed a symbol of his success, a jewel in his showcase. Thus, the wife of the master, who had previously shared the farm work, 'was slowly transformed into an expensive, delicate, impractical pet' (136). But the pet's or jewel's value must be maintained by its inaccessibility, and so the white woman was placed high on a pedestal for all to see and none to touch. This formed no great difficulty for the white master's sexual needs, for he had access to alternative partners, his African women slaves.

The discourse of racialized sexuality derives from the white master's strategy of avoidance. As JanMohammed points out, the white master's violation of the racial border, his rape of the female slave, was that discourse's 'open secret.' 'The need to deny the "open secret" leads, moreover, to the formation of an internally contradictory juridical discourse around racialized sexuality.' For, the white man's desire 'implicitly admits the slave's humanity' and thus 'undermines the foundation of the border – the supposed inhumanity of the black other, her putative ontological alterity' (JanMohammed 104). The pathological discourse of racialized sexuality, then, avoids its open secret by creating a new mythological story: the red-herring story of the black rapist's lust for the white virgin deflects attention away from the hidden deeds of the white master rapist.

What happens, then, to the African man? How does he read himself in relation to the continuously dissembling discourse of racialized sexuality? The woman he lives with in the backyard cabins, with whom he loves and raises children, can be ripped away from him at any time. She is the lowest of slaves. The white Lady, high up in the big house, is a distant and

beautiful ideal. She represents the master's success, the sign of his manhood. In such a situation, who signs the black man's manhood? The
African woman is made to represent servitude in this symbolic mythology. She cannot certify male dignity for the African man. So how does he
represent his masculinity to himself? 'Out of the blackest part of my soul,'
writes Fanon,

> across the zebra striping of my mind, surges this desire to be suddenly *white*.
> I wish to be acknowledged not as *black* but as *white*.
>
> Now ... who but a white woman can do this for me? By loving me she proves
> that I am worthy of white love. I am loved like a white man.
>
> I am a white man. (63)

And so, in the pathological discourse of racialized sexuality, a charge is
created between the poles of the virginal white woman and the paradoxically emasculated and super-potent black man. Across the taboo of their
separation, these two figure for each other the possible sexual fulfilment
from which each has been disqualified.

The missionary woman's letter to the Ethiopian man fell into Dad's hands.
Somehow.

Is it coincidence that one of my incriminating letters fell into Dad's hands
too? Grade nine. I was fifteen years old. Delighted and disturbed at my
emerging sexuality. Full of fantasies and confusion. I speculated in an airform
letter to Phillip, who had recently returned to Adelaide with his family, about
whether our boarding-school's track coach, just married in the States, had, and
I quote myself, 'screwed his wife yet.' Adolescent vulgarity, uncertain of how
to talk about these new bodily possibilities.

The airform sealed with a gluey flap that you licked and stuck down at one
end. The two sides were open on the sealed pocket. I left it on the table to be
mailed when Dad went in to the office. Did he squeeze it end to end so that it
would bow out and read the offending words? By whatever method, his
discovery produced an awkward discussion about the word 'screw' – one in
which he was as much embarrassed as I was. 'Screw,' he told me, 'is a dirty
word, taken from the shape of a pig's penis to make sex vulgar. Would you like
someone to talk of "screwing" your sister or your mother?' No I wouldn't. 'So
don't use the word yourself.' He didn't want sex to become a dirty thing for
me. He wanted me to see it as something lovely and beautiful, not polluted.

All I could think about was his reading my sealed letter. Had he read any
others? Was I under surveillance? Is this what my new sensations meant, that
someone was watching me, and I must be careful?

My sister has heard the story of the missionary woman and her Ethiopian lover more recently than I. She says they had already spent the weekend together in the hotel. There was a quick consultation between Dad and HQ, likely by the public telephone in the little telecommunications building in Woliso town, since there were no lines to our house in the country. The woman was confronted. Told to pack up and stuck on a plane to Canada within a matter of days. End of story. I don't know where she went, whether she protested, whether there was a scene, whether she took it quietly. Nothing. Did it end there? Did she send for her lover to join her wherever it was she went? Did she come back to him on her own terms?

HQ's job was both to care for the woman and to administer the mission's activities in Ethiopia. To get missionaries' visas renewed by the Ethiopian government, the mission administrators needed to distinguish themselves from the various Europeans who had come to Ethiopia during the 'scramble for Africa' – particularly the Italians before and during the occupation of the 1930s who had 'carried on' with Ethiopian women until the invaders' abrupt defeat. What would Ethiopians think of missionaries who had affairs with their parishioners? What kind of Christian witness is that? And what about the woman herself? Did the man really love her, or did the liaison with her write him a ticket to emigration or a North American education? How would he provide a livelihood for her? And what about her vocation as a missionary? Was she going to throw it off for romance? And what about their children? Would they remain Ethiopians? Would they become Canadians? Both? The men at HQ would have had lots of questions to consider before sending her home.

Throughout *How to Make Love to a Negro*, Vieux parodies not just the obvious figures – the white master, the white virgin, the black stud – but also the complex pathology of the discourse of racialized sexuality itself, as well as its analysts. Who is to say that Fanon himself is not included in the swipe Vieux takes at the psychopathology of race? 'Is a psychoanalysis of the black soul possible?' he asks in one rhetorical outburst:

Is it not truly the dark continent? I'm asking you, Dr. Freud. Who can understand the crisis of the black who wants to become white, without losing his roots? Can you name me a single white who one fine day decided he wanted to be black? ... I'd like to be white. Let's say I'm not totally impartial. I'd like to be a better kind of white. A white without the Oedipus complex. (59)

But, of course, Vieux's outburst indicates no deep existential crisis, for, in true picaro form, he switches back and forth throughout the novel from self-despair to self-delight, particularly delight in the sexual opportunities afforded by the mythology of black studsmanship. For, in this novel, which is 'more like fantasies,' *it* does come along. And, in the spirit of the Black Panther from Harlem, Vieux arrogates his philandering by 're-siting' it as colonial revenge. 'This house breathes calm, tranquility, order,' he says during a liaison at one of his girlfriends' well-appointed Outremont family home.

The order of the pillagers of Africa. Britannia rules the waves. Everything here has its place – except me. I'm here for the sole purpose of fucking the daughter. Therefore, I too have my place. I'm here to fuck the daughter of these haughty diplomats who once whacked us with their sticks. I wasn't there at the time of course, but what do you want, history hasn't been good to us, but we can always use it as an aphrodisiac. (76)

Vieux's slippage from his own French colonial history to a British one phases him not at all. The multinational genealogy of the discourse of racialized sexuality is turned simultaneously into an aphrodisiac and an opportunity for colonial vengeance.

This use of sex for racial–colonial revenge, linked with the Black Panther figure above, alludes to another phase in that discourse's genealogy. I stated earlier that the mythical story of the black stud's lust for the white virgin was a disavowing projection of the white master. Rape, says JanMohammed, came to signify the multiple tensions along the racial border (109). If the master's rape of the black woman is the subtext for the discourse of racialized sexuality, the black man's putative rape of the white woman serves as its pretext. The historical narrative of the subtext, bell hooks explains, has gone largely unexamined, having been replaced by the myth of the pretext, the story of the black man's overwhelming desire to violate the white woman. 'It is the story of revenge, rape as the weapon by which black men, the dominated, reverse their circumstance, regain power over white men' (hooks, *Yearning* 58). The power of this discursive pretext over African men's struggle for self-actualization evinced itself in the tendency among leaders of the Black Power movement in the 1970s (particularly after the murders of Martin Luther King, Jr, and Malcolm X) to take on that mythic story with belligerent literalism. If they were feared for the fantasy of their sexual ferocity, then they would utilize whites' own terror by turning up the testosterone in their battle against white domination (Segal 194). Who can forget Eldridge Cleaver's notorious statements in *Soul on Ice*?

Rape was an insurrectionary act. It delighted me that I was defying and tram-
pling upon the white man's law, upon his system of values, and that I was
defiling his women – and this point, I believe, was the most satisfying to me
because I was very resentful over the historical fact of how the white man has
used the black woman. I felt I was getting revenge.

I became a rapist. To refine my technique and *modus operandi*, I started out by
practicing on black girls in the ghetto ... and when I considered myself smooth
enough, I crossed the tracks and sought out white prey. I did this consciously,
deliberately, willfully, methodically. (14)

According to Wallace, the emergence of this extreme machismo among
black men, and the way in which its violence routed itself through black
on its way to white women, destroyed the liberatory potential of the
black movement (69). Focused intently on the masculinist rivalry with
white men, African men disregarded their strongest allies, African women.
In other words, the phallocentric economy of the discourse of racialized
sexuality contained angry black men's liberatory imaginations.

   Even a radical novel such as Richard Wright's *Native Son* remains well
within the terms of the phallocentric discourse established by white men.
In Wright's novel, the protagonist, Bigger Thomas, throws a kind of
rebellious black male power in the face of white domination, but that
rebellion expresses itself through violence towards, first a white woman,
and later his black girlfriend. The novel may hold up a mirror to the
'structure and economy of phallocractic society,' writes JanMohammed,
'but it is unable to escape or undermine them' (111). 'In inventing such a
protagonist,' Wallace observes, 'Wright seemed much more concerned
with making a lasting impression on whites than he was with self-
revelation or self-exploration. The black man could only come to life in
the act of punishing the white man' (55). In this way, she says, the black
revolution of the 1970s played itself out within the terms of the pretext
established by white men during and after slavery. By setting the terms
of what constitutes manhood, claims Wallace, 'by controlling the black
man's notion of what a black man was supposed to be, [America] would
successfully control the very goals of his struggle for "freedom"' (32).

*'Buck Island Sail and Snorkle': it's one of the shore excursions Wendy and I
have selected during the cruise of the eastern Caribbean that her parents have
taken us on. This morning we had a submarine ride. This afternoon, sailing
and snorkelling. About thirty of us tourists lounge about the trampoline of the*

catamaran as we skim over the aquamarine waves towards a small, barren island about a mile out from St Thomas harbour. Buck Island – no trees, bushes, buildings. Nothing. You could walk around it in fifteen minutes. It's a pile of rocks jutting from the Caribbean blue.

'Wasn't there a Buck Island off Tortola too?' a big guy with an Indiana Jones hat and a sunburn asks one of the crew. 'How come there are so many islands called Buck Island?'

'All these Caribbean islands had a Buck Island,' says the tanned crew member who's been videotaping the trip so we can buy mementos of our adventure. 'It's from slavery days. When a buck – ya know, male slave – wouldn't work or was rebellious. Ya see, a slave was worth lots of money. Two or three thousand bucks. Takes more 'n a buck to make a buck, eh? Ha. Ha. Slaves cost more 'n a cow. Ya couldn't kill 'em. Worth too much. So what ya do is, ya take'm out to this island, see, where there ain't nothin'. No water. No shade. No nothin'. And ya dump'm off for four or five days, maybe a week. Then when ya come back, ya ask'm if he's ready to work again. Nice 'n' civilized 'n' everything. Ya don't lose a slave or have ta beat the shit outa'm, and ya git a new slave all ready ta work.'

I'm looking around at the startling blue-green of this water. The golden sunlight. The green hills of St Thomas encircling the harbour where our white Regal Princess is anchored. And there's a Buck Island lying in the heat near each and every Virgin Island.

How do we read Laferrière's parody in relation to these more menacing elements of the discursive history of racialized sexuality? As comedy, Vieux's narration reduces all the human subjects of the discourse of racialized sexuality to stock figures. 'For all intents and purposes,' he informs Miz Bombardier in one of his imagined interviews, 'there are no women in my novel. There are just types. Black men and white women. On the human level, the black man and the white woman do not exist. Chester Himes said they were American inventions, like the hamburger or the drive-in' (111). The ridiculed figures include not only the mythology-duped white liberal female, the medicine-dropper–sexed white male, and the super-potent black stud, but also the Black Power movement, the Nation of Islam (through the many re-sited quotations from the Koran: 'Allah is great and Freud is his prophet,' 15), and black intellectual leadership. (Vieux hopes his writing will put James Baldwin out to pasture, 69.) But it also includes Vieux himself, for example, when he misjudges Miz Cat's taste for 'African' savagery and gets himself expelled from her apartment for asserting that people in his country eat cats; cannibalism, he reflects ruefully, would have been the better myth to get him into her bed (98ff.). And, if the parody includes Vieux, does it not also reach, through the metafictional slippage I mentioned earlier, to Laferrière himself, who may or may not have misjudged his choice of mythologies with a book titled *How to Make Love to a Negro [Without Getting Tired]*?

In fact, it is impossible to locate Laferrière's intentions in the multi-levels of his parody with any certitude. And it is this indeterminacy that makes the novel *meta*parody. 'The audience of a parody,' writes Morson, 'knows for sure with which voice they are expected to agree.' He goes on to define metaparody as that kind of multi-voiced parody which is so designed that readers do not know.

In texts of this type, each voice may be taken to be parodic of the other; readers are invited to entertain each of the resulting contradictory interpretations in potentially endless succession. In this sense, such texts remain fundamentally open, and if readers should choose either interpretation as definitive, they are likely to discover that this choice has been anticipated and is itself the target of parody. (81)

Laferrière's text is not a simple one-to-one parody in which Vieux inhabits and subverts slavery-era stereotypes of black men; it is a metaparody because it re-sites and ridicules not just the original discourse of racialized sexuality, but also its many responses and variations throughout its etiology, including its opponents and resisters. The moment readers settle on a certain interpretation of Vieux's narration, they find themselves anticipated by the text's own metafictional commentary (recall Bouba's dismissal of 'disabused, used-up critics who don't have any more juice,' 47).

The sex scene between Vieux and Miz Literature offers a rich example of the proliferating and shifting vectors of parody at work in Laferrière's text. Vieux introduces the scene in the interracial-sex-as-vengeance-for-colonialism mode: 'Miz Literature climbs into my bed. I put the book down at the foot of the bed, next to the bottle of wine, then bring her down to my level. Europe has paid her debt to Africa' (35). The book and the wine, on one level, represent Vieux's aesthetic and literary sophistication: 'a black with a book denotes the triumph of Judeo-Christian civilization! ... True, Europe did pillage Africa but this black is reading a book' (34). But since the wine also signifies romantic seduction and the book he is reading is by Charles Bukowski, author of such works as *Erections*,

Ejaculations, Exhibitions and General Tales of Ordinary Madness (1972) and
Notes of a Dirty Old Man (1969), Vieux's reading hardly realizes the
sanitizing hopes of the European civilizing mission. So, at this stage, the
reader is led to believe that Vieux's seduction of Miz Literature uses the
tools of a colonial education against the descendants of the colonizers
themselves.

Aware of the salacious energy generated around the eroticized discourse of racialized sexuality, Vieux proceeds to warn the reader, 'If you
think you're about to be served up a hot slice of Miz Literature's sexual
proclivities, think again.' But, in true stand-up–comic fashion, he goes on
to undercut the high moral tone his warning implies with the punch line:
'You've got your choice of porno novels for that. I recommend the
Midnight series.' (37). He and Miz Literature have sex. Afterwards, she
holds him in her arms while he dozes. 'I am her child. An untrusting
child, so hard sometimes. Her black boy. She strokes my forehead. Happy,
gentle, fragile moments. I am more than Black. She is more than White'
(37). Vieux's reverie projects a utopian dream where, through sex, human
differences evaporate and racial antagonism is transcended; yet the phrase
'Her black boy' indicates that such dreams often participate in a nostalgia
for an era when all black men, despite their age, were called 'boys.' And
his next line identifies that era with chilling precision: 'If she had been
giving me a blow job. I would have had my cock lopped off. Oof! Cut
clean off!' (37). The required diminution of the black male links directly
with the black man's lynching and castration in the pathological logic of
racialized sexuality.

Vieux's meditations are interrupted by a sexual storm bursting overhead in the apartment upstairs, where the neighbour Vieux and Bouba
have nicknamed 'Beelzebub' is making love like one of the galloping
'Horsemen of the Apocalypse' (37). Vieux tries to resist his tumescent
response by mentally reviewing the warnings of the Koran, '"Tell me, if
the scourge of Allah overtook you unawares or openly, would any perish
but the transgressors?" (Sura VI, 47)' (37). This latter allusion to the black
consciousness movement of the Nation of Islam cannot help but remind
the reader of Malcolm X's autobiographical confessions of his own dalli-
ances with white women before his conversion to the faith. But Vieux's
lust overrules any religio-racial commitments, and his member continues
to rise. So he turns his thoughts to philosophy and *The Critique of Pure
Reason* by Immanuel Kant, but Kant also 'becomes porno. *The Critique*
gives me a hard-on' (38). The many literary references in this scene (to
Bukowski, Henry Miller, the Bible, the Koran, and Kant), in addition to

the brief commentary on Matisse's painting *Grand Intérieur rouge* that he manages to squeeze in, parody not only the intentions of the civilizing mission, but also the posturing of the young black intellectual himself who makes sexual mileage out of playing his aesthetic cultivation off against the mythology of his barbarity.

Thrown into a trance by the overhead ululations, Miz Literature commences the most exciting fellatio of Vieux's life. 'I knew that as long as she hadn't done it, she wouldn't be completely mine,' he says, launching a direct parody of Fanonian-style analysis of racialized sexuality's hierarchy of subjects:

That's the key in sexual relations between black and white: as long as the woman hasn't done something judged degrading, you can never be sure.

Because in the scale of Western values, white woman is inferior to white man, but superior to black man. That's why she can't get off except with a Negro. It's obvious why: she can go as far as she wants with him. The only true sexual relation is between unequals. White women must give white men pleasure, as black men must for white women. Hence, the myth of the Black stud. Great in bed, yes, but not with his own woman. For she has to dedicate herself to his pleasure. (38)

In the midst of his rapture, however, his cultural memory will not leave off. 'I think of the faraway village where I was born,' he says with a sigh; 'Of all those blacks who travelled to a white man's land in search of riches and came back empty-handed' (38). And then he adds:

I don't know why – it has nothing to do with what's going on – but I think of a song I heard years ago. A guy in my village had a Motown record. The song was about a lynching. The lynching in St. Louis of a young black man. He was hanged then castrated. Why castrated? I'll never stop wondering about that. Why castrated? Can you tell me? Of course no one wants to get involved with a question like that. (38)

Immediately following the parody of the hierarchies of racialized sexuality, a parody which includes in its scope the black-activist scholars such as Fanon, Wallace, and the others I have cited above who delineated such hierarchies, we are brought back to the historical violence to which Vieux's parodic representations refer. His claim that the haunting memory of a song about lynching 'has nothing to do with what's going on' we know is facetious, but how are we to evaluate the disjuncture between the seriousness of his questions and his mockery of those who have tried to address them? Truly, Vieux's 'world has grown rotten with ideologies' (39).

After the simultaneous climax of his meditative soliloquy and the fellatio, Miz Literature proceeds to take her pleasure, riding him like her own version of the apocalyptic horseman. In the throes of orgasm, she growls two completely uncharacteristic epithets: 'Fuck me!' and later, 'You're my man.' Vieux apostrophizes, 'that's the limit! Here I am worrying about that animal Beelzebub who reduces sexuality to the animal level, and all the time he was just screaming out loud what Miz Literature always wanted to say' (40). Bouba has nicknamed Vieux's girlfriend 'Miz Literature' because she is doing a PhD in literature and belongs to a feminist literary club at McGill ('So as not to get Gloria Steinem on our case we say "Miz"' 23). But in the intertextual context of the multiple allusions that run through this scene (and throughout the novel), one cannot help but connect Miz Literature's exclamations to Vieux's literary ambitions. As the young, would-be writer makes love to Miz Literature (a figure much reduced from the traditional literary muse), his passion is ignited underneath, under the influence of, the preceding devilish amours upstairs. This young reader of the virulent writers of male eroticism (Bukowski and Miller in this scene, but elsewhere Chester Himes, James Baldwin, and Richard Wright) hears Miz Literature shout his mastery: 'You're my man ... I want to be yours' (40). In eclipsing these older writers, he congratulates himself that he has enabled her to say what she has always wanted to say. In this parodic scenario, the young black writer puts the entire older generation 'out to pasture' (69). The hyperbole of Vieux's fantasized success mocks the grandeur of his ambitions.

How, then, do we sort through such a mass of postures, the erotic energy, the tragicomedy, the anger and sheer exuberance of such chaotic metaparody? As metaparody, Laferrière's text does not settle into a simple oppositional relationship with the discourse of racialized sexuality; instead, it inhabits and mimics a whole array of contradictory positions and utterances throughout that discourse's etiology. Neither does the target discourse, in all of its complexities, remain the passive object of parody; rather, it actively complicates the metaparody with what Mikhail Bakhtin, in *Problems of Dostoevsky's Poetics*, calls 'hidden polemic.' 'When parody senses a fundamental resistance, a certain strength and depth to the parodied words of the other,' writes Bakhtin, 'the parody becomes complicated by tones of hidden polemic ... The parodied discourse rings out more actively, exerts a counterforce against the author's intentions.

There takes place an internal dialogization of the parodistic discourse' (198). When the parody registers an awareness of its target's trenchancy, it loses its composure. It becomes a hidden polemic which is 'agitated, internally undecided and two-faced' (198); at the same time that it makes 'digs' at the other's speech, and employs barbed words and phrases, it also tries to anticipate the other's responses: an 'element of response and anticipation penetrates deeply inside [this] intensely dialogic discourse' (197).

The anxiety of hidden polemic appears throughout *How to Make Love to a Negro* in Vieux's many comments about his novel that double as metafictional commentary on Laferrière's text. They work as a defensive strategy (the best defence is a strong offence) which allows Laferrière to anticipate and manipulate the responses to his novel; and, since they emerge from Vieux's mouth, they allow Laferrière to avoid the appearance of stooping to self-defence. Literally, these passages are, in good Bakhtinian fashion, two-faced and double-voiced. Vieux's imagined interview with Miz Bombardier after the publication of his novel is the most extended example of these metafictional moments. In the passages that lead up to the interview, we are introduced to various reviews of Vieux's book in the Montreal papers. All the reviewers' names happen to be those of real-life review writers in Montreal. Jean-Ethier Blais is reported to have written: 'If what this young man says is true, then we must conclude that our brand of liberalism is the most incredible hogwash that ever existed (something I've always suspected)' (109). Réginald Martel is rumoured to have said that 'the book is the first in a search for new literary forms,' while Gilles Marcotte is supposed to have called the book 'a filter of lucidity through which violence and eroticism of the most explicit sort acquire a certain purity' (110). (In their separate reviews of Laferrière's novel, Martel and Marcotte both chuckle at encountering themselves in Vieux's narration.)

In Vieux's conversation with Miz Bombardier – herself a caricature of the real-life talk-show host Denise Bombardier – Laferrière has the opportunity to anticipate a whole range of objections to his novel. 'I read your book and I laughed,' begins Miz Bombardier, 'but it seems to me you don't like women.' 'Negroes too,' quips Vieux, effectively derailing her feminist opening (110). And, just to make sure that she cannot then label him an intraracial misanthropist too, he adds: 'there are no women in my novel. There are just types ... On the human level, the black man and the white woman do not exist' (111). So he is making fun, but not of real people. The people do not exist, just the types. But the interviewer will not settle for such a disclaimer. Observing the close similarity between his narrator and himself, she cannot resist asking him, 'Did all those things really happen to you? I ask because, in your real life, you live in the same neighbourhood, off the Carré St. Louis. You live with a friend and you're a writer, like your narrator' (111). 'Pure coincidence,' Vieux replies, sidestepping again for himself as well as his author any definite relation between himself and the 'types' represented in his text. So Miz Bombardier tries a different tack: 'Your novel is the first portrait of Montreal from the pen of a black writer. Admit that you were a bit harsh.' 'The ones in my novel never stop complaining,' Vieux protests. 'Yes,' she replies, 'but the tempo is different. They're tougher, sharper, more pugnacious. They're complainers, but they know how to hit back. Humour is their most effective weapon.' She said it, saving Vieux or Laferrière the trouble of offering the cliché. 'That's the way life is,' Vieux philosophizes. 'You parry the blows and you strike back' (111) – identifying, perhaps more precisely than anywhere else in this novel, the reactive paradigm of its metaparodic form and the defensive struggle of its hidden polemic.

'Their weapons are quite different,' pursues Miz Bombardier. 'Generally, blacks appeal to Africa, but your characters never do. Why not?' Despite the fact that they appear to be Moslems, Vieux explains, 'their culture is totally European. Allah is great, but Freud is their prophet' (111). Vieux here anticipates criticism from black activists who would object to his glib sell-out to Euro-American cultural domination. He is not interested in a nativist, return-to-Africa politics. He seems happy to exploit the opportunities of life in the contemporary African diaspora. And he goes on deliberately to antagonize those who lobby for black solidarity. 'When a black man and a white woman meet, the lie is the predominant feature,' he says. He launches into an anecdote about an incident in a bar in which he heard an African acquaintance feeding a white woman the barbaric-savage pick-up line.

He was all but telling her he was a cannibal, fresh out of the bush, that his father was the big medicine-man in his village. The whole mythology. I watched the girl: she was nodding, in total ecstasy at finding a real bushman, homo primitivus, the Negro according to *National Geographic*, Rousseau and Company. I know the guy and I know he's not from the bush. He's from Abidjan, one of Africa's great cities. He lived in Denmark and Holland for quite a while before coming to Montreal. He's an urban man, a virtual European. But he'd never admit that to a white girl for all the ivory in the world. In the white man's eyes, he wants to be a Westerner; but with a white woman, Africa serves as his supernumerary sex. (112)

Vieux divulges the black pick-up artist's lie, but we should recall that he himself has used it to some degree of success in his own fantasized adventures. 'How have blacks reacted to your book?' Miz Bombardier's interrogative bombardment continues. 'They want to lynch me,' he replies, choosing his punishments carefully. 'Because I let the cat out of the bag ... They say I've sold out, that I'm playing the white man's game, that my book is no good and the only reason it was published was because whites need a black man around to carry on and give whites a clear conscience' (112–13). 'Is that your opinion?' she asks, trying to get some solid ground under the interview. 'I have no opinion,' says Vieux on behalf of his metaparodist author, 'I make no statements without consulting my lawyer – unless they're about writing. That's not what the Moral Majority thinks. They say my book is the kind of trash that pollutes the reader, whose only goal is to debase the white race by attacking its most sacred object: Woman. You see, I've hit the jackpot' (113). 'Doesn't that bother you?' interjects Miz Bombardier. 'Your black readers' opinion'? And Vieux comes back with this summation of Laferrière's non-position in this novel: 'To be a traitor is every writer's destiny. I hope that's the first cliché in this interview' (113). The many shifts and reversals, the braggadocio and self-deprecation of this passage remind us of Morson's warning that if readers of metaparody 'should choose [any] interpretation as definitive, they are likely to discover that this choice has been anticipated and is itself the target of parody' (81).

How then are we to understand this traitorous re-sitation of the de-meaning discourse of racialized sexuality and its stereotypes? As I have shown above, it accomplishes an exposure of that discourse's history of avoidance and displacement. By so doing, Laferrière's metaparody works what critic of postcolonial literature Helen Tiffin would call a counter-discursive strategy. In re-siting the discursive genealogy of racialized sexuality, *How to Make Love to a Negro* takes some of the subversive steps Tiffin identifies: 'Post-colonial counter-discursive strategies involve a mapping of the dominant discourse, a reading and exposing of its underlying assumptions, and the dis/mantling of these assumptions from the cross-cultural standpoint of the imperially subjectified "local." ('Post-Colonial' 23). But, as Tiffin observes, since 'post-colonial cultures are inevitably hybridised ... [d]ecolonization is process, not arrival; it invokes an ongoing dialectic between hegemonic centrist systems and peripheral subversion of them' (17). She goes on to explain:

Post-colonial literatures/cultures are thus constituted in counter-discursive rather than homologous practices, and they offer 'fields' of counter-discursive strategies to the dominant discourse. The operation of post-colonial counter-discourse is dynamic, not static: it does not seek to subvert the dominant with a view to taking its place, but to, in Wilson Harris's formulation, evolve textual strategies which continually 'consume' their *own* biases' at the same time as they expose and erode those of the dominant discourse. (18)

Applying her theory to Samuel Selvon's *Moses Ascending*, whose protagonist-narrator performs a hyperbolic black studsmanship similar to Vieux's, Tiffin claims that 'Selvon destabilises the dominant discourse through exposure of its strategies and offers a Trinidadian/Caribbean post-colonial counter-discourse which is perpetually conscious of its own ideologically constructed position and speaks ironically from within it' (27). Anti-colonial, anti-racist readings of Laferrière's novel might interpret it, then, as an excellent example of this implicated but subversive kind of counter-discursive postcolonial writing.

However, other critics are not so optimistic about the subversive effects of counter-discursive or parodic discourses, especially when these discourses take up the overdetermined discourse of racialized sexuality. One of the remarkable distinctions about this discourse, contend these critics, is its power to contain potential dissidents. Endlessly elaborated over the last century and a half, it resembles a vast oil spill: sodden, sticky, heavy. If you enter into its contaminated landscape, you will find it very difficult to traverse, almost impossible to escape. For this reason, some critics committed to racial and postcolonial liberation think it best not to wander heedlessly into its terrain. In reference to the deployment of the metaphor of rape in contemporary critiques of colonialism in India, Sara Suleri has written that 'the anxieties of empire are only obscured by a critically unquestioning recuperation of the metaphor of rape'; indeed, this trope for the act of imperialism 'has been in currency too long for it to remain at all critically liberating' (*Rhetoric of English India* 16–17).[4] In specific reference to the eroticized myth of the black man and the white woman, African-American cultural critic Michael Dyson insists that even subversive attempts to deploy the myth often serve to 'reinforce pernicious stereotypes about black men, increasing the already rampant sociosexual fear that continues to exist between black men and white women, and especially in the minds of many white men' (178).

In his discussion of the subversive function of the broad-talker's scandalous performances in Creole cultures, Abrahams asserts that, while the broad-talker provides a 'channel for anti-social community motives' (58), the feeling of 'liberation is short-lived, for no real social transformation occurs in such playful occasions' (75). We need to remind ourselves, as Peter Stallybrass and Allon White put it in *The Politics and Poetics of Transgression*, that 'it would be wrong to associate the exhilarating sense of freedom which transgression affords with any necessary or automatic political progressiveness' (201). The social function of Laferrière's metaparody depends upon whom it circulates among and their positions relative to one another in social power and authority. No utterance, no matter how transgressive in tone or intention, 'can be intrinsically or essentially subversive,' writes Jonathan Dollimore.

Likewise the mere thinking of a radical idea is not what makes it subversive: typically it is the context of its articulation: to whom, how many and in what circumstances; one might go further and suggest that not only does the idea have to be conveyed, it has also actually to be used to refuse authority *or* be seen by authority as capable and likely of being so used. (13)

Among whom, we might then ask ourselves, does Laferrière's parodic discourse circulate, and in what context, under what conditions?

We can address these questions on two levels. First, the discourse circulates on the diegetic level, that is, within the narrative of the parody itself, among the four typological figures of racialized sexuality's discourse: black and white men and women. Second, the discourse circulates in the complex economy of the publication and reception of the novel itself. In Laferrière's case that economy is particularly complicated because it involves the translation of a French text into English by a Montreal-based translator for a Toronto-based publisher; and that text parodies a discourse elaborated largely in American terms.

Freud throws useful light, I think, on the circulation of Laferrière's parodic comedy on the first level, on the level of the parody's diegesis. A sexually aggressive joke, Freud writes in *Jokes and Their Relation to the Unconscious*,

calls for three people: in addition to the one who makes the joke, there must be a second who is taken as the object of the hostile or sexual aggressiveness, and a third in whom the joke's aim of producing pleasure is fulfilled ... When the first person finds his libidinal impulse inhibited by the woman, he develops a hostile trend against that second person and calls on the originally interfering third person as his ally. Through the first person's smutty speech the woman is exposed before the third, who, as listener, has now been bribed by the effortless satisfaction of his own libido. (100)

The male teller and listener and the silent woman form a triangular configuration identical to the homosocial economy identified by Eve Kosofsky Sedgwick according to which the bonds between men are expressed through a traffic in women. Drawing on ideas from Claude Lévi-Strauss and Gayle Rubin, Sedgwick describes phallocentric hetero-sexuality as an economy in which 'the use of women as exchangeable, perhaps symbolic, property [serves] the primary purpose of cementing the bonds of men with men' (*Between Men* 25–6).

It happened while I was presenting an earlier version of this chapter as a conference paper in Ottawa. I was doing my best in front of the twenty-or-so scholars from across Canada assembled in a classroom at Carleton University. Renée, who was from McGill University and was hosting the session, had introduced herself and the panel of speakers, and I was on deck. I had met her at a previous conference and was glad to have a friend in the room. Standing at the podium in my summer-weight green cotton suit and my luxurious wine-coloured tapestry shirt, I was trying my hardest.

I came to the part in my discussion of Laferrière where I mention that white 'girls' from McGill are primary targets of his parody. I don't know where the impulse came from. Had I been premeditating it somewhere in my uncon-scious? Or was it completely spontaneous? At the mention of 'McGill girls,' I looked up and glanced significantly at Renée. It just occurred to me then that she was a white woman student at McGill, the very group Laferrière was hitting on! My meaningful glance brought a laugh. I got what I wanted. A contact with my audience, a sense that they were with me, confirmation that they were keeping up.

But I got it at Renée's expense.

She told me later when I was grovelling through my apology that my glance was the closest thing Daniel Coleman had to a leer. She also said that she herself laughed nervously.

So here it is. In the middle of a paper about the exchange of women between men in the discourse of sexual humour, I pull off an eye-glance joke at my friend's expense.

Okay, so I'm nervous. I'm standing up there in my finery, looking out at a roomful of Canadian scholars. Some of their names appear in the bibliography of the paper I'm presenting. Why do I decide that it's worth making Renée a

*target of my humour to get their approval? Especially when I don't know her
well enough to know whether or not it'll embarrass her, even offend her? When
I'm tense like that, I'm halfway into something before I've even thought about it.*

*And how did I know without premeditation that the joke would work? What
structure, what habit, what knowledge of how to create humour, how to elicit
an audience's response, informed me? What need in me decided that their
laughter was more important than Renée's comfort?*

*I would not have thought, to draw a contrast, to level that kind of glance at
George Elliott Clarke, an African-Canadian scholar and poet who was also in the
room. Laferrière pillories gifted young black writers. But I would never have
glanced at George with the same significant leer. If I had, no one would have
laughed (except perhaps George himself). So why was it so easy to glance at
Renée? Why did it bring the laughter I was playing for, even from female
members of the audience?*

Clearly, the rivalry/attachment between white and black men in *How
to Make Love to a Negro* traffics in women. Sex with the daughter of the
white colonist enacts Vieux's revenge upon the white father. And, as
Sedgwick suggests, this exchange need not always be antagonistic. Sometimes, white and black men construct a solidarity among themselves in
their need to maintain their ascendancy over women. This is what occurs
in the scene where the white union man steps in to defend Vieux from the
skin-head woman's verbal attack in the post office. The woman had
observed Vieux 'cruising' another woman in the line ahead of him, and,
when she gives him a piece of her mind, a middle-aged union-looking
man steps in to say, 'You can't be prejudiced ... lots of guys hassle women
and not all of them are black ... Sure, coming onto a woman is degrading
for her, but it's an innocent game compared to the slave trade' (44).
Defending themselves against the perceived threat of the lesbian – Vieux
is sure she must be a lesbian – who might beat them at their own game,
the black and white man band together.

But Freud's and Sedgwick's models both assume a triangular configuration of three characters, whereas Laferrière's model, following the
typology of racialized sexuality, deploys four. It is not difficult to understand the relationship between black and white men in the novel according to the homosocial paradigm, but how do the two women figures fit
in? Are they both lumped together into the category of the silenced
woman who is the object of male exchange? Certainly, the black woman
is a silent figure in Laferrière's text. How are we to interpret Vieux's

silence about her? Why do black women play no significant roles in this text? Are they too sacred to be submitted to parody? Or are they so insignificant in Vieux/Laferrière's paradigm that they merit no attention? How, for that matter, should we understand the role of the white woman? Is she merely an object of exchange in the male libidinal economy? Could it not be that Laferrière's text, in broaching the taboo of miscegenation, liberates the white woman's desire from the white patriarch's discourse that had confined her to the pedestal of virginity? Is there no possibility that Laferrière's satire does in fact enable a conspiracy between black man and white woman against the prohibitions of the white man?[5]

Freud wrote that 'every joke calls for a public of its own and laughing at the same jokes is evidence of far-reaching psychical conformity' (151; see also Fine, 'Obscene Joking Across Cultures' 134). To participate in the humorous mockery of *How to Make Love to a Negro*, then, you have to identify yourself within the economy its parody recites; you have to share in its far-reaching psychical conformity. Vieux makes a joke of the 'great roulette wheel of the flesh' that forms 'The Great Mandala of the Western World'; it turns through the cycle of the coloured races: 'Red, Black, Yellow. Black, Yellow, Red. Yellow, Red, Black' (19); what he does not point out is that the wheel revolves around the hub of white desire. The problem rises out of the nature of parody itself: to produce its satire, it reproduces the original. In the present case, the parody recites the phallocentric economy of the discourse of racialized sexuality. And it is often hard to tell in its various performances whether the parody repeals or repeats the original.

I have deliberately returned to Judith Butler's terminology here because, as I said at the start of this chapter, I think Laferrière's text provides a significant opportunity to re-evaluate Butler's theory of the destabilizing potential of performative parody, subversive repetition. Perhaps, as suggested above, Laferrière's metaparody does liberate the sexual subjectivities of black men and white women, but its dismissal of the subjectivity of the black woman participates in the silencing of the primary victim of the original discourse. In other words, the performance that may generate subversion or liberation on one axis may recaptivate and recuperate in another. On the diegetic level of the parody itself, Laferrière's text circulates among its four major figures in such a way that it replicates the original allegory's suppression of the African woman.

But we can also evaluate the effects of Laferrière's metaparody on the level of the novel's publication and reception. Just as Vieux dreamed, a novel about white women and black men did turn out to be a jackpot (113). *Comment faire l'amour avec un Nègre sans se fatiguer* made Laferrière a Montreal celebrity, where he became a regular on talk shows (including Denise Bombardier's) and literary interviews. Within two years his novel was translated by a white man into *How to Make Love to a Negro* for English audiences, and in another two years it was made into a feature film that enjoyed wide circulation (a friend of mine found it in a video shop in Tokyo, in French with Japanese subtitles). Laferrière went from an underclass life in St Denis to being a lionized jet-setter who now divides his time between Miami and Montreal (see Demers's author profile). Most early (white) reviewers read with the comic grain of the novel, interpreting it as a social satire that contains serious protest against systemic racism and colonialism. 'In this book,' Laferrière declared in an interview with Homel, 'I'm interested in resistance between cultures ... It's the minority question seen in a new light' (38). By and large, Canadian reviewers have read him on his own terms.[6] *How to Make Love to a Negro* has given Laferrière what Vieux said he wanted: fame and fortune. He has read the Canadian public accurately; there is indeed a market for parodies of the erotically charged discourse of racialized sexuality.

Laferrière has capitalized upon a consumer desire. But there are problems once again, for his eroticized parody works on the basis of his hyperbolic performance of the black stud of racialized sexuality. It repeats what African-American sociologist Calvin Hernton, in *Sex and Racism in America* (1965), calls a kind of self-exploitation: 'many blacks exploit the exploitable. In the process, the blacks exploit themselves. They parade and display their Negroness. No, no, it is the *nigger* in them that they display, the stereotype' (76). Not only does Vieux's parody repeat the silencing of the African woman, it also reiterates the sexualization – the phallicization – of the African man. Hernton predicted that such a reiteration would continue, for, he wrote, the 'racism of sex in America ... stems from and is maintained by an economic-political-social system that has made it and still makes it *profitable* for the majority of white Americans' (178–9). What Laferrière's socio-economic success masks is that he has made a commodity of the metaparody itself. 'Should we not be suspicious of the way in which white culture's fascination with black masculinity manifests itself?' asks bell hooks in her critique of images of black males purveyed in contemporary rap music, videos, and movies. 'Commodification of blackness that makes phallocentric black masculinity marketable makes the realm of cultural politics a propagandistic site where black people are rewarded materially for reactionary thinking about gender.' Such representations fit readily into the political agendas of white supremacists, she adds, who evoke exactly these images in their bid for public support for a genocidal assault on black men (*Black Looks* 109). The novel's astounding success, then, points towards the discomfiting possibility that, regardless of its potential for parodic subversion, the economy in which it is consumed will contain its transgressive potential. It is no wonder, therefore, that black writers and critics have been less than enthusiastic about Laferrière's novel. In his essay on the implications of Laferrière's reception in mainstream literary institutions in Canada, Cameron Bailey notes that the 'novel's glibness, its complete exclusion of black women and, above all, ... the sense that its satire is played mainly to white male readers' have given African Canadians plenty of cause for discomfort (87).

But who is the readership implied by Laferrière's text? The novel's artistic and literary references identify an audience as conversant in American literature, European philosophy, jazz discography, and Hollywood cinema as in the situation of immigrants of African descent in Montreal. Indeed, despite the fact that *How to Make Love to a Negro* makes strategic use of the class register of Montreal neighbourhoods such as Westmount, Outremont, and St Denis, and despite the way the ridicule of English-speaking McGill women plays to a *péquiste* anglophobia, the novel is much more concerned with the global than it is with the local. It is more a novel about the figure of the black man in generalized cosmopolitan culture than it is about, say, French-speaking Haitians in Montreal. In this sense, it is a novel of diaspora.

Shirley Geok-Lin Lim distinguishes diasporic from immigrant thematics by noting that, whereas immigration is oriented towards assimilation into the nation, diaspora 'denotes the condition of being deprived of the affiliation of the nation' (297). Ien Ang adapts Benedict Anderson's formulation of the nation as an imagined community to the concept of diaspora by asserting that diasporas imagine themselves as a dispersed communities: 'Diasporas are people, creating imagined communities whose blurred and fluctuating boundaries are sustained by real and/or symbolic ties to some original "homeland"' (5). I would suggest that Laferrière's parody of the discourse of racialized sexuality constitutes a dissident retracing of the pathology that has come to dominate the symbolic ties members of the African diaspora have to the lost homeland.

The diasporic address of the novel explains why its parody does not settle clearly on specifically Canadian situations. Had Laferrière wanted, for example, to mount an attack on Canadian racism, he could have garnered plenty of literary allies among African-Canadian writers such as Austin Clarke, M. Nourbese Philip, and Dionne Brand, not to mention fellow Haitian-born Montrealers such as Emile Ollivier and Joel Des Rosiers. The novel is saturated with allusions to Chester Himes, James Baldwin, John Coltraine, Charlie Parker, Ella Fitzgerald, and Tina Turner; never once does it mention an African-Canadian figure, not even Oscar Peterson or Oliver Jones, black jazz greats who hail from Vieux's adopted home town. The novel does not address Canada in any overt fashion; nor does it directly address Quebec.[7] Perhaps, the diasporic purview also explains why so little is made of the French–English conflict that runs throughout Quebec's political history. Aside from the targeting of McGill girls as daughters of the white Anglo dominant class, the novel does not elaborate the kind of analogy between the oppression of Africans and that of Québécoises developed in Pierre Vallières's *Nègres blancs d'Amérique* (1968).

This does not mean that Canadians cannot be included in the scope of Laferrière's metaparody. Perhaps one vector of the parody targets Canadians' belief in their distinction from the mass culture represented by America. 'I want America,' Vieux quips. 'Not one iota less. With her Radio City girls, her buildings, her automobiles, her enormous waste – even her bureaucracy. I want it all ... America is a totality' (27). Does one vector of the metaparody target Canadians' denial of our American envy? And does another expose our hunger for images of the rapaciously sexed black stud, while yet another pillories our tendency to project such objectionable tastes onto brash Americans? Perhaps Laferrière wants to expose the smug Canadian hypocrisy that dismisses racism as a phenomenon unique to populations south of the forty-ninth parallel. Whatever his intentions, the popularity of this novel in both its French and its English versions, despite its diasporic address, raises disturbing questions about the commodification of African male sexuality in Canadian society. As Bailey puts it, 'For better or worse, Laferrière has learned the compromised skill of how to make love to a nation – with your eyes open' (87).

The question of the success or failure of Laferrière's metaparody to effect a transgression or intervention in discourses of racism or sexism remains, I believe, unresolvable. The novel operates on too many levels, behind too many screens of evasion and self-protection, to settle comfortably into any single interpretive track. What the novel does demonstrate with remarkable clarity, however, is the tenacity with which a social discourse such as racialized sexuality continues to exercise powerful constraints upon the representations and performances of human beings. And *How to Make Love to a Negro* does do the innovative, counter-discursive work Tiffin identifies; it does map a dominant and oppressive discourse's etiology, and it does expose the illogic and avoidance underlying that discourse. In her discussion of the similar double-voiced narrative mode of irony, Hutcheon claims that 'irony is ... a way of resisting and yet acknowledging the power of the dominant.' We might think of Laferrière's metaparody when she writes that 'irony allows a text to work within the constraints of the dominant while foregrounding those constraints as *constraints* and thus undermining their power' (*Splitting* 81). Certainly, *How to Make Love to a Negro* foregrounds the constraints of the dominant. One wonders, however, how far that foregrounding goes towards effective subversion. The phallic stereotype of the black stud persists even in the site of transgression, for, to borrow words from 'Black Machismo,' a poem by African-American gay writer Essex Hemphill,

> it drags behind him,
> a heavy, obtuse thing,
> his balls and chains
> clattering, making
> so much noise
> I cannot hear him
> even if I want to listen. (130)

Moreover, the *commercial* success of Laferrière's parody indicates how the persistence of a social discourse such as racialized sexuality is financed and reproduced within an economy that makes a traffic of that discourse. 'It is the book of a traitor!' shouts the Nigerian cab driver in yet another of Laferrière's metafictional commentaries, this time in his sequel, *Why Must a Black Writer Write About Sex* (1994). 'All writers are traitors,' replies the Laferrière in the story. 'The competition is fierce ... When you're not a genius, strip-tease is the only thing that'll bring in the customers.' 'Why do you keep exploiting these clichés about blacks?' demands the cab driver. 'I don't want to destroy America,' Laferrière retorts. 'I just want my piece of the pie' (63–7; rptd. from 'Why Must a Negro Writer Always Be Political?'). Laferrière's troubling metaparody re-sites the economy that trades in the exoticism of black studsmanship in such a way that it hands him personally a generous slice of that pie.

But because the novel is metaparody, one can never be sure where to find Laferrière himself among his parodic voices. This radical indeterminacy is clearly evident in George Elliott Clarke's distinction between the voices of Vieux, the narrator, and Laferrière, the author. 'Despite his [black] nationalist moods ... Vieux is an avowed individualist,' Clarke writes. 'The novel concludes, not with a communal call to arms, but with a truly American-style declaration of pragmatic self-interest' (69). In contrast, Clarke points out that 'Laferrière mouths the credos of individualism, but lobs black nationalist barbs at North American society' (72). This is a finely nuanced distinction, and it is one that puts its finger on the question at the heart of this novel: which voice are we most likely to hear?

3

Resisting Heroics:
Male Disidentification in Neil
Bissoondath's *A Casual Brutality*

If Joshua and Vieux consciously engage with certain social codes of masculinity, Dr Rajnath Ramsingh, the narrator of Neil Bissoondath's first novel, *A Casual Brutality*, tries to resist socially prescribed perform-ances. Whereas Joshua and Vieux overperform different kinds of man-hood in the face of alienating, and even hostile, social circumstances, Raj underperforms his masculinity. Whereas their parodic performances are given to hyperbole, his actions tend to a sincere variety of understate-ment. Bissoondath's novel, then, presents a very different kind of mascu-linity from those with which I began this study. In the previous two chapters, I traced two types of assertive masculinity that respond to disenfranchisement by trying to bend dominant masculine ideologies to their own ends. In this chapter, I examine a retiring masculinity: one which distances itself from the prescribed rituals of aggressive masculine performance, one which does not want to participate in the competition in the first place.

A Casual Brutality tells a sad story. Narrated through Raj's reflections, the novel opens at the story's end with the young doctor in transit back to Canada upon the failure of all his efforts in the fictional island of Casaquemada. After years in Toronto, where he trained in medicine, opened a practice, married, and started a family, he moves back to his Caribbean birthplace with his Canadian wife, Jan, and their son, Rohan. But the return is plagued with difficulties from the start. Jan does not like Casaquemada; their marriage begins to crumble; Raj's family is not the supportive unit he had imagined; and the political situation on the island slides quickly into frustrated violence when the multinational oil compa-nies that had fuelled a brief era of prosperity begin to curtail their investments. In one of the moments of casual brutality that give the novel its name, Jan and Rohan are murdered. The doctor has been unable to heal any of the dis-ease around him, let alone in himself, and in the end he retreats to Toronto in despair at his utter failure. He has performed no noble acts, displayed no remarkable courage, done nothing that would give him tragic dignity. Raj's version of the 'been-to' narrative – the story of the postcolonial subject who has been to an imperial metropolis and returned to a troubled relationship with his or her birthplace (see William Lawson) – belies the kind of nostalgia I noted earlier in Montgomery's gesture to the certitudes of his pre-migration home. Raj's attempt to pass back through the lens of cross-cultural refraction meets only with loss, helplessness, regret.

So what can we gain from such a bleak narrative? David Richards finds that Bissoondath's writing 'constantly reaches for the negative form. Not what is, but what is not: denial, negation, the mirror's reflection,' and this makes Richards ask whether 'Bissoondath's work [is] an exercise in negation' and if it is 'possible for fiction to emanate from a place which is always a "not"' (56). I think it is. I will address Richards's question, however, by reframing the concerns he raises in reference to postmodern and postcolonial aesthetics of dislocation and disjuncture within a meditation upon passive masculinity.

I am interested in Raj's passivity because his reluctance to identify himself with images of dominant masculinity is relevant to the experiences of many contemporary, middle-class men whose sensibilities have been trained in an era of multiculturalism, feminism, anti-racism, gay and lesbian politics, and anti-imperialism.[1] The retiring male, the man who declines various performances of domination, raises important questions about the possibility of passive resistance. Is it possible for a man to resist the discourses of phallocentrism or patriarchy or neo-imperialism simply by refusing to repeat their prescribed performances? Is it possible to exempt oneself from the cycle of compulsory recitation? Butler claims that social practices are in fact affected, even altered over time, when people *fail* to repeat the socially regulated script. Is failure, then, a kind of momentary exemption? If the vagaries of certain people's histories render them unable to perform according to society's gender regulations, or if their ex-centric, refracted experience excludes them from full participation in a dominant set of social codes, are they excused from the performative requirement? Is the *via negativa* of failure, of grief, of what Michel Pêcheux terms 'disidentification' – that is, the inability to either espouse or reject a given ideology's subject position – a possible mode of opposition or resistance?

I raise these questions here because Raj as narrator presents himself as a version of what Kaja Silverman in another context has identified as the 'male subject of historical trauma.' Such a subject is the product, she explains, of 'any historical event, whether socially engineered or of natural occurrence, which brings a large group of male subjects into such an intimate relation with lack that they are at least for the moment unable to sustain an imaginary relation with the phallus, and so withdraw their belief from the dominant fiction' (55). Raj sees himself as subject to trauma, historical and continuing. Dreadful circumstances have overpowered him, and he presents himself as a failed man. This chapter explores the effects of the passive man's evasion of dominant forms of masculinity. It studies what we might call the 'anti-performance' of the man who accepts that the power to determine his own life has been taken out of his hands.

Close to the end of the novel, Raj looks down at his hands, which are resting on his lap. The scene is one of the last that takes place on the island. He sits in his car, parked on the grounds of a long-abandoned British colonial fort. Nearby, two ancient, black cannons overlook the Lopez city harbour. Columbus paused here briefly in his quest for India almost five hundred years earlier. However, Raj, a descendant of indentured Indian labourers brought to the West Indies by the British after 1838 to replace recently emancipated African slaves, has not come to this abandoned place to contemplate the colonial past; he's come to grieve the murders of Jan and Rohan. But colonial history and his present anguish are closely linked, for the traumas of colonial history spawned the sociopolitical conditions for the novel's contemporary casual brutality. 'I liked my hands,' he thinks to himself,

had always liked them; they were not weak, were hands of finesse, formed for fine work. One of my professors, watching me carve my cadaver, had called them the hands of a surgeon. 'Or of a pianist,' he had said, walking away, dissatisfied with my wielding of the scalpel. But now, looking at them lying palm downward, I thought them absurd, ineffectual. They had helped save no one, had soothed much simple distress, had prolonged the inevitable with some, had gestured feebly or sat helpless before others. My wife, my son, my grandfather, even my pet project: they had all proved, in the end, to have been beyond my reach. And these hands, instruments of apparent possibility, had shown themselves in the end to be finely wrought trappings fashioned solely for display, like handsome theatrical props of papier-mâché. (364)

Raj's hands have disappointed him. He used to like the vital feeling they gave him. But they have failed in every way. When protection was needed, they did not protect. When a cure was needed, they procured nothing. They are empty, as he himself is empty. 'Trappings,' he calls them, 'solely for display.' They are 'theatrical props' of a failed performance. Equipped with the hands of a physician, he stood helplessly by while all around him was death: the literal deaths of his wife, his son, his grandfather; and the metaphorical deaths of his identification with his family, his belief in the political and social potential of his island birthplace, and his own attempt to find a home by returning to the island. His are the hands of an impotent man, of an emasculated male.

March 1992. Five of us from the University of Alberta have driven to Vancouver for a conference on postcolonial theory. Saturday afternoon and we're at one of the most enthusiastically attended sessions: Linda Hutcheon on irony in postcolonial contexts. She focuses her talk on the fiasco at the Royal Ontario Museum's 1990 'Into the Heart of Africa' display of African artefacts and photographs. The items on display were originally gathered by nineteenth- and early-twentieth-century soldiers and missionaries. Toronto's African community, under the umbrella group Coalition for the Truth about Africa, rose up in protest that any such exhibition could claim to uncover anything resembling Africa's 'heart.' The museum's gaff, Hutcheon suggests, has to do with its attempt to employ irony.

Then, with a squeeze on the forward button, Professor Hutcheon flashes a slide on the screen. The slide reproduces a black and white photograph in which four African women in wrap-dresses and head-scarves crouch nonchalantly around a washtub. They are paused for a moment to gaze upon the photographer before returning their attention to the lumps of soapy cloth in their hands. In the foreground and to the right, a white woman stands in an ankle-length, checked dress collared with white lace. The fringy leaves of a banana tree and several thatched-roofed houses tell you we are in tropical Africa; the standing lady's fulsome skirts and hair pinned up in a bun tell you these are Victorian times. The museum's caption reads: 'Mrs. Thomas Titcombe offering "a lesson in how to wash clothes" to Yagba women in northern Nigeria about 1915. (Photo: Courtesy of the Titcombe family).' The African women's names do not seem to have been recorded.

Superior laughter ripples around the conference room. As if African women had never thought of washing clothes before starched-white Victorian women came along to teach them how! Silly white missionaries. Tricky white Victo-

rian missionary-colonialists who taught Africans how to become servants.

But I don't hear the rest of Hutcheon's talk. My mind is racing, spine prickling up to my neck. MRS THOMAS TITCOMBE!

It's a famous name in my family history.

Dad traces his early decision to become a missionary in Africa to a charismatic missionary preacher who was often billeted in Grandma Coleman's home – Tommy Titcombe! Titcombe was an early pioneer with the Sudan Interior Mission (everything south of the Sahara was 'Sudan' to Europeans back then). Dad recalls sitting in the living-room as a teenager in awe of this energetic little man who had braved the wilds of Africa on the adventure of Christ's mission.

My mind leaps to a segment of the Titcombe story Dad once told me. It's a story the Royal Ontario Museum neglected to weave into its ironical web. According to the cosmology of the nineteenth-century Yagba the Titcombes lived among, twins were of the devil. The doubling was unnatural, monstrous. When a woman gave birth to twins, the two babies were taken from the mother and left to the animals overnight. Mrs Titcombe, that Victorian lady standing so regally near the washtub, was horrified at the practice. Determined to prove the innocence of these victims of superstition, she took in several sets of twins and raised them in her home. Then, as if this were not a strong-enough statement, 'God gave her twins of her own.' These are Dad's words. Every villager who saw her adopted and home-born twins, brown and white, playing together in front of her house had a daily lesson in the humanity of twins.

Stories like this convinced my teen-aged father that he wanted to be a missionary. Grandma was in full support.

And now, about half a century later, here I sit, in a conference on postcolonial theory, listening to a lecture that describes the outrage felt by African Canadians against the likes of Mrs Thomas Titcombe and her attempts to teach African women how to wash European-made clothing. And I'm thinking: This woman, or her husband anyway, shaped me. Not just in determining that I was born in Addis Ababa, but also – and here's how things get sticky – in my being here at a conference on postcolonialism.[2]

Unlike Joshua or Vieux, Raj is self-consciously sincere. There is no humour in him, no evasive trickery. He is self-critical, aware of his failures, of his impotence. In narrating his own story, he confesses frankly his social and political ineffectuality, his inability to please Jan sexually. He is a well-intentioned, de-horned, straight man.

Basically, Raj is a good guy with no proactive goodness. He is passively good, based on the evil he does not do. He has lived in Canada long enough to have internalized the rule of golden negativity that Jan says is typically Canadian: 'do not do unto others as you would not have them do unto you' (287). This good Canadian guy does not kill people; he does not commit rape or family violence; he does not dominate people or inflict injury. His goodness consists of hesitancy, lack of direction, passivity. His goodness *is* his empty hands.

Repeatedly, Raj rejects the law of the gun, the brotherhood of violence. In elementary school during his Casaquemadan childhood, he feels disgusted by the petty masculinity of the cadets performing military manoeuvres in the school yard. He admires his grandfather's self-possession in firing a shotgun over a threatening drunk's head to scare him away, but will have nothing to do with finishing off the dove his irascible cousin Surein wounds with his pellet gun. He rejects outright the would-be dictator, Madera's, law-of-the-male-jungle assertion that 'you have to have the balls to do whatever necessary. And you have to cut off theirs before they cut off yours' (245). Everyone else carries a gun: Surein, Grandpa, Madera, even the civil-rights lawyer, Kayso. Surein tells Raj to take a gun and defend himself and his family against the vermin of a degenerating society. But Raj refuses. He sees through Surein's talk of self-protection: 'Surein needed something to fear, he needed someone to hate, and it was only through these passions, their stir and their consequence, that he could fashion an image of an unassailable self' (88). Raj does not want to construct a self out of hatred, fear, violence. He prefers the image of the 'soft' man of a gentler masculinity.

Raj does not want to act out the old roles. He hates performing, wants to live genuinely, sincerely: no phony pretensions; no fake certitudes. Particularly, he resists playing at heroics. This resistance shows itself in Raj's assessment of the theatrics of young medical students in Toronto:

The popular, modern imagination makes much of medical school, more, probably, than there is to it ... As students we complained of fatigue, of endless hours trudging the shining halls in our running shoes, of insufficient time for overabundant work ...

There was, in all of this, only a little exaggeration, just a touch of the playacting that had us a little more frazzled, a little more hustling than we actually were. But there was, too, another element, one acknowledged only in brief moments of respite and reverie when, alone in the silence, hunched into a corner of the library or dreaming at our desks in our flat, we awed ourselves with visions, embarrassingly heroic, of the enterprise in which we were engaged, our own, quiet machismo. (269–70)

Medicine, Raj believes, fosters a kind of performative hypocrisy; as a doctor he 'learnt, as unspoken corollary to the certainties of medical delivery, the greater uncertainties underlying the bravado' (269). Early in the novel, he sits across his desk from a woman dying of cancer. He knows he is putting on a brave face to encourage her to fight for her life. 'But it remains a lie,' he admits; 'there comes a time, always, when one must acknowledge this to oneself, even though the temptation is to embrace the theatre and turn away from the inevitable despair' (19).

The scene is crucial, for it pinpoints Raj's central conflict: his struggle to be honest, *real*, under no illusions, against his need to interact meaningfully with the people who make up his social world. The trouble is that social interaction requires adherence to social niceties; it demands that a person perform cultural scripts that others can understand and appreciate. Yet every performance assumes a certain amount of artificiality, the art of social intercourse, of crafting one's way in society. Raj feels uncomfortable with the various roles his circumstances require him to play. He rejects the we're-all-one-big-happy-family game with his island relatives because he would have to countenance their racist, class-conscious, parochial scripts. He does not play the game of the loyal-native-son because his status as orphaned child of Indian indentured pedigree has left him without allegiances either to the island or to his family. He does not play the returned-from-abroad-to-save-my-country role because he has no quixotic illusions about himself or his medical expertise. He does not play the husband-father-provider-protector because he never really chose to be a husband and because, lacking a father himself, fatherhood is problematic for him. So, since all the roles are phony, he tries not to perform at all.

And the feeling I had at the postcolonialism conference was an old, familiar trouble. The discomfort of wanting to be there, but not fitting in. Belonging and not belonging at the same time.

Pre-school, down at Woliso in rural Shewa province, my siblings and I were the only white kids we knew. My Ethiopian playmates' parents would pet my flimsy blond hair to see if it was real. If I was real. When we went to market in town, the car Mom and Dad left us in became a zoo, Marianne and I featuring as exotic creatures. A circle of curious, coffee-coloured people would gather around the windows, making faces and pounding on the glass to get a response from us albino monkeys. We were cute, cuddly, Other.

Later, in my teens, we moved to Addis. One day, during the hysteria after Haile Selassie was deposed, Yared and I went shopping in the piazza. We were walking down the sidewalk, when a guy elbowed Yared in the side and cursed at him for walking with a white kid, for walking with me. Whites were imperialists. Hanging around with a white person was consorting with the enemy. I realized with a shock that my friendship was dangerous to Yared.

If I was not a cute little monkey, I was the oppressor's progeny.

Visits to Canada were a different version of the same thing. Mom and Dad spent their furlough doing 'deputation' – which meant touring across Canada visiting family, friends, churches, and drumming up spiritual and financial support for their missionary work. We'd come into each town, each home, each church as a travelling show: slides, songs, stories of Ethiopia, pitches for support. The kids I met in church basements, in people's rec rooms, and at backyard barbecues from Ontario to Alberta thought us exotic. We came from the 'dark continent,' went to boarding-schools with names like 'Bingham Academy,' lived without electricity and running water. 'Here's our running water,' Mom would say during the slide show, 'trotting in on donkey-back.' A picture of our two donkeys with jerrycans loaded on their backs always brought a chuckle.

We were weird; our parents didn't have regular jobs; they came and went from their Canadian families' lives every four or five years. They had more invested in the Lord's work than in retirement savings plans. And Mom and Dad used us, too, in their deputizing: we kids sang, and played guitars, trumpets, pianos. We provided the human-interest stories between the slide show and Dad's sermon.

I grew to hate my strangeness, the expectations of exotica I had to meet. Mad at my parents for giving me this strange upbringing; mad at myself for being miffed at the parents I loved. I grew to hate the question 'Where do you come from?' After finishing high school and moving to live in Canada permanently, I'd opt for the short answer: 'Oh, from Ontario. A little place called Wheatley. It's down near Windsor.' It was my Dad's home town. With major detours, it's where I could be said to come from.

But it is not so easy to opt out. The decision not to perform these various scripts does not free Raj from phony performances. Even his refusal itself can be understood as the solipsism of an upper-class snob,[3] or an iconoclast, or a coward. The point is that there is no escaping the social stage; even leaping off into the audience or into the wings makes a kind of performance. Here we find the basis for a severe interrogation of the passive male: virtuous negativity, the refusal to participate in various social evils, does not absent the refuser from his social system. Raj's 'goodness' may consist of his passivity. But, as the novel shows on many levels, his faults, rather than being the stereotypical male ones of aggression and violence, or of bigotry and dominance, involve *omission*: he lets violence destroy people around him; he betrays others – and himself – by inaction.

It should be no surprise that Raj's sense of futility and lack signals itself most distinctly in his sexual relationship with Jan. His social and political ineffectuality registers as that greatest of masculine anxieties, the spectre of sexual impotence. The marriage itself occurs without Raj's input. He doesn't *get* married; it happens to him by default. He meets Jan at the Riviera strip club, where he goes regularly to indulge a voyeuristic pleasure. She works there as a waitress and they talk. She invites him to a party at her apartment. A snow storm forces him to stay overnight, and there is nowhere else to sleep but Jan's bed, where she takes revenge on her unfaithful boyfriend with Raj. She makes something like love to him and gets pregnant. An orphan himself, he cannot bear the thought of the child's having no legal father. They marry, and Jan miscarries.

In each of the sex scenes between himself and Jan, both when they meet in Toronto and later on, in Casaquemada, Raj cannot bring Jan to orgasm. She always brings herself. Raj is always too late, too early. We should remember that Raj's impotence is not physiological – they conceive twice: the first, a miscarriage and the second, Rohan – it is relational. Raj cannot give Jan pleasure, cannot enter with her into a mutual intimacy, into a shared delight. 'Absolutely the worst thing a man can be is impotent,' writes Paul Hoch. 'Indeed to be in this condition is regarded – even by oneself – as being something less than a man' (65). Raj's sense of sexual failure accompanies his emotional withdrawal from Jan. The detachment that marks his relationship with her parallels his feelings towards the island and towards his family. The distance between him and all collective involvements occurs most devastatingly in marriage. 'Curiously,' Raj says of their first meeting, 'the conversation Jan and I had at the party was the first time and the last that we spoke with any intimacy' (295). Ever since, he confesses, 'Jan and I lived our individual obsessions ... less in a life together than in lives parallel' (318). In a trope that Pamela Mordecai identifies as common among the writings of West Indian men, the male character's relationship to a woman indicates the possibilities (or lack thereof) of the male's connection with community (641). The fact that Jan is Canadian, however, highlights as much the distance Raj feels from Canadian society as it does his detachment from Casaquemada. He is aloof from everyone.

Furthermore, true to patriarchal convention, the man's marital impotence is linked to his inability to protect his woman. In the scene when Raj walks into the bedroom and finds Jan masturbating under the comforter, he has just refused to buy a handgun from Surein. 'You did good, Raj,' Jan says huskily, having overheard his refusal, 'Damned good.' 'You didn't want it, either?' he asks, fumbling to get out of his pants. 'But I did, I did!' she responds, coming to climax just as he enters her (100). The scene plays upon the illogic of patriarchal phallocentrism: refusing the handgun metonymically figures his sexual impotence. Would not buying the gun be a sign of his commitment to Jan? Had he bought the gun, might he have protected her and Rohan from death? A 'real' man would at least have tried. According to patriarchal convention, a man's entry into the crucible of violence tests his true mettle. He proves himself by being willing to handle the machinery of death, even if it ultimately destroys him. This is what it means to protect, to be a real man.

But the situation need not be stated in such extreme terms. Surely, a man can prove his effectuality without a gun in his hand. Perhaps Raj could not have saved Jan and Rohan from the police wearing the light-ning insignia and wielding the automatic weapons. Maybe he could not have saved them from death, but he does nothing to save his marriage or his parenting from death while Jan and Rohan are alive. He never exerts himself in any positive direction. It is this passivity, this indisposition to act, that makes him and his family completely susceptible to violence. And, in its own way, the passivity is itself a kind of violence. Raj and Jan violate each other by refusing to affirm each other; they negate each other by their lack of interest, their inattention. Bissoondath shows carefully that Raj and Jan participate equally in this destructive passivity, but since my interest here is in the passive male, I will trace his side of the relationship.

The passive heterosexual man is a common male figure that either is ignored by feminist descriptions of masculine empowerment or gets elevated by gender reformers into an idealized 'new man.' He rarely undergoes concerted analysis,[4] because he is the one who backs out, who fades into the background. He calls attention to himself by neither hero-ism nor notoriety. He thinks passivity relieves him of accountability. Like Raj, he does not want to see that being married, having a son, being a member of an extended family bring responsibilities whether he wants them or not. Refusing to admit or attend to those responsibilities is a kind of violence. Wilful ignorance – 'a part of me didn't want to know about the multiplying violence, was unwilling to acknowledge it' (93) – imposes negation on others.

In this sense, then, *A Casual Brutality* interrogates the 'soft male' who denies his responsibilities, who hesitates to be the domineering male and so becomes the morally vacuous one. Both types of men deny interrelation, but they deny it oppositely. The domineering male operates from the assumption of power: if he admits relation to others at all, he asserts that their rightful relation to him is one of subordination. The passive male denies his access to power to escape accountability to others. He denies others' validity by denying his role in their constitution. The domineering male destroys others by crushing them underfoot; the passive male destroys them by denying their significance, their existence.

Raj's story demonstrates, however, that avoidance constitutes an action anyway. Humans are already implicated in social interactions simply by being born into a family, a history, a culture. There is no way of not being implicated. The fact is that we give and receive the gift – or curse – of selfhood through interaction with others in every social interaction (Bakhtin, 'Author and Hero' 49); we must act intentionally in each instance to ensure that it is a gift and not a curse. There are no social sidelines. The negativity of the passive male who does not want to perform the received modes of masculinity is too easily recuperable, too weak to provide any escape from social implication and interpellation.

I remember sitting on my bed in my leopard room in Addis – I'd painted it myself, canary yellow with dark brown splotches all over – and thinking: 'I don't care what they say. I'm going to write poetry and play guitar if I want to. I don't care if they do think I'm a sissy.'

I was fifteen. Class president for the tenth grade at Good Shepherd High School. I was on the track, soccer, and basketball teams. I had a leading role in the school play. You'd think I would be as full as a fifteen-year-old can be of self-confidence.

So who was 'they'? And why did I think they'd mock my love of music and poetry? Where did I get the idea that it wasn't manly to love these things?

I was in the 'in' crowd at school, not a social on-looker. Plenty of friends. But a need grew in me for more than the public stuff. I wanted the private, too – writing poems and songs in my leopard room. And I felt, accurately or not, that the friends who hugged me after a soccer victory might mock those poems and songs. I couldn't trust them with some parts of me.

The 'they' whose disapproval I'm scared of changes, but the private/public split remains with me still. I read feminist discussions of the many ways men dominate women, excluding them from language, from good salaries, from controlling their own bodies. The functions of patriarchy, phallocracy, to

organize everything from the House of Commons to the family to capitalism.
And I agree.

I see that there are more male than female professors in my department. That
the senior ministers at my church are men. That women's bodies are used to
sell cars, televisions, diet sodas. I agree that there ought to be affirmative-action
hiring procedures, even if they jeopardize my own chances of getting a job; that
we need to learn gender-inclusive language; that we should try to feed the male
gaze something other than the ubiquitous tits-'n'-ass of every other billboard,
magazine cover, film, commercial.

But what's this excitement? The thrilling tumescence? The sweaty palms,
rushing blood, nerves like piano wires, when I flip through the Penthouse
magazine in the corner store? Why does my eye linger over the curvaceous
limbs of the calendar girls by the check-out counter? One part of me celebrates
their beauty; another looks around to see who's watching. How can I be these
two people at once? the feminist sympathizer and the red-eyed voyeur? What
would my feminist friends think if they really knew about me?

I know I'm not a male stereotype: not a macho iron man, not overly ambi-
tious, not a deft wielder of power, not even a strong silent guy. Yet I know that
I am the stereotype in other ways. In the way I see a woman's legs and breasts
before I hear what she says, in my susceptibility to competition, the way I
admire independence and exertion, my assumption that heterosexual is normal,
my interest in adventure, action.

So I am and I am not a Typical Man.

Writer and critic M. Nourbese Philip interprets Raj's malaise as having
much more pernicious effects than merely those of masculine disavowal.
She calls Bissoondath's novel 'immoral fiction' because it 'pimps' the
Caribbean to the Canadian reader by exploiting the exoticism of third-
world violence and disorder without calling the reader's attention to the
first world's involvements in fostering that violence and disorder in the
first place. 'There is a fundamental immorality at work in writers like
Naipaul and Bissoondath,' she writes. 'It is the immorality that manifests
itself in a writer shitting on his country of birth, yet using the image of
that country or place as Other in the psyches of Western and Northern
countries, to fuel their writing and to enrich themselves' (198). Fundamentally, Philip wants Bissoondath's protagonist to exhibit a nationalistic consciousness. She wants him to represent a more positive
Casaquemada, to have some dignity and not 'sell out' to a myth of
Canadian 'first world' superiority. She objects to his lacklustre attitude,
his unwillingness to identify with his place of birth. She dislikes

Bissoondath's choice of a modernist anti-hero. She wants writers from Caribbean countries to defy Canadian racist, neo-colonial stereotypes by presenting admirable figures who throw those stereotypes back in their faces. She wants someone stronger than Bissoondath's empty-handed man; someone with the chutzpah of Joshua or Vieux; someone like the questing traveller at the centre of her own novel, *Looking for Livingstone*, who has the inner strength to re-create her own African cultural heritage despite, and even within, the silences imposed by the violent ruptures of colonial history. Bissoondath's passive male has no place in her anti-racist, anti-colonial politics; she wants someone with a backbone.

Philip's critique assumes the priority of national solidarity over internal divisions. It values the political efficacy of a unified discourse of nation over a diffusive discourse of heterogeneity and fracture. Philip laments that 'Bissoondath, because of his social amnesia, fails to see that the sad spectacle of his character as an individual filled with self-loathing, unable to attach himself anywhere, is very much a product of that experience of colonialism' (197–8). Clearly, she has chosen to disregard the chilling presence of the marines, who, in an obvious allusion to Reagan's invasion of Grenada, remind us of the contemporary neo-imperialist willingness of wealthy nations to enforce with violent brutality the continuing exploitation of the 'West Indies.' In addition, she disregards Raj's repeated reflections on how it is the colonial system itself, the one that brought slaves to the West Indies and then replaced them with indentured Indian labourers, that has deprived him and the islanders at large of a shared sense of heritage, of cultural dignity. She has chosen to ignore Raj's bitter reflection that the British soldiers who had those cannons put in the fort 'were in no small measure responsible for the fact that my wife and my son were dead, that my home was a shambles, that Madera, gun in hand, was down there somewhere satisfying his blood-lust' (367). Instead, she notes that Raj omits the fact that it was African slaves, or possibly Indian workers, and not British soldiers who would have sweated to put the cannons in place in the old British fort. Her emphasis upon the history of African slavery causes her to subsume the Indian history of indenture to the former, creating identity out of diversity. The struggles for power between the largely African People's National Movement and the mostly Indian Democratic Labour Party since Trinidad's independence in 1962, for example, demonstrates clearly the extent to which internal racial divisions undermine the national solidarity Philip wants Bissoondath to affirm (Bissoondath, *Selling* 13). But the particular history of Indians in the Caribbean prevents Bissoondath, and his character Raj, from such affiliations.

So why does this traumatic history of indenture disqualify Raj from positive identification? And why does it have such demoralizing effects? Surely, the Africans who were taken from their homes, packed into cargo ships, and then forced to labour under the overseers' whips on West Indian plantations experienced more severe trauma than the Indian labourers who at least had the appearance of choosing to make the journey, the tenuous promise of return passage at the end of their contracts, and some remuneration, if scanty, for their work?

'Loss. It stays with you, informs your every attitude, your every decision, your every act,' Raj says, pondering the maps on his study walls and trying to imagine the route his Indian ancestors must have followed across the *kala pani*, the black water, from the Indian subcontinent around Africa and north to the Caribbean (42). What motivated these 'faceless ancestors,' he wonders, to undertake such a perilous journey on the strength of so little knowledge of the conditions of their arrival? What were they fleeing? What desperation pushed them? 'I had none of the answers,' he realizes, 'and those who could tell me without frill or fantasy were long dead' (313). When his grandfather, in the senility of old age, begins to slip into Hindi, the language of his childhood, Raj declares,

I understood none of it, this my ancestral language, but I felt no loss, no nostalgia, little curiosity ... I understood that, in the migration of my ancestors, I had been not so much unmade as remade ... I felt no special affinity for Indian miniatures; was bored by Indian music; caressed no dream of visiting India. There was in me no desire to resurrect the ancestral. That I understood nothing of what my grandfather said in his periods of forgetfulness was of little consequence to me. It failed to move me. I had been taken too far ..., become a mere witness to the end of what I saw to be a disintegrating culture. (127)

What remains is loss, but his loss is that he feels no loss.

In her survey of Indo-Trinidadian and Indo-Fijian writing, Helen Tiffin observes that the atrocious histories of African slavery and the annihilation of the Arawaks in Trinidad have absorbed the history of indenture in such a way that, even in writings by the descendants of indentured labourers, these previous histories seem 'to have outweighed the vocabulary and metaphors that might have arisen out of Indian indenture itself' ('History' 91). Indian writers, when they do refer to the narrative of indenture, employ the metaphors and history of slavery to describe it. In this sense, the dominant national discourse of Trinidadian history – as we saw in Philip's critique – subsumes the Indian narrative to the African, and a language has not yet emerged which articulates adequately that

Indian narrative. It is as though, beside the greater horrors of African slavery and aboriginal genocide, the history of indenture has no justification of its own. 'They have become people without a past,' declared V.S. Naipaul in a 1975 speech on Indians in the Caribbean. 'Most of us can look back only to our grandfathers, after all. Beyond that is a blank' (Introduction 4). And, as Ottawa writer Cyril Dabydeen has written about his growing up as an Indian in Guyana, the interracial post-independence struggles for political power have only further increased the alienation and fracture of what he calls the Indo-Caribbean imagination (110). This sense of double marginalization (exiled from India, peripheral to the larger traumas of Trinidadian or Guyanese history) keeps Indo-Caribbean writers on the edges of cultural identification. Even those who desire to assimilate into Creole culture, writes Victor Ramraj, 'are perpetual *arrivers*, who find themselves at the harbor contemplating the enigma of their arrival' ('Still' 84).[5]

And I am and I am not a Christian.

I agree with the postcolonial critics who point out how Christian missionaries, like the Tommy Titcombes, were the left hands of European imperialism. I don't like the links between Christianity and colonialism, Christianity and patriarchy, Christianity and capitalism. Don't like the churchy prudishness, the readiness to make moral judgments. The smugness of considering oneself among the 'chosen' and the corresponding exclusion of others. The tendency to create factions, usually on some theological basis that masks issues of race, class, gender, ethnicity. I don't like the institutional-mindedness that quashes spiritual vitality. The cocksureness that's conceited but goes by the name of 'faith.'

But another part of me, a part I don't wave around very much at postcolonial conferences, loves being Christian. That is, Christian in the sense of 'follower of Christ,' not as adherent of orthodoxy. I love the radical Christ. His alternative manhood: his powerful humility, leadership through service, skirting the hierarchies of his times, preference for healing over judgment, anger at hypocrisy, and compassion for the disadvantaged.

Once, just once, I admitted to the Christian in me during a conversation over coffee with one of the conference's speakers. I had really enjoyed his paper on postcolonial theory and pedagogy and, in my enthusiasm, relaxed my usual reticence. 'I know that's one of the reasons I'm here at a conference on postcolonialism,' I heard myself say. 'The old Christian virtues I learned as a missionary's kid. You know – love your neighbour, set the prisoners free, feed the hungry – all that stuff feeds right into anti-colonial politics.'

He erupted in protest. Christianity has never found or even attempted a more equal distribution of wealth, he said. And its institutions have always squelched the beginnings of any such attempt. 'I'll always have in my mind that image of Ernesto Cardinal before the Pope,' he continued. 'There's Ernesto Cardinal – a priest, a leader in a popular revolution, one of the world's greatest poets – kneeling to request the Pope's blessing. And what does the Pope do? He refuses! Wags his finger at him because of his commitment to liberation theology! There's Christian virtue for you – the refusal and rejection of its own poor.'

My face flushed hot, and I fell silent. What could I say? How do you respond to the stupidities of your own religion?

It wasn't until I got home several days later that I realized it all depended on who you thought represented Christ in the tableau. If John Paul II represents Christ, then Christianity crunches the poor once again. But what if the Christ-figure turns out to be the kneeling poet-priest? I want it to be the latter. But what do you do when most of the public institutions and structures of the faith you love keep on clamouring after the former?

Raj's sense of alienation, of dismembership, is most poignantly signalled in his lack of parents. Too young when they were killed in a car crash on the island to remember them now, he can only guess what his father was like by observing the gestures, features, and intonation of his aunt. Raj's lack of parents fundamentally structures his own experience of alienation. Particularly, his lack of a father. 'Lacking a Father Is Like Lacking a Backbone,' declares therapist Guy Corneau in *Absent Fathers, Lost Sons*:

The father's absence results in the child's lack of internal structure; this is the very essence of a negative father complex. An individual with a negative father complex does not feel himself structured from within. His ideas are confused; he has trouble setting himself goals, making choices, deciding what is good for him, and identifying his own needs ... Basically he never feels sure about anything. (37)

Raj's negativity, his resistance to decisive action, to positive identification, can be traced in part, then, to his lack of paternity. But what of the other men around him? Of necessity the orphaned infant grew up in the home of his grandparents. However, the perspectives of their generation ensure that Raj will not identify with them as he grows up. His grandfather works hard in the store, not so Raj can learn the business and eventually inherit it, but so he can get the foreign education that will release him from the confinements of his grandfather's difficult life. Nor do any of the male figures around him provide models of a masculinity with which he can identify. Grandfather goes senile after his store is fire-bombed. Grappler, the most promising father-figure, is stripped of political influence by a harsher, leaner generation, leaving him feeling irrelevant and helpless. Raffique, the neighbour next door, loses himself in compulsive philandering and then returns to a marriage for which he has no heart. Cousin Surein represents a new and cynical generation when he puts his training at law to use in gun-running and the black market. Wayne, the black man who works throughout the years for Raj's family, remains admirable in his physicality and faithfulness; however, he is forever unreachable across Raj's family's barriers of race and class.

When he first returns to Casaquemada, Raj entertains vague notions that his extended island family may serve as a kind of support system, a safety net for him and his wife and son. He believes it will be good for Rohan to know his great-grandparents, his aunts and uncles. But the extended family turns out to be more confining than comforting, more stifling than supportive. The petty bigotries and fitful rivalries of Casaquemadan politics that disgust Raj manifest themselves in his own island family. Members of the Brahman Indian merchant class, they lift themselves above the poorer Indian peasants by accusing them of laziness, deriding them for being too stupid to do anything but remain 'cane-cutters' like their indentured ancestors. His family members polish their racial superiority with the cloth of socio-economic success. Every new lawyer or doctor or successful businessman among them reinforces the belief that blacks are lazy, Chinese dirty, Moslems malicious, mulattos impure (313). Raj and Jan find themselves sitting apart during family get-togethers, cynically listening to the uncles, aunts, and cousins pontificate upon the island's improvement while each one continues to build up the foreign nest-egg that guarantees an eventual escape from Casaquemada.

But in setting themselves apart from the family gossip, Raj and Jan make themselves the objects of suspicion, and even derision. In his chapter on the community-forming function of 'commess,' or gossip, in island culture, Abrahams notes that commess guarantees 'a certain level of homogeneity of ideals and even of social practices' among participants. The person who remains distant from the loquacious community, then, is seen by the participants as an unfriendly person: 'Not only is this lack of communicativeness held against him, but imputations of greed and lack of cooperativeness may also be voiced' (84). And, indeed, the family members mock Raj for trying to help an alcoholic Indian by calling Sagar his 'pet project.' Raj realizes that his attempt to help Sagar by giving him a job at his medical office is becoming a nervous family joke 'for in helping Sagar I ran the risk of becoming Sagar' (193). Commess circulates that Sagar must be an illegitimate cousin or uncle. Why else would a rich Indian help a poor one? And, in the end, Sagar himself rejects Raj's efforts, junking the medication, the job, and the place to live, in a fit of rage. So, Raj's experience of alienation is the product of a complex combination of circumstances, including a lack of parents, the dislocations of Indian indenture history, the further dislocations of his own migration to and from Canada, the local antagonisms of class and race, and a dysfunctional marriage. It is no wonder that these circumstances have produced in him an unendearing tendency to uncommunicative introversion. On all fronts, Raj experiences only alienation, loss, the impossibility of belonging.

Let us return, then, to the reframed version of David Richards's question with which I began this chapter: what kind of masculinity can possibly emanate from negativity, from a place which is always a 'not'? And can such a negative masculinity do anything but comply with domineering forms of phallocentrism and patriarchy? At this point, I believe Michel Pêcheux's theory of disidentification becomes useful. Pêcheux engages Althusser's theory of interpellation by observing that three kinds of subjects are distinguished by their responses to the impositions of ideology. There is the good subject who 'freely' accepts interpellation under dominant ideology, and there is the good subject's opposite, the bad subject, who 'counter-identifies' against dominant ideology. Pêcheux insists that both good and bad subjects reinscribe or reinforce the dominant ideology since both live and act in response to the same determining system. But in a third modality which he calls 'disidentification,' contradictions in the 'inter-discourses' under which a subject lives cause that subject neither to espouse nor to reject dominant discourse completely. This disidentifying subject, he says, is the potential site where new forms of subjectivity can begin to emerge. A Marxist of the Althusserian school, Pêcheux gestures towards Lenin in an example of how disidentification separates the third modality from that of the 'good' and 'bad' subject. In a time of war, he says, good subjects will say 'our country is at war. Loyalty demands that I enlist,' while bad subjects will say 'war is evil. Morality demands that I assert myself as a pacifist.' Disidentification shifts the discourse altogether. After Lenin, the disidentifying subject says that the proletariat has no nation, but is part of an international community of workers. Thus, the decision to go to war or not in the national sense must be decided on the basis of its role in the class struggle of the proletariat (165–6). According to the Marxist ideal, the interdiscourse of proletarian class-consciousness dislodges that of patriotism or nationalistic morality; it causes the subject not just to reject one side or the other of the debate, but to disidentify with the entire debate itself.

In any given social formation, there are multiple and uneven interdiscourses that have a similar potential to refract dominant identifications. Pêcheux refers, in classic Marxist orthodoxy, to the interdiscourse of class, but social formations are composed of many other complex discursive combinations which include colonial history and family systems as well as gender and sexuality. In the previous two chapters, I have shown how both Joshua and Vieux intentionally inhabit specific traditions of male performativity in order to gain for themselves certain social advantages. In both cases, their innovative inhabitations work *within* and *against* the discursive parameters of those traditions themselves. Raj's masculine practice operates differently: the discursive contradictions of his traumatic history cause him to disidentify with received traditions of masculine performativity altogether. His history, which includes not just the discursive histories of colonialism, indenture, and modern-day neo-imperialism, but also a private family history of orphanhood and dysfunction, has derailed him from such conventional masculine identifications as father, husband, political hero, and loyal son of family or nation. His fractured inheritance has rendered him a subject of disidentification.

Same kind of trouble with my position in the university system. The Academy. I really dislike the élitism. The we're-all-in-the-know stuff that pats itself on the back for not making the Royal Ontario Museum's blunders. The smug brilliance that didn't need Hutcheon to explain the curator's ironies, that knew without being told that missionary ladies in Victorian dress had nothing to teach the African women.

At coffee breaks during the conference on postcolonialism, people clustered eagerly around Homi Bhabha, the plenary speaker, lapping up the brilliant crumbs that fell from his table. Meanwhile, off to one side, Lenore Keeshig-Tobias, who had given the opening talk, watched her toddler careen around the carpeted floor. The only Canadian Native speaker at the conference, she had challenged postcolonial scholars to listen first to voices of aboriginal people; speak, write, analyse later. No one engaged her during question period; the only person I saw leave the Bhabha circle and go over to speak with Keeshig-Tobias was my friend Catherine.

I didn't go over to talk with her myself. I hadn't come to hear aboriginal stories, full of metaphor, about listening and not listening. I'd come to hear about 'cultural incommensurability' and the 'politics of ambivalence' from the Big Names.

But I didn't like the incommensurability in the coffee room. It made me think that university life had done something to me. Handed me a loss. Made me unable to hear language not paraphrased for the theoretically élite.

On the other hand, it's at university that I learned I had a brain – a respectable one, too. It was at university that I found out I could trust my own intelligence, that a whole world of ideas, perspectives, came to me. I learned new ways to think about my own experiences, my own life. And in the classes I've taught, I've seen it happen to others too. The lights going on. The newfound self-respect. The awareness of one's own relation to people of other cultures, languages, geographies. The development of tolerance for others alongside a re-evaluation of what is one's own.

And so, once again, I am and I am not an academic, just like I am and am not Christian, masculine, Canadian, Ethiopian.

Two of Pêcheux's comments about disidentification are particularly relevant to Raj's situation: first, he insists that disidentification operates 'retrospectively' (162) or 'in reverse' (196), that it functions with reference to history and the constellation of social structures under which the subject has lived; and, second, he claims that disidentification 'is never, in any concretely existing thought, definitively achieved. It is all "a question of tendency"' (198). Pêcheux's observation about the retrospective mode of disidentification reminds us that *A Casual Brutality* is narrated in hindsight. Readings such as Richards's that focus on the story of Raj's negativity fail to reflect upon that story's structure. These readings focus on the diegetic level of the novel, on its *content* rather than its *process* or narration. They base their commentary on what happens in the story, and they do not take into account how it is told. For Raj narrates the whole thing in reflection. The novel starts at the story's end. Raj is leaving Casaquemada after the funerals, heading, without luggage, without any clear plan for the future, back to Toronto. Grappler and Ma have come to see him off. In the airport's departure lounge, Grappler gives Raj a parting gift. It is a little black notebook and a fountain pen. 'You're your own best listener, Raj,' he says. 'Use them' (12). Minutes later, after the plane has taken off, Raj, eyes moistened by his awareness of the empty seat beside him, opens the notebook and uncaps the pen. We are to believe the novel that follows is composed of his reflections recorded in Grappler's notebook. We are reading his self-therapy, his attempt to sort through his experiences, to understand what happened, to understand himself. This retrospective self-examination makes *A Casual Brutality* more than a Naipaulese allegory of Caribbean degeneration, more than a pessimistic critique of postcolonial malaise.[6]

The narrator's process of meditation and self-evaluation gives some credence to Bissoondath's claim that we can read the ending of the novel optimistically. 'It is not an easy optimism,' he tells Bruce Meyer and Brian O'Riordan in a 1989 interview; it offers no trumpets blaring on the hero's exit. Instead, it is the kind of realistic optimism in which the character catches sight of the 'possibility of possibility' (22). In writing out his discomfort with his various roles – as doctor, as postcolonial returnee, as husband, as father, as orphan of the Indian diaspora, as sensitive male – Raj puts himself through the strenuous first paces of self-assessment, one which may point the way, through a never fully achieved disidentification, towards alternative masculine practices. 'What are the possibilities,' Butler asks in a brief aside in her recent *Bodies That Matter*, 'of politicizing *dis*identification, this experience of *misrecognition*, this uneasy sense of standing under a sign to which one does and does not belong?' (219). Raj's first-person narration performs his unease, his discomfort with the identifying signs under which he stands. His narration exposes, elaborates upon, the incoherencies and struggles of an identity in turmoil, a masculinity under fire.

Clearly, Raj feels disidentified from his heritage, his island birthplace, his extended family, his marriage, his fatherhood, his chosen career. Pretty well everything up to the point when he starts to write his story has been misrecognition: 'I have spent my life polishing shadows,' he confesses (370). But the process of writing itself, the process of reflection, of meditation, is an *effort* towards recognition, towards honest self-appraisal. 'To go forward is to return,' writes Michael Dash in his assessment of loss and exile in Caribbean literature; 'the past holds the key to the future; retrospection is vision' (22). This process of reflection holds out the possibility of reconstitution, of healing. Raj rejects nostalgia's rosy illusions. He is bluntly honest about his failings, his inabilities to comprehend his situation, his incapacity to act, his emotional impotence. We, however, can interpret his process of narration itself as a creative act, because it elaborates his sense of standing under a sign – a whole series of identity signs – to which he does and does not belong. This elaboration of discomfort or self-disidentification produces more than negative ground. We can read Raj's course of self-assessment not only as confession and self-critique, but also as an attempt to sketch the social and historical conditions of his failures. In attending to Raj's reflections, we can, with him, try to imagine how this unheroic male could learn to live differently.

This said, it seems to me that, in his reluctance to overemphasize the optimistic potential of Raj's self-reflections, Bissoondath misses the opportunity to give depth or richness to the 'possibility of possibility' in this novel. He never defines the distance between the present, reflecting Raj (the narrating subject) and the previous, acting Raj (the subject of narration) by giving us scenes of the man writing in Grappler's notebook. Such a distinction would allow for a clearer separation between the diegetic and the meditative parts of the narration and would emphasize a critical distance between the two. By calling greater attention to the scene of writing, Bissoondath could also have avoided the naïve readings which, as Philip warns, may see Raj's narration as a 'transparent' depiction of endemic West Indian 'chaos and backwardness.' He could have kept his readers more aware of the partiality and provisionality of Raj's perceptions. To have given Raj Grappler's notebook in the opening pages and to have produced the whole of the narration through hindsight and then not to call attention to the process of the narration itself constitutes the major flaw in this novel.

None the less, despite Bissoondath's failure to develop this potential in his own narrative structure, we can still sketch the possibility of its possibilities. The possibility of a healthier form of masculinity, for example, reveals itself in Raj's present grief. I return to the scene I opened with: Raj sitting in his car on the grounds of the old British fort. 'The pain, lancing from within, pulled my eyes shut,' Raj writes, 'to a darkness behind the lids that was peopled: faces I did not wish to see, expressions known too well contorted now ... into expositions of pain all the more powerful for not having been witnessed' (363). He blames himself, his empty hands, for not trying to save Jan and Rohan. Raj finally confronts his own emotions. His belated pain tells him how much he did care about them. How much he loved them. It takes the murder of his wife and son to put him in touch with his own passion. Before their deaths, he was noncommittal. Their loss makes him grieve. Grief makes him *feel*. The sad and problematic thing is that it takes the death of woman and child to do this. It takes violence against the man's intimate others to wake him to his intimate self. As I noted earlier, Raj's story shows that the passive male's denial of involvement with others too readily complies with forces of violence and destruction. His story is about the break-up of such self-protecting denials. 'So this is how the world shatters,' he thinks, 'with a peep at the soul' (367). Raj has always avoided this glance within.

In this scene of complete devastation, we realize, paradoxically, Raj's hands are no longer empty. From the seat beside him he has picked up Jan's blouse, ripped from her corpse by the military police and thrown on the roadside in front of their house. 'I raised the blouse to my face,' he says, 'rubbed it against my cheek – the fabric caught on the stubble, scraped sharply like sandpaper – then spread the frilled pocket on my open left hand. The bullet hole, neat, singed, the corona of dried blood stiff and crusted, was large enough for my index finger to pass through. Just around the heart, I estimated' (370). His empty hands are filled, overwhelmed, with the symbol of his grief. And, having recognized its personal significance to him, he lays it to rest where it belongs: on the wall of the old British fort, to which, in the global scheme of things, his agony can be traced.

In a passage on male grief, Corneau claims that depression can play a role much like the father's in structuring the son's psyche. Just as, according to the Oedipal scheme, the father forms his son's unconscious by preventing him from acting out his incestuous desires, so depression 'confronts the individual with his inner workings.' It forces a man to confront his own inadequacy. 'Because our fathers are missing,' Corneau states in metaphoric language borrowed from Robert Bly, 'we must cover ourselves with the ashes of depression in order to experience rebirth' (166; cf. Bly 85, 88). There is another way to say this: Grief and depression are the symptoms of the subject aware of limitations, of failures, of loss. This awareness, says Silverman, founds the possibility of alternative masculinities. 'Our dominant fiction,' she reminds us, 'calls upon the male subject to see himself, and the female subject to recognize and desire him, only through the mediation of images of an unimpaired masculinity. It urges both the male and the female subject, that is, to deny all knowledge of male castration' (42). In her discussion of how an elaboration of alternative masculinities can contribute to feminist politics, she registers her wish 'that the typical male subject, like his female counterpart, might learn to live with lack' (65). Raj's delineation of his own failures, his reconsideration of his own historical trauma, his disidentification with ideologies of domineering masculinity, I believe, constitute the narrative of a man who attempts to do just that: learn to live with his own lack.

4

Michael Ondaatje's Family Romance: Orientalism, Masculine Severance, and Interrelationship

Like *A Casual Brutality*, Michael Ondaatje's fictionalized memoir, *Running in the Family*, constitutes a narration of loss. Ondaatje's narrative, like Bissoondath's, traces an emigrant son's return from Canada to the island of his birth and his failure to connect satisfyingly with his past. Like Bissoondath, he outlines the alienation that derives from a traumatic family history of displacement and migration. The similarities continue in that the son's alienation is most poignantly figured in his lost father: the emigrant son's severance from *patria* is emotionally intensified through his severance from *pater*. But the parallels stop there, for, whereas Bissoondath's protagonist, Raj, believes the only intelligent response to his sense of alienation is to withdraw from social interaction (*Casual* 89), Ondaatje responds to the loss running in his family by immersing his narration in the ethos of his extended family and its stories. Accordingly, Ondaatje composes *Running in the Family* from his relatives' anecdotes and bits of gossip, and from snippets of journal entries, poems, photographs, and newspaper clippings he gathered during two visits to Sri Lanka in 1978 and 1980. As a result, the 'historical trauma' at the root of this narrative's sense of loss has a much more intimate locus than that conveyed in Raj's narrative. Ondaatje's narration registers the turmoil of Sri Lankan colonial and postcolonial history in the social decline of his own family, in the divorce of his parents, in his migration with his mother to England when he was eleven years old, and in the sad story of his father's dipsomania and eventual death by alcohol poisoning.

In this chapter, I examine Ondaatje's retelling of his extended family's self-explaining stories – which I am calling, after Freud, his relatives' collective family romance. 'I would be travelling back to the family I had grown from,' Ondaatje declares at the outset of his journey. 'I wanted to touch them into words' (22). What we discover, though, is that they already have plenty of words of their own. The focalization of Ondaatje's narration *within* this family romance produces yet another instance of the tension between innovation and constraint I have been tracing throughout *Masculine Migrations*. Adapting Freud's concept of the family romance to the situation of Ondaatje's extended family, I show how the family narratives the Ondaatjes compose to compensate for their traumatic decline resist and redirect Michael Ondaatje's desire for reconnection with *pater* and *patria*. Specifically, the Ondaatjes' family romance makes use of a form of Orientalist discourse whose upper-class register produces and maintains the alienation against which Michael Ondaatje's text rebels but never breaks free: the desire for reconnection with *pater* and *patria* remains unfulfilled. None the less, Ondaatje's immersion in the family's stories – his narrative of return to Sri Lanka and to the network of aunts, uncles, cousins, and family friends – constitutes a masculine innovation insofar as it breaks with the ideology of male autonomy. While the desire for reconciliation with the father in *Running in the Family* meets with failure, the necessity to pursue that desire through interaction with the surviving members of the extended family produces an image of relationally dependent masculinity that belies the myth of self-sustaining masculine independence.

In an earlier article on *Out of Egypt* and *Running in the Family*, I described the male emigrant's distance from his own family's past in terms of the masculine complex of Oedipal severance evident in Ihab Hassan's and Michael Ondaatje's autobiographical texts. Masculine severance, I argued, often reinforces the estrangement from the colonial past that emigration involves, and this estrangement merges easily into an Orientalist discourse. In this way, I attempted to 'demonstrate how certain discourses of masculinity and Orientalism cooperate with and mutually enforce one another' (62). My intention here is to elucidate in greater detail the intimate workings of that cooperation and enforcement. By relocating Freud's concept of the family romance – which he outlines within the nuclear-family triad of father–mother–child – in the wider ethos of the extended family, I hope to show how the Ondaatjes' family romance inevitably incorporates elements of the social and political into the intimate structures of the family itself. I want to demonstrate how an Orientalist discourse, specifically, can operate as a 'family system,' as the discursive formation within which the Ondaatje family understands itself.

In his brief article 'Family Romances,' Freud describes the process by which children deal with the unhappy discovery that their parents are neither omniscient nor omnipotent. To compensate for this disillusion, the child begins to make up 'pseudo-biographies' which discard or replace the disappointing parents. Generally in these stories, the child imagines that his parents are not the people who feed and clothe him. (I use the male pronoun here not only because Freud himself asserts that the family romance is more commonly a male mode, but also because I am among those who question the applicability of psychoanalytic models to female development.) Since the child wants to compensate for his own loss at his parents' 'fall' from perfection, he creates for himself noble parentage, usually modelled on whatever examples of aristocracy he has observed (the Lord of the Manor, the rich neighbours next door, etc.). In other words, the family romance becomes associated with early ambitions for social power and upper-class status. Paradoxically, the child dismisses his real parents through a fantasy that exalts them above their actual status.

Around the age of puberty, Freud says, the child's family romance takes on specifically gendered modifications. As the child learns about the distinct sexual roles played by the parents in his own procreation, he comes to realize that maternity is provable and certain, while paternity is not. Thus, the pseudo-biography undergoes a revision whereby the mother's status becomes settled, while the father's remains the object of speculation. In other words, the mother is disqualified from the fantasy while the father remains at its centre. The family romance 'contents itself with exalting the child's father,' Freud writes, 'but no longer casts any doubts on his maternal origin, which is regarded as something unalterable' ('Family' 239). Furthermore, the projection of the father into the fantastic story at once *exiles* and *exalts* the father. Freud asserts that in

the replacement of both parents or of the father alone by grander people, we find that these new and aristocratic parents are equipped with attributes that are derived entirely from real recollections of the actual and humble ones; so that in fact the child is not getting rid of his father but exalting him. Indeed the whole effort at replacing the real father by a superior one is only an expression of the child's longing for the happy, vanished days when his father seemed to him the noblest and strongest of men and his mother the dearest and loveliest of women. ('Family' 240–1)

The child's self-assuring story, therefore, is regressive in so far as it is based on loss and nostalgia. But it has future effects too. In her discussion of the ways in which the structure of family romance shapes the novel-writer's fictionalizing impulse, Marthe Robert claims that the exaltation of the father can become a kind of cult. The child storymaker, she explains,

relegates his father to an imaginary kingdom beyond and above the family circle – a form of tribute, maybe, but in fact an exile, since this royal, unknown father who is forever absent might just as well not exist for all the part he plays in everyday life; he is a phantom, a corpse, who may be the object of a cult, but whose vacant place cries out nevertheless to be filled. (26)

In this way, the child's family romance constructs an intimacy with the mother and a dismissal of the father without requiring the Oedipal patricide. In the family romance, then, the cult of the father involves his simultaneous exile and exaltation. And, as Robert points out, the child's reliance upon material from his own real-world experiences to create his imaginary family romance lies at the heart of the tension between realism and fantasy which structures the genre of the novel – a genre which she argues has its roots in the family romance, so that the novel is its 'sequel' (40).

The songs we sang told our collective story:

This world is not my home, I'm just a-passin' thru
My treasures are laid up somewhere beyond the blue
The angels beckon me from heaven's open door
And I can't feel at home in this world anymore.

Our voices, thin and high, bright as birds, rose in the late-afternoon air in the chapel at Bingham Academy, boarding-school for missionaries' children. I remember the songs and the ten-cent pieces. We were handed a coin on the way into Loyal Ambassadors for Christ (LAC), the Sunday-afternoon chapel service, and if you rubbed the coin hard with your thumb, you could make a shiny new version of Haile Selassie's bust appear in the copper before you deposited it in the collection plate. If you sucked on the coin for a minute first, the grime loosened easier, and you could make your teacher turn green if you let her see you do it. 'This world is not my home,' said Timmy Murray, rubbing spit across Haile Selassie's profile. The old negro spiritual was one of our favourites. What did we know about African slaves in the American

South? Next to nothing. This was a song that explained to us where we were,
and why we were there.

Just like Abraham in the Bible, our parents had heard the call of God to leave
kith and kin and go to a land God would show them. My mother was nineteen
when she left Canada for Ethiopia, my father in his early twenties. They gave
up the care of their own parents for the care of God. The story was simple.
Once you'd been 'saved,' you realized that this world was not your home and
that you were passing through on your way to heaven. This realization
changed your whole life. You abandoned the ways of the world, and committed
yourself to the ways of God. You became charged with the responsibility to
'witness' to others, to help them realize the spiritual journey they were on. In
order to witness properly, you needed to know the message well yourself. So
you went to Bible school. After three or four years of study, you emerged, ready
to carry the great evangelical commission to the ends of the earth. This was our
parents' story. We sang:

> *Far, far away, in heathen darkness dwelling*
> *Millions of souls forever may be lost.*
> *Who, who will go, salvation's story telling,*
> *Looking to Jesus, counting not the cost?*

The good news of salvation, of forgiveness for sins and healing for wounds, was
the message our missionary parents bore. They conveyed it through hospitals,
mission schools, leprosariums, orphanages. They preached it in thatched-roof
churches in the countryside and tin-roofed churches in the cities. And we were
the children of their adventure. Even before I was old enough to read the words
in the hymnal, I mimicked the vowels and consonant-clusters while the older
kids sang the LAC theme song every Sunday afternoon. The students old
enough to read sang,

> *I am a stranger here within a foreign land*
> *My home is far away upon a golden strand*
> *Ambassador to be of realms beyond the sea*
> *I'm here on business for my king,*

while I sang,

> *I am a strain-er here withinna foar-in laan*
> *I ho is far away ah-pawna old-en straan*

Am ass a door teebee of relmsby on da sea
I'm here on biss-niss or I'm king.

Eventually, we sang the song enough times for me to pick out the words. I learned that 'golden strand' meant heaven, but I also thought it might mean Canada, which was the mythic 'home' my parents talked about. I learned, too, we were singing about God the King, not a real king, but that didn't keep me from thinking of Ethiopia as the foreign land in which I was a stranger dwelling in heathen darkness.

And how were we kids to understand ourselves? Sent away to boarding-school at the age of six, seeing Mom and Dad for a weekend once every month or six weeks. I loved school: the dorm was like a permanent slumber party with twenty friends your age. There were lots of books to read; the teachers and dorm parents were kind and conscientious. After weekend visits, my parents were often teary-eyed when they waved goodbye and drove out the school gates. They loved my siblings and me and wanted to be with us. But God's work came first. Family second. We were loved, but not as much. I understood – just like many kids in Canada know Mom's business or Dad's day-shift has to come first. The evangelical story was the air we breathed. I didn't resent it because I didn't know you could live a different way.

And the gospel adventure had compensations for us kids, too. If heaven was our real home and we were merely travelling through this earth, so, too, our real Father was God. If our earthly parents had to be absent, our heavenly Father was just a prayer away. And this father was a King, Creator of the Universe, Potentate of Time. It gave you a real edge when you got into the old my-dad's-bigger-than-your-dad routine with a kid whose father lived in town. 'He owns the cattle on a thousand hills,' we sang,

The wealth in every mine.
He owns the rivers and the rocks and rills,
The stars and sun that shine,
Wonderful riches, more than tongue can tell –
These are my Father's, so they're mine as well.
He owns the cattle on a thousand hills –
I know that He will care for me!

The family romance provides a useful structural paradigm in which to examine the relations between the nostalgic storytelling, the sense of loss, the cult of the father, and the generic slippage between biography and fiction that are all significant features of *Running in the Family*. To apply the paradigm to Ondaatje's family memoir, however, we will need to make several adaptations to Freud's theory. First of all, the parents' 'fall' from perfection in the present case is not simply a matter of a child's private disillusionment. The original fall for which the Ondaatjes' family romance attempts to account was public, political, and social. With the collapse of British colonial rule in Ceylon after the Second World War, the burgher class of which the Ondaatjes were members lost its privileged comprador position in the colonial social structure and either accepted an increasingly déclassé existence in the new Sri Lanka or emigrated – generally to Australia or Britain. The trauma of this social decline coincides with the dysfunction and eventual dissolution of Mervyn Ondaatje and Doris Gratiaen's marriage. 'They had come a long way in fourteen years,' writes Ondaatje, 'from being the products of two of the best known and wealthiest families in Ceylon: my father now owning only a chicken farm at Rock Hill, my mother working in a hotel' (172). So it is that at puberty, when Freud says the child's impulse to compose the family romance is at its height, the eleven-year-old Michael was taken by his mother, Doris, to live in England, where he never saw his father again. This family romance, then, deals not with an imaginary exile of (or from) the father, but a real one. As well, Doris's custody of Michael meant that he remained in that close intimacy with the mother which Freud posits as the norm.

Furthermore, since the parents' 'fall' is public and social, it stands to reason that other members of the family will be affected by the disappointment. They, too, will have their own motives for telling themselves and each other compensating stories. And, since that family is an extended family – a network that includes grandparents, aunts, uncles, nephews, nieces, and cousins, as well as close family friends – the number of stories that account for the disaster is limited only by the number of imaginative tellers. When Ondaatje returns to the dining-rooms and verandas of his relatives in Sri Lanka, he encounters an endlessly proliferating family romance, told in contradictory and competing versions by a variety of narrators. In other words, in the public and social context of the extended Ondaatje family, the romance is already running in the family when Michael Ondaatje decides to compose his present version of it. 'No story is ever told just once,' he writes, describing his relatives' gifts for endless elaboration: 'Whether a memory or funny hideous scandal, we will return to it an hour later and retell the story with additions and this time a few judgements thrown in. In this way history is organized ... [A]ll day my Aunt Phyllis presides over the history of good and bad Ondaatjes and the people they came in contact with' (26).

'There are so many ghosts here' (26), he says, as much of the storytelling as of the Jaffna mansion in which he and his family members are residing. 'That night,' he adds,

I will have not so much a dream as an image that repeats itself. I see my own straining body which stands shaped like a star and realise gradually I am part of a human pyramid. Below me are other bodies that I am standing on and above me are several more, though I am quite near the top. With cumbersome slowness we are walking from one end of the huge living room to the other. We are all chattering away like the crows and cranes so that it is often difficult to hear. I do catch one piece of dialogue. A Mr Hobday has asked my father if he has any Dutch antiques in the house. And he replies, 'Well ... there *is* my mother.' My grandmother lower down gives a roar of anger. But at this point we are approaching the door which being twenty feet high we will be able to pass through only if the pyramid turns sideways. Without discussing it the whole family ignores the opening and walks slowly through the pale pink rose-coloured walls into the next room. (27)

This chattering family pyramid, with its sharp witticisms and cavalier disdain for the practical function of doorways, provides Ondaatje's conscious and unconscious mind with an overabundance of stories. 'She belonged to a type of Ceylonese family,' he says of his mother, 'whose women would take the minutest reaction from another and blow it up into a tremendously exciting tale, then later use it as an example of someone's strain of character.' In this way, the family continuously produces and revises its own history, even as that history unfolds. 'If anything kept their generation alive it was this recording by exaggeration,' he continues. 'An individual would be eternally remembered for one small act that in five years had become so magnified he was just a footnote below it' (169). Thus, a resetting of the Freudian family romance in the loquacious ethos of the extended Ondaatje and Gratiaen families, requires a more communal, less individualistic conception of the discursive field in which the son formulates his pseudo-biography.

Indeed, the conviviality and dynamism of Ondaatje's extended family disallow in his self-narration the kind of isolationism that characterizes so many men's autobiographical writings. 'Roots,' scoffs the emigrant Ihab Hassan at the outset of his autobiography *Out of Egypt*; 'everyone speaks of roots. I have cared for none' (4). Conscious of the continuing influence of family roots, Ondaatje, despite his sense of severance from the past, does not respond to that alienation by committing himself as Raj and Hassan do to the 'fierce intricacy of asseveration' that Hassan claims is an inescapable element of human self-definition' ('Parabiography' 595, 612); instead he returns, after twenty-five years' absence, to explore the family interrelations that have shaped him. In this regard, *Running in the Family* represents an intervention in the gendered conventions of the autobiographical genre. Feminist poetics of the genre assert that the drive to define the self by severance from the other is masculine. Mary G. Mason claims that 'the disclosure of female self is linked to the identification of some "other"' (210), while Susan Stanford Friedman shows that the female subject represents herself in relation not just to one other, but to a community of others. Friedman takes issue with the masculinist assumption in Georges Gusdorf's influential essay 'Conditions and Limits of Autobiography' when she insists that the female autobiographical self, contrary to Gusdorf's (male) individual, 'does not oppose herself to all others, does not feel herself to exist outside of others, and still less against others, but very much *with* others in an interdependent existence' (56). Ondaatje's text heartily endorses Sara Suleri's assertion in *Meatless Days*, a memoir of her own convivial, extended family in Pakistan, that 'living in language is tantamount to living with other people' (177).[1] *Running in the Family* breaks the masculinist illusion of autonomy (reflected in Freud's individualized formulations, as well as in male conventions of autobiography) with a vivid depiction of a male character who pursues a living reconnection with his familial community of language. As I have tried to emphasize in previous chapters, this kind of masculine *innovation* or intervention results, not so much from any kind of authorial intention, but from the way in which one culture's conventions can be refracted when filtered through another culture's traditions. The cultural disjuncture between European and American assumptions of the nuclear-family triad and the Ondaatje family's extensive network produces in Ondaatje's text a variation from the gendered conventions of the autobiographical genre.

We must not forget, however, that despite the family's delightful sociability in Ondaatje's memoir, his narration is motivated by loss and severance. And, that severance itself can be traced in the discursive structure that I am calling the Ondaatje family romance. Freud's suggestion that the child's imaginary biography has upper-class ambitions is significant here, for, the Ondaatjes' family romance is the product and reproducer of an upper-class sensibility. In their privileged position as mixed-race managers and agents for British-owned tea estates during the colonial era, the burghers of Ceylon were separated both from the colonial rulers and from the Sinhalese and Tamil denizens of the island. They were Ceylonese by birth, but usually British by education. And that education separated them further from local society. 'An English education ... tended, by its very nature, to cut a Sri Lankan writer off from his indigenous culture,' explains the writer and critic Yasmine Gooneratne in her survey of the island's literature. Gooneratne is herself a member of the British-educated, Sri Lankan upper class (she is a descendant of the Bandaranaike family, whose commitment to Sinhalese hegemony secured three prime-ministerships between the 1950s and the 1970s). This intellectual severance, Gooneratne claims, was complete and disastrous for the 'Sri Lankan, who took enthusiastically and, on the whole, uncritically, to the new ways of living and thinking introduced by the British to the island' (102). Moreover, if the native Sri Lankan was deprived of his or her heritage even while living *within* the culture, the expatriate descendants of Sri Lankan emigrants were even more profoundly cut off, to the extent that Suwanda H.J. Sugunasiri says that one might as well not call them 'Sri Lankan,' not just because they represent the bourgeoisie that fled the 1971 revolution, but because 'they are ignorant of the history, culture and myth of the land and its people' (75). Ondaatje himself, who left Sri Lanka at age eleven and never returned until the writing of *Running in the Family*, registers this loss after meeting Ian Goonetileke, librarian at Peredeniya, who 'knows history is always present' and has had to publish his books on the 1971 insurgency overseas to avoid government censorship. Goonetileke, writes Ondaatje in a wistful moment, knows the 'voices I didn't know. The visions which are anonymous. And secret' (*Running* 85). Ondaatje's severance from his own national and cultural past, then, is an effect of the combined history of his élite burgher-class ancestry, his British colonial education, and his own family's history of divorce and emigration.

Bingham Academy gave us kids a different kind of family. There, we had dozens of brothers and sisters whose parents had made the same choices ours had. In the cultural island of that school, we belonged; we were not strangers in a foreign land. But it was an island which separated us from immersion in Ethiopian culture. It separated us from Ethiopian life. We did not study Amharic, nor did we learn Ethiopian history or geography. The curriculum was loosely American, and we expected to graduate and go to the Bible schools our parents had attended. The number of my schoolmate-siblings who are now missionaries themselves speaks to the strength of the narratives in which we were educated.

I got a letter this week from my brother John who has taken his young family to Ethiopia, where he teaches in the same Bible college in Hosa'ina my parents did. 'I've been getting to know one of the Ethiopian teachers here,' he says. 'His name is Demmesee. I think he's going to be another Negusee to me.'

A complex wave of envy and guilt rolls through me. Negusee. I never kept close ties with Negusee like John did, writing letters back and forth, even during the years when Negusee was in prison. I never maintained a close Ethiopian friend, not even Negusee. The anti-foreign sentiment under the revolutionary government of Mengistu Haile Mariam during the 1970s and 1980s made it difficult to make or keep Ethiopian friends; made it dangerous for them to be our friends; made us more paranoid than usual about our outsidership. Older than me by three years, John had already gone to Canada for high school and college when the revolution took place, so he'd missed those years of fear and estrangement.

In some ways, my trip back to Ethiopia in 1993 after the change of governments was an attempt to bridge the internalized divisions. I had hoped that I could talk with an old family friend like Negusee, try to understand what his life had been like, hear how he would tell the story of what our family meant to him after all he'd been through. I wanted to speak with an Ethiopian friend who could give me some sense of what life was like outside the island of white expatriates' kids that was Bingham Academy.

But it was not to be. I got to see him once. He had been horribly sick and was lying on a temporary bed in a clinic, awaiting diagnosis. I embraced his feverish body, stroked the hands painfully swollen from kidney malfunction, whispered his name, stammered words of attempted assurance. Three days later he was dead. By then we were far down in the southern part of Shewa province and could not get back to Addis for the funeral.

It made no sense to me. He had survived so much – TB of the spine as a child, seven years of imprisonment complete with torture chambers and brutal interrogations – and now he had died in a time of peace.

He had been a kindly, patient figure in the landscape of our family for as long as I can remember. One of the mission nurses had found him, during my pre-school years, when we lived at Woliso, bent double on a cot in his parents' house and unable to stand straight. She put him in a body cast, and, months later, he was able to stand and walk normally despite the hump he would always carry on his back. He enrolled in the mission school. Mom and Dad welcomed him not just into the classroom, but into our home, where he became like another member of the family. He was a legendary Monopoly player and a teller of local lore that kept us kids spellbound. He taught us yard games that remained with us years later. Mom and Dad gave him his start on the evangelical narrative. He got saved, went on to teacher's college in Addis Ababa and then Asmara, got a job as a teacher, and hoped to be able to afford someday to attend Bible college and seminary. He wanted to become a minister in the Ethiopian evangelical church.

While he was working as a teacher, he was arrested as a suspected 'counterrevolutionary,' an imperialist collaborator. The evidence: his Amharic Bible and a couple of letters in English from members of our family. It was such a stupid charge that it would have been ridiculous if it weren't for the beatings he suffered in Woliso prison and the seven years of incarceration without trial that he endured after he was transferred to the jail in Addis popularly known as 'Alem Bucka' – 'the End of the World.' He was arrested during those early, chaotic years of the Mengistu government when some people used the extremist rhetoric of the day to carry out personal vendettas. Maybe someone wanted Negusee's teaching job. Or maybe the sincerity of his Christian faith grated a colleague. Whatever it was, his Bible and his association with our family were enough to put him in prison for seven years.

Since the Ethiopian prison system does not feed inmates, relatives must supply the prisoner's meals. So John wrote from Canada to Negusee's aunt and fiancée, and they delivered his letters along with the food. For a time, John even considered contacting Amnesty International about Negusee's case. But the problem with involving Amnesty is that you don't know whether the foreign pressure will make the local authorities release the prisoner or send him back to the room with the bamboo canes and electric wires.

Suddenly, after seven years, and without apology or explanation, Negusee was released. Maybe the prison was too full and they needed to make room. Maybe his good behaviour got him an influential somebody's favour. Of course, after his release and with the record of an ex-con, he found it hard to get a job. With some money cobbled together from mission friends, our family, and a scholarship from his church, he went to Kenya to attend Bible college and seminary, so he could later return to Ethiopia, trained to work in the church he loved. It was in Kenya that he got the mysterious disease that eventually took his life.

What is it about the colonial intellectual ethos that produces such alienation? How does a British education sever the student from indigenous culture? In her 1980 essay collection, *Diverse Inheritance*, Gooneratne identifies two varieties of 'Orientalism' – a discourse more famously analysed in a Middle Eastern context by Edward Said at about the same time. The first kind of Orientalism is that written by European travellers to the East, a discourse which became 'a powerful literary convention of the "oriental", the "eastern" and the "picturesque" [that] still dominates [the Sri Lankan writer's] approach to the description of the local landscape' (104). This Orientalism gave the island the legendary names of 'Serendip' or 'Taprobane': source of exotic spices, fabulous tales, unearthly beauty, fecund vegetation; goal of adventure and desire; site of myth and mystery. In contrast to this imperialist production of what we might call *desirous knowledge* – that is, knowledge produced to confirm and elaborate Europe's desire for the exotic Orient – Gooneratne identifies an opposed kind of 'politicized' Orientalism such as that produced by Sinhalese scholar and statesman James Alwis (1823–1878). Alwis used his training in English schools, not to mimic European exotic visions of his homeland, but to resist them. By producing translations of ancient Sinhalese and Pali Buddhist texts, and then writing critical analyses of these texts in English, Alwis asserted the pre-existence of a tradition of native aesthetics that need not give way to British literary standards of taste. Gooneratne explains that this nineteenth-century scholar 'was inviting his countrymen to refuse to accept judgments of their society that were based on irrelevant standards, and to rediscover their self-respect as a nation through an intelligent understanding of their own history and literature' (137). The tragedy of colonial and postcolonial history is that, as Said has shown, the first kind of Orientalism contained and overshadowed the second. The Orientalist discourse about the East produced by and for the West (*Orientalism* 12, 5), a discourse which confirms the 'otherness' of the Orient for the Occidental subject (65) and operates even today as a 'latent' or unconscious constraint upon Western and Eastern thought (42, 206), has rendered the efforts of Orientalists such as Alwis largely unknown to successive generations of Sri Lankans. As a result, the graduates of the colonial school system most often themselves reproduced the desirous epistemologies of the West. 'The accommodation between the intellectual class and the new imperialism,' writes Said, 'might very well be accounted one of the special triumphs of Orientalism' (322).

In many ways, the Ondaatjes' and Gratiaens' family stories are products of the exoticized Orientalism that dominated the discourses of Sri Lanka's colonial history. 'Here. At the centre of the rumour,' Ondaatje writes in his catalogue of fantastical maps by which colonial Ceylon mirrored the desire of each wave of colonizing Europeans, emerged his own family history. 'At this point on the map' arrived the first Ondaatje from India in 1600, 'a doctor who cured the residing governor's daughter with a strange herb and was rewarded with land, a foreign wife, and a new name which was a Dutch spelling of his own. Ondaatje. A parody of the ruling language' (64). From this fabulous story of origins to the Gatsby-like excesses of the 1920s and 1930s, the entire family narrative is rife with the exotica of textbook Orientalism. Tellingly, the exoticism takes in not just Ceylon's fecund plant and animal life, but also the characters who people the collective family romance. The nineteenth-century Ondaatjes were not only members of a privileged class, but also active writers of the growing collection of aesthetic, scholarly, economic, and philological texts that opened Ceylon's natural and social eccentricities to the desirous inspection of English readers. Dr William Charles Ondaatje, as director of the Botanical Gardens, wrote books about the island's luxuriant flora and fauna, including one on the hundreds of varieties of natural poisons; his brother, Matthew, was an expert in matters of finance and military; another brother, Philip de Melho Jurgen, was master of law and scholarship; and the fourth brother, Reverend Simon, was the last Tamil colonial chaplain of Ceylon, serving in the venerable parish of St Thomas in Colombo (67). 'Almost every Ondaatje of the second and third generation,' writes Michael's brother, Christopher, in his own version of the family romance, 'seems to have contributed something to the well-being of the island, particularly as professionals, intellectuals, and Christians' (19). Each of these distinguished ancestors' occupations made a vocation of over-writing Ceylonese civilization and culture with their education in the desirous epistemologies of the Occident. The family history is both product and reproductive of an exoticized Orientalist discourse.

The next generations, rather than writing learned treatises on Ceylon's curiosities, became exotic curiosities themselves. 'This charmed group was part of another lost world,' writes Michael Ondaatje of his parents' circle during the 1930s. 'The men leaned their chins against the serene necks of the women, danced a waltz or two, slid oysters into their partner's mouths' while the 'waves on the beach collected champagne corks' and 'men who had lost fortunes laughed frantically into the night' (51). The discourse of Orientalism determines more than the 'facts' of the family history; it also shapes the way in which that history must be told. Always, the Ondaatje storytellers reach for the dramatic, the eccentric, the carnivalesque, the cavalier in their anecdotes and recollections. 'Sissy,' one of them tells Michael, 'was always drowning herself because she was an exhibitionist' (51). Family lore insists that Ajoutha, the eight-hour card game Lalla, his grandmother, was playing with her brother Vere just before her death, was a pastime 'the Portuguese had taught the Sinhalese in the 15th century to keep them quiet and preoccupied while they invaded the country' (126). Family gossips use Lalla's travesty of court-room protocol to sum up her character, citing the time when, as a witness in a murder trial, she called the judge, her bridge partner, 'My Lord My God' and received a standing ovation from the gallery (116).

Michael Ondaatje's own contributions to the family narrative follow suit. Lalla's death by alcohol poisoning (see Christopher Ondaatje, 50) becomes, in Ondaatje's narrative, a magical and poetic ride in the flood waters high above the town of Nuwara Eliya until she comes to her rest in the 'blue arms of a jacaranda tree' (113). Even Mervyn's self-destructive dipsomania plays its part in what Douglas Barbour calls the 'grand black farce of his father's life' (153); Mervyn's repeated drunken commandeer-ing of the Trincomalee–Colombo train makes for some of the most enter-taining reading of the entire book. The cumulative effect of these narratives of delightful chicanery, unimpeded eccentricity, perfectly timed witti-cisms, and charming deviousness is an image of an Orientalist's Ceylon, that devious and inscrutable civilization where, as Ondaatje himself puts it, 'a well-told lie is worth a thousand facts' (206). The seductions of such a discourse are so powerful that critics find themselves swept up in its current: Urjo Kareda, for instance, calls *Running in the Family* an 'elegant, superbly woven Eastern wall hanging' (50); and Bernard Hickey admires the 'striking combination of the sensuous, the sensual, the exotic and the erotic ... redolent of the perfumes and smells of the balmy tropics' (38).

This heady family discourse, however, masks deep pain. Lalla does indeed die by drowning, but she drowns in the flood of alcohol that destroys several generations of Gratiaens and Ondaatjes, including Mervyn; and these destructive currents flow perhaps even in the Michael Ondaatje whose certitude about the necessity of his return journey emerges most forcefully when he dances drunk at his own farewell party in Ontario (22). In addition, the idyllic life of the burghers masks the painful divisions of class and ethnicity that have escalated over twenty years into full-scale civil war in Sri Lanka. The burghers' fantastic existence paral-lels the unreality and isolation of the house at Kuttapitiya on the tea and rubber estate that Mervyn managed during Michael's childhood: 'House and garden were perched high above the mist which filled the valley below like a mattress, cutting us off from the real world' (144). As the family declines in dysfunction, alcoholism, and debt, its performances of the exotic discourse of Orientalism become a method of keeping a brave face amidst the general collapse. 'Even in poverty,' writes Ondaatje's brother Christopher of their mother's years working as a housekeeper in Chelsea, England,

she was the star on her own stage. Many of her friends from Colombo came to visit, staying in the rooming house to be near her, and the place was always full of life. Despite her reduced circumstances, she instilled in us a pride and purpose that were infectious ...

Of course, we were still snobs. Though we'd been knocked off our perch as wealthy and pampered colonials, God help the person who treated us as inferiors. Indeed, we all put on a new front as extrovert bohemians who knew everyone and had a great time. (80)

The front may have felt new to the young Christopher, who was just launching his career in banking and finance, but one cannot help seeing it as the current adaptation of an old family narrative.

Indeed, the continuing strength of that Orientalist discourse reveals itself powerfully in Christopher's own book of return to Sri Lanka and the ghosts of his father. For *The Man-Eater of Punanai: A Journey of Discovery to the Jungles of Old Ceylon* uses the extended metaphor of hunting for a man-eating leopard as the vehicle for Christopher's journey back in 1990 to a politically dangerous Sri Lanka and to the psychologically threatening memories of his father. The intertexts to which Christopher returns again and again in *Man-Eater* are those of Sir Richard Burton, Sir Samuel Baker, Harry Storey's *Hunting and Shooting in Ceylon*, and Captain Shelton Agar's account of the hunt for the original leopard in the colonial village of Punanai in 1924.

The discourse in which the two Ondaatje brothers search for their past is inevitably the Orientalist one they inherited through the extended family's romance. In both cases, as Linda Hutcheon observes of Michael Ondaatje's text, the returning Ondaatje is not just the 'recorder, collector, organizer, and narrator of the past, but also the subject of it' (*Canadian* 86). Produced by the self-alienating discourse of his family's Orientalism, Michael Ondaatje confesses, 'I am the foreigner. I am the prodigal who hates the foreigner' (79). Like the Karapotha beetles of the white spots who came but never became native to the island, he remains foreign to the place where he passed his childhood. So, at the same time that *Running in the Family* portrays a male-emigrant subject in intimate relation with his family, it also highlights his severance from the place of his birth.

In the end, Negusee's monkey was an impossible pet, and we had to let it go into the forest. Of course, the problem was that it had lived its whole life with humans, and I doubt it had the survival skills to last very long in the wild. But Mom and Dad didn't know what else to do. It had bitten Bobby Bowers three times, it had sunk its teeth into Colin Creighton's leg once, and it had left me with incisor marks on my chin that I occasionally nick with the razor even now when I shave. The monkey was too high-strung to make a good pet. And we kids were too curious to keep our distance. It was an impossible combination. You could never predict when one of our sudden movements, a startling voice, a thoughtless gesture, might send Tota (we'd simply given him the Amharic word for 'monkey' as a name) into a rage of fear and sharp teeth.

The thing is – I'd wheedled the pet out of Negusee. Negusee was older than me by six or seven years, so would have been in his early twenties when he came down from Addis on a break from teacher's college to visit us. This would be about three or four years before his arrest. We'd gone on a picnic outing to the hot springs at Wando Valley, and the sight of the black-leather, white-fringed faces of the Vervet monkeys waiting for food scraps around the pool reminded me of Tota. Negusee had found the infant monkey when its mother had been killed in a maize field, and he'd raised it as a pet. The idea of having a monkey of my own possessed me with images of Swiss Family Robinson, and I begged Negusee to let me have Tota.

I was twelve or thirteen at the time, aware, but not fully aware, of the power of my begging. With all his feelings of gratitude for what my parents had done for him – the TB cure and the entry into school, as well as his delighted conversion to the Christian faith – I tapped in to feelings of generosity and obligation which I knew how to direct to my own ends but which I didn't consider carefully. I didn't think, for instance, how he would need to convince his young nieces and nephews with whom Tota now lived to give up their pet to his white friends. (On the other hand, maybe his nieces and nephews were tired of getting bitten by the little bugger too.)

And it was all a fiasco. Tota bit me as we were getting him into the car on the way home. He bit me again after we got home. By the end of a couple of weeks, the number of bitten kids in the neighbourhood required Dad to load Tota in the car and take him out to a forested spot near a creek and let him scamper into the trees. He probably didn't last a night before some farmer killed him with a stone for trying to steal food from the cookhouse.

Michael Ondaatje's side-stepping of a fulsome discussion of Sri Lankan politics indicates his severance from *patria* most tellingly. Arun Mukherjee braved the hero-worship that has characterized much Canadian Ondaatje criticism when she took him to task for his 'unwillingness or inability to place his family in a network of social relationships' ('The Poetry' 57) and said that, by not drawing explicit attention to his family's involvements in the colonial tea plantations of pre- and post-independence governments, he naturalizes, even takes sides with, the colonizers. As Mukherjee notes, Ondaatje does not take up the challenge of the lines he quotes from the Sri Lankan poet Lakdasa Wikkramasinha:

Don't talk to me about Matisse ...
the European style of 1900, the tradition of the studio
where the nude woman reclines forever
on a sheet of blood
Talk to me instead of the culture generally –
how the murderers were sustained
by the beauty robbed of savages: to our remote
villages the painters came, and our white-washed
mud-huts were splattered with gunfire. (85–6)

Although the quotation from Wikkramasinha constitutes a significant gesture towards the history of Sri Lankan politics, *Running in the Family* does not talk of 'the culture generally.' In Sri Lanka–born critic Chelva Kanaganayakam's words, Ondaatje's book 'shares the shortcomings of the majority of Sri Lankan writing in English which, for the most part, has stayed clear of the upheavals that have transformed a kindly, generous nation into a cruel and mindless battlefield' (41).

Ondaatje does mention in passing the student insurgency of 1971, but he makes no attempt to address its significance in Sri Lanka's history. He does not explain that young Sri Lankans tried to force the postcolonial government to redistribute the land more equitably and to offer more opportunities to the poor; nor does he divulge his own plantation-owning family's comprador relation to political power during that turbulent time. He does not mention that some of the insurgency's bloodiest battles were fought at Kegalle, where Rock Hill, his ancestral home was located (Kanaganayakam 37). The few references he does make to the rebellion portray his family members as outsiders to the conflict whose popularity and accomplishments excluded them from the insurgents' resentment. During a raid on the Ambepussa rest-house for food, for instance, none of his cousin Rhunie's friends were harmed because they were all members of the Chitrasena dance troupe, of which the young rebels were great fans. Or, in another example, when the insurgents came to collect guns from the Ondaatje estate at Rock Hill, not only did they leave the family in peace because Mervyn had donated a playground to the public some years before, but they invited Michael's step-sister Susan to join them in a game of cricket on the front lawn (100–1).

Such cheerful representations of the family's political position, however, leave significant gaps. 'Was the break-up of inherited wealth only something which affected the Ondaatjes and Gratiaens,' asks Leslie Mundwiler of the earlier generation of the 1920s to 1940s,

or were there deeper social reasons for the generation of 'flaming youth' which Ondaatje describes? What was the relation of the social group he characterizes to the colonial administration and to other groups and classes in Ceylon? If this social group stood outside the many political currents in its time (as Ondaatje seems to suggest), why did it do so? (139)

Of course, the truth is that the group was not apolitical: no social group can be. With the removal of the British in 1948, the fortunes of the burgher class collapsed; and when the Bandaranaike government replaced English with Sinhalese as the country's official language in 1956, there was a mass exodus of burghers to Australia. Many of those who remained, however, involved themselves in a disastrous *coup* attempt in 1961 (MacIntyre 316–17). They wanted to regain the privileges they had lost. Ondaatje's grandfather provides an example of what those privileges had been.

Philip Francis Ondaatje built the Rock Hill estate from the fortune he made when the British 'opened up' the tea plantations – which, Christopher Ondaatje explains, was the technical term for the buying of large tracts of land for tea companies. 'What with the Portuguese and the Dutch and the inadequate village records,' Christopher writes,

the titles to land up in the hills or out in the jungle weren't very clear. A lawyer with cunning and a grasp of the local language was obviously useful, and 'Bampa' was such a lawyer. He worked for various tea agencies, and sometimes he acted for his own account, accumulating badly titled property and selling it cleaned up. In the process he became extremely wealthy. (20)

What even the more politically-minded Christopher fails to mention, of course, is that hardly any of the land of such a densely populated island could be considered 'empty' and available for such 'cleaning up.' This dedication of great tracts of land to cash-crop plantations and estates is precisely what the insurgents of 1971 protested. In light of considerations such as these, Sugunasiri goes one step further than Mukherjee's assertion that Ondaatje sides with the colonizer, claiming instead that 'he *was* (through his community and class) the colonizer!' (64). *Running in the Family* consistently bypasses such recognition. In so doing, it reproduces the ignorance the Ondaatje family discourse wishes to maintain. Burgher poet Peter Scharen's poem, 'Fathers,' explains:

Bringing bread and canon, chain, pike and halberd,
Came my stately fathers, gowned and booted,
Zealous but unfanatical, with book and fortress
Of squared stone, coat of arms on the great door,
Warm as home, sweating greed, my fathers,
Whom I do not know
    Whom I do not wish to know ... (quoted in Gooneratne, 169)

Despite Ondaatje's silence about his family's comprador position in pre- and post-independence politics in Sri Lanka, none of the Sri Lankan writers I have quoted above agree wholeheartedly with Mukherjee's attack. Sri Lankan playwright Ernest MacIntyre claims that Ondaatje's representation of his burgher ancestors conveys accurately the unreal, solipsistic existence of these people in the 1920s and 1930s (317); Christopher Ondaatje suggests the book presents a poeticized truth (50); while Sugunasiri and Kanaganayakam agree that the picture of the burghers is accurate, though, in Sugunasiri's words, 'it is a picture without a frame' (63). My claim here has been that this sociopolitical frame is exactly what the family's upper-class Orientalist discourse excludes. Linda Hutcheon has identified *Running in the Family* as an instance of historiographic metafiction, which includes among its values, she says, quoting Terry Eagleton, those of 'ideological fiction, taking ideology as meaning "those modes of feeling, valuing, perceiving and believing which have some kind of relation to the maintenance and reproduction of social power"' (*Canadian* 72). The Ondaatjes' family romance of high exploits, ingenious repartee, devious brilliance, and tragic grandeur obscures the very real social relations upon which their life-story depends,

and by so doing serves the ideological function of maintaining and repro-
ducing the social power of the discourse of Orientalism.

*Mom and Dad are retiring this summer after more than thirty-five years
working in Ethiopia. Dad's most recent letter outlines some of the final
arrangements they want to make before they leave. One of them involves
Fantaye, Negusee's widow. It's two years since Negusee died, and she's finding
it difficult to make a living. But she's got an idea. She wants to open a day-
school kindergarten in Addis Ababa, and she is wondering if our family would
like to help her get started. Dad says that Negusee's church and the mission
would put up some money, and private donations would be gladly received. Of
course we'll help; it's the least we can do.*

*Somehow, anything to do with Negusee cuts me somewhere deep. But in a
different way than it does John. He and Negusee promised each other as kids
they would one day serve the Lord together in Ethiopia. John kept his pledge,
arriving back there just ten or twelve months after Negusee's death. Now, he's
fulfilling the promise through his friendship with Demmesee. I never made
those kinds of promises. Somehow, I missed the family path of the missionary
narrative. Call me a black sheep, though, and you'd have the wrong impression. I wasn't an active rebel. I didn't reject anything; it just happened.*

*Was it the bodies lying in the street during the Kai Shebbir (red terror)
phase of the Mengistu government's violent suppression of dissidents between
1976 and 1978? The crumpled forms in bloody clothing I saw from the school-
bus window in the mornings? Was it the shock on Mekdes's face when she told
Mom she couldn't work in our kitchen for a week while she buried her husband, father, and brother who'd been shot in her home when men in army
uniforms burst through the door? Was it the way people averted their eyes
when we foreigners walked by on city streets? Was it the knowledge that our
friendship was used as an excuse to put Negusee in jail? Whatever it was, I
could not continue telling myself the inherited story.*

*But each time I see the photograph of Negusee and Fantaye among the
family photos that clutter the top of my bookshelf, I wonder what it would have
been like not to have gone to Bingham Academy, not to have sung those
missionary songs, not to have left the violence of the Mengistu government for
the predictability of Canada. More than anything else, I wonder what kind of
narrative Negusee would have told – what story of his relation to the Coleman
family – had he lived long enough to tell it, and I the ears to hear it.*

I have been arguing that the public and social nature of the Ondaatje family's decline means that a communally composed family romance predates Michael Ondaatje's own retelling. I have also argued that the family's Orientalist discourse reinforces the class-position of the narrative Ondaatje inherits, alienating him from an intimate reconnection with the country and its people. Furthermore, the severance from *patria* is given increased emotional intensity through its metonymic association with the severance from *pater*. The inheritance of the Ondaatje family romance becomes even more complicated when it comes to the cult of the father: for, as Freud indicated, the family romance produces simultaneously the father's *exile* and his *exaltation*. Mervyn Ondaatje thus becomes a scandalous romantic hero whose self-destruction places him beyond reach, beyond comprehension, amid the series of rumours and myths that eddy around him. After his death, for example, he reappears as an old grey cobra which defies shotguns fired at point-blank range, returning and returning to visit the family until finally 'one of the old workers at Rock Hill told my stepmother what had become obvious, that it was my father who had come to protect his family' (99). Thus, as Freud says, the father is exalted to legendary status, while the mother in *Running in the Family* copes with the real-world problems of poisonous snakes and an alcoholic husband's gin bottles. 'They were both from gracious, genteel families,' Ondaatje says of Doris and Mervyn, 'but my father went down a path unknown to his parents and wife. She followed him and coped with him for fourteen years, surrounding his behaviour like a tough and demure breeze' (149).

The mythology that surrounds Mervyn removes him from intimacy with his children. 'My father's body was a globe of fear,' writes Ondaatje in a poem entitled 'Letters & Other Worlds.' 'His body was a town we never knew / He hid that he had been where we were going / ... He hid where he had been that we might lose him' (*There's a Trick* 44). This is the complex cult of the father with which Michael and Christopher must somehow come to terms. (I take it as a sign of the particular complex of the father–son relation that Mervyn's two sons publish books about their struggles to understand him.) And the cult haunts both sons' narratives of return to Sri Lanka. 'Everywhere I went, my father's ghost kept reappearing,' writes Christopher in *Man-Eater*, which is dedicated 'For my father, Philip Mervyn Ondaatje.'

... my whole life may have been haunted by my father's ghost. It had followed me – driven me – from England to Canada, from hardship to wealth, and back once more to the island where I had been born.

The more I thought about it, the more it seemed as if the entire history of this island was a variation on the theme of fathers battling sons ... The lesson seemed clear, like a universal law of nature: if you don't come to terms with the ghost of your father, it will never let you be your own man. (165)

The problem is, however, that there is no direct access to the deceased father. 'My loss was that I never spoke to him as an adult,' writes Michael Ondaatje (179). The only way to learn of him is through the haunting family stories.

'What began it all,' Ondaatje says of his return journey to Sri Lanka, 'was the bright bone of a dream I could hardly hold onto ... I saw my father, chaotic, surrounded by dogs, and all of them were screaming and barking into the tropical landscape' (21). The nightmare image derives from one of the many surreal stories of Mervyn's dipsomania – 'a story about my father,' Ondaatje admits, that 'I cannot come to terms with' (181). According to this story, Mervyn's friend Arthur finds him walking naked in the jungle, holding with superhuman strength five ropes with a black dog dangling on the end of each one. 'The dogs were too powerful to be in danger of being strangled,' the son explains. 'The danger was to the naked man who held them at arm's length, towards whom they swung like large dark magnets ... He had captured all the evil in the regions he had passed through and was holding it' (182). The super-human strength, the deluded attempt to master the world's evil, the threat of self-destruction are all masculine modes in their most extreme form: isolation and violence; the super-man stripped of his social garb and struggling to master a threatening world. This is the Ondaatje family romance's legendary father, who, to borrow lines from Ondaatje's poem 'White Dwarfs,' has 'sail[ed] to that perfect edge / where there is no social fuel' (*There's a Trick* 68). Now, the son wants to reach through the multiple refractions of the exalting–exiling cult that surrounds his father so he can try to understand him. As Smaro Kamboureli indicates, such an understanding is difficult to achieve, given the scandalous instability that the figure of Mervyn represents in *Running in the Family*. 'Mervyn Ondaatje is not the father figure as legislator,' Kamboureli writes; 'his is the law of scandal ... [H]e is a scattered center, a figure that deconstructs his own paternal (patriarchal) authority' (88).

Mervyn's remoteness and insanity remind Ondaatje of Gloucester and Edgar on the edge of Shakespeare's imaginary cliff. 'I long for the moment in the play where Edgar reveals himself to Gloucester,' he writes, 'and it never happens. Look I am the son who has grown up. I am the son you have made hazardous, who still loves you' (180). But, unlike the moment in Shakespeare's play, the *éclaircissement* never takes place. Despite Ondaatje's imaginative and sympathetic reconstruction of Mervyn's 'thanikama,' his bitter isolation after his divorce and the dispersal of his children, the son is forced to admit: 'There is so much to know and we can only guess. Guess around him. To know him from these stray actions I am told about by those who loved him. And yet, he is still one of those books we long to read whose pages remain uncut. We are still unwise' (200). Ultimately, then, the family romance, which compensates for the tragic story of Mervyn's self-destructive fall through a cult which exalts and savours the stories of his eccentric brilliance and theatricality, proves impervious to the son's desire for reconnection.

And this discursive family system severs Michael from *pater* – as it does from *patria* – through its ultimate imperviousness to his quest for truth. 'Truth disappears with history and gossip tells us in the end nothing of personal relationships,' he writes (53).

Individuals are seen only in the context of these swirling social tides ... Where is the intimate and the truthful in all this? Teenager and Uncle. Husband and lover. A lost father in his solace ... After the cups of tea, coffee, public conversations ... I want to sit down with someone and talk with utter directness, want to talk to all the lost history like that deserving lover. (54)

'The rumours pass on,' Ondaatje writes in his poem 'Taking,'

> the rumours pass on
> are planted
> till they become a spine. (*There's a Trick* 57)

So the rumours and legends solidify into a family discourse that cannot bend to the returning son's inquiries, will not readmit him to the intimate, curling Sinhalese vertebrae of the alphabet of his past (*Running* 83). The discursive genealogy of the Ondaatje family romance, invested in an upper-class Sri Lankan Orientalist narrative mode that tries to recuperate the family's loss of status through the elaboration of an exotic, self-exalting theatricality, resists the emigrant son's desire for reintegration with his father and homeland.

An awareness of the specific social and historical contexts of this genealogy demonstrate how postcolonial critique, with its willingness to name political and historical referents, can supply a corrective to the kind of 'easy' postmodernism which names only aesthetic antecedents. Much of the criticism of *Running in the Family*, despite Mukherjee's intervention, restricts its focus to the generic experimentation, the deliberate toying with historiography, and the fragmentation and piecing of self-representation that make Ondaatje's writing so amenable to postmodernist analysis. John Thieme, for example, reads the book as a 'quintessentially Canadian text' (40) because of its postmodern resistance of unitary classification, closure, and essentialism, along with what he calls its suggestion that 'both individual and national identities are formed through a series of random, and frequently bizarre, accretions' (41). A postcolonial awareness of the political genealogy of the Ondaatje family romance demonstrates how far from 'random' is the logic of the 'bizarre' history of the self Ondaatje produces in *Running in the Family*. An attention to the specific historical and social context of the Ondaatje family romance shows that postcolonial identities are neither haphazard nor coincidental in their formation, but are often composed under colonialist discourses such as Orientalism, which, in turn, shape family relations that are also often grimly predictable: alcoholism, alienation, divorce, family dysfunction, emigration, and the exile (or death) of the father. Ondaatje's text allows us to see how the predominant and wide-ranging ideologies of colonial and imperial history continue to exert their defining influences within family systems so that Orientalist discourse can define and de-limit the whole of a family's self-sustaining narrative.

We should not allow ourselves to forget, however, that despite the fact that the Ondaatje family romance produces Michael's severance from *patria* and *pater*, it also has positive effects. Freud claims that the family romance constitutes an arena in which the child develops a highly imaginative storytelling capacity. And Marthe Robert has expanded on Freud's suggestion with her theory that the family romance is the psychological origin of the genre of the novel (31). She claims that the 'pseudo-biographical' mode of the family romance introduces the 'dialectic of "invention" and "reality"' which 'the novel inherits long before it is transcribed' (33). Thus, it could be that the family romance which determines Michael Ondaatje's severance also nourishes his writerly imagination – a theory that parallels Lacan's schema whereby Oedipal castration facilitates the subject's entry into the symbolic. On the genealogical level, certainly the family romance's endless elaboration and recitation provides Ondaatje with a wealth of story-starters, so that it represents, at one and the same time, the source of plenitude and of alienation. Furthermore, despite the fact that the son's desire for reconnection with the father meets with failure, the necessity that he pursue that desire through renewed contact with his extended family means that the male subject represented in *Running in the Family* breaks with the tradition of autonomous masculinity and instead celebrates an interdependency which is, despite the paradigm of male severance, a form of masculine innovation.

5

The Law of the Father under the Pen of the Son: Rohinton Mistry, Ven Begamudré, and the Romance of Family Progress

In chapter 4, I argued that the extended family's desire to recuperate from its traumatic past – from social decline and internal dysfunction – mobilizes the family romance that Michael Ondaatje inherits and re-writes in *Running in the Family*. This chapter traces Rohinton Mistry's and Ven Begamudré's inheritance of a more forward-looking type of family narrative, one which I will call, echoing some of the concerns of the previous chapter, the romance of family progress. Like the Freudian romance, the romance of family progress responds to disillusion through the construction of a family fantasy, and, like the Freudian version, this fantasy expresses itself in terms of upper-class ambition. But whereas Freud's family romance involves the child's (usually the son's) nostalgic invention of a *grand past for himself*, the romance of family progress involves the parents' invention of a *grand future for themselves through their child* (usually the son). This chapter studies how the father–son struggles in Mistry's *Such a Long Journey* and Begamudré's *Van de Graaff Days* take up and challenge the romance of family progress. And, as in the previous chapter, on *Running in the Family*, the postcolonial context of Mistry's and Begamudré's narratives highlights the social and political determinants of these families' self-perpetuating narratives.

According to the romance of family progress, your place of origin is a dead end. In this place, there is no future: it is too backward, too impover-ished, too corrupt for you to make anything of yourself here. Especially if you are young. It is different for the old; their roots are sunk too deep in this overtilled soil to pull up now. But the young must leave this hopeless place and make a name for themselves in the big world. Two paths, often intersecting, lead to that glorious future: education and emigration. And it is the glad duty of the old to set their children's, usually their sons', feet upon one or both of these paths. For, according to patrilineage, the son's success is the father's success, the child's achievement the parents' achievement.

The postcolonial version of the romance of family progress in Mistry's and Begamudré's novels follows the ancient pattern of migration from country poverty to reputed city wealth that I derived, in the introduction to this book, from Raymond Williams. According to Williams, the ancient pattern of rural-to-urban migration has evolved through twentieth-century imperialism into a pattern whereby the stories of 'first world' wealth and security induce colonial and postcolonial people to abandon their homes in the 'third world' for the El Dorado of the imperial metropolis. This version of the romance of family progress flows steadily in what we in Africa used to call the 'brain-drain,' whereby the intelligentsia leave their homes for better jobs and paycheques in Europe or America (since moving to Canada, I have learned that Canadians resent a similar current to the United States). It flows in the movement of people, products, and capital from the poor East and South to the rich West and North. This intergenerational romance, in its particularly patrilineal form, runs in the heart of Rohinton Mistry's and Ven Begamudré's first novels;[1] it is the restless current that carries these characters on such a long journey. But romances are easier dreamed than lived, and, as the fathers in both novels discover, the journey is fraught with upsets, the current dangerously unpredictable. Here, then, is the focus of this chapter: the author-son's questioning of the father's authority. Whereas *A Casual Brutality* and *Running in the Family* address the haunting absence of the colonial-era father, *Such a Long Journey* and *Van de Graaff Days* address his troublesome presence. Both Mistry and Begamudré are emigrant sons, and both have written novels in which sons defy the romance of family progress and, with it, the plans of their fathers; none the less, I also argue that each of these books constitutes an attempt by a son who bailed out of his father's narrative of progress to write his way towards a resolution of that filial betrayal, and thus to salve an inner pain.

But first of all, two stories, one as old as the ancient Indian epic the *Mahabharata*, and the second as recent as 1991. Early in Begamudré's *Van de Graaff Days*, Krishna, soon to be a father, comes upon a calendar picture of the popular Hindu god Ganesha. We listen as he mentally rehearses the story:

Ganesha's father [Shiva] often surprised his wife [Parvati] while she bathed. One day she mixed the scurf of her body with ointments. She formed a boy and brought him to life with water from the Ganges. Setting him outside her door, she hoped Ganesha would guard her. His father found his way blocked. Not realizing Ganesha was his own son, the father cut off Ganesha's head. Ganesha's mother grieved so bitterly, her husband sent messengers to find another head. The first creature they saw was an elephant. It willingly sacrificed its head, which the father then attached to his son's neck. (64)

These are the bare bones of a story that refracts the impulse of the Oedipal story. The initial situation is generally the same – the rivalry, the contest for possession of the mother, the deadly violence – but the emphasis differs here from that of the Freudian narrative: the Indian story draws our attention to the anxieties and violence of the father, rather than those of the son.

But there is more. One variant of the story tells us that, later on, while Shiva and Parvati were making love, the god Krishna came to the door to return Shiva's battle-axe. There, he engaged in combat with Ganesha, who was on duty at the entrance. Ganesha had the upper hand in the struggle, but when he saw it was his *father's* axe that Krishna was preparing to hurl at him, his 'enmity was disarmed' and he submitted to a blow that broke off one of his tusks. It is this tusk, broken in submission to the father and the father's peer, that, according to another narrative fragment, Ganesha later uses to take dictation from the scop-poet of the *Mahabharata* itself. In other words, the work that carries his own story is written out of the very wound inflicted by the father. And this story, rather than ending with Oedipus's mutilation and exile, leaves us with Ganesha, fat and jolly god of wisdom and remover of obstacles, enjoying in perpetuity an endless supply of sweets (Ganesha-legend variants appear in Bonnefoy 896–910, Mercatante, Keith 181–2, and Kearns 212–13).

The second story was written by Marwan Hassan, who came to Canada from Lebanon. His 1991 novel, *The Memory Garden of Miguel Carranza*, makes a haunting allegory of a grieving father's anguish. Two suicides have cast Dr Miguel Carranza, a Toronto neurosurgeon, into deep sorrow and self-doubt. The suicide within the novel's present time-frame occurs when one of the doctor's patients, a victim of phantom-limb syndrome, finds Carranza's cure impossible to endure and takes an overdose of alcohol and barbiturates. The other suicide occurred some years before the novel's events, but it has taken up permanent residence at the centre of Carranza's own mind. Ever since his fifteen-year-old son, Jaime, slashed his wrists at the family cottage north of Toronto, Carranza has been plagued with guilt, nightmares, self-reproach. In dream after waking dream, he grieves for his lost son, searching through the rooms of the house and through his memories for clues to Jaime's whereabouts, hints to his own despair. Carranza cries for his lost son, mourns for his own inability to understand him, for the possibility that this lack of under-standing drove Jaime to suicide. The loss of his son is a loss from his own body. The illusory pain of damaged nerves has entered his own cortex. Jaime has become his own phantom limb. For all his professional poise, the genuine brilliance of his surgical skill, the deep compassion that makes him outstanding as a practitioner and physician, Carranza cannot cure himself. Despite his own achievements and successes, the father's whole identity depends upon the love and acceptance of his son. Without these, he feels hollow, purposeless, a failure.

These two stories, ancient and modern, urge us to study the Oedipal story in another direction, as it were, to examine the beginning of the story, the story of what American psychologist John Munder Ross has called 'the Laius complex' (32, 22). These stories refer us to the conflicts and anxieties of a father who loves and fears his son, who comes to see his son as inheritor and disinheritor, friend and rival, comrade and traitor. In so doing, they identify the central narrative current of *Such a Long Journey* and *Van de Graaff Days*. For in drawing our attention to the father's anxieties, they bring into view the trouble that drives both novels: the insecurity of the father who depends upon the love and obedience of his son. And by exposing the dynamic instability at the base of the paternal régime, by showing how the father's authority competes with many other social forces, these two novels, *Such a Long Journey* and *Van de Graaff Days*, provide a resituation of the Lacanian Name-of-the-Father in spe-cific social relations that complicates the negotiations of the classic, nuclear self–mother–father triad of psychoanalysis. 'Citizenship, class, ownership, wealth and debt, gender, community, the social relations between men and women, ethnicity and race, forms of power and so on – all these features of the social world are found *in* the Oedipus complex,' writes John Brenkman in *Straight Male Modern: A Cultural Critique of Psychoanalysis*. 'I suspect that Lacan reduced the moral universe to un-conscious desire and paternal Law to avoid the consequences, theoretical and therapeutic, of having to make psychoanalysis address this dispa-rate, volatile field of relationships' (245–6). By delineating the ways in which the Indian father's authority is challenged and limited by colonial and ethnic history; by the natural process of ageing; and by postcolonial politics, Westernization, marital breakdown, and emigration; these novels refract the symbolic authority of the Name-of-the-Father. They trouble the self-justifications of the paternal law.

It stands to reason that such troublings of paternity would take place in immigrant writing. In an article entitled 'Italo-Canadian Poetry and Ethnic Semiosis in the Postmodern Context,' William Boelhower claims that 'the ethnic subject produces difference ... by questioning the original project of the immigrant fathers and mothers. In effect, ethnic semiosis as *poiesis* means recounting a rival story, what we might call a mapping exercise in ethnic tracing, an attempt to recount a series of micro-differences' (175). This tracing of divergence from the parents' romance constitutes the 'genealogical project' that, according to Boelhower, distinguishes 'ethnic semiosis.' His Sausserian-derived term sounds like some kind of ethnic disease, and as such it is well chosen, for, as *Such a Long Journey* and *Van de Graaff Days* reveal, the emigrant son's retelling of the intergenerational family narrative conveys profound dis-ease, especially for the paternal law.

Some little kids are cuddly on your lap; they nuzzle your neck, circle your shoulders with their arms, snuggle close to your warmth. Others stand on your thighs, stiff-arming you in the solar plexus so they can keep their balance while they look around. The cuddling and stiff-arming take different forms as the child ages.

I stiff-armed Dad with a briefcase when I was twenty-one. He gave John and me matching briefcases for Christmas the year we all started school in Regina – Dad and John at seminary, me at university. That was seventeen years ago, and John still has his. I've seen it, filled with sermon notes, Sunday-school lessons, missionary correspondence. The briefcase, one of those stiff, rectangular, pressboard cases with the leatherette finish and pop-up clasps, was too big to fit in my locker.

I was disappointed Dad hadn't noticed that university students carried their books and papers in backpacks, not briefcases. You saw the students everywhere – on city buses, bicycles, sidewalks – packs slung casually over their shoulders, hands free for something else. Anything else. But then, when would he have had the chance to notice that university-types carried backpacks? He'd never seen where I spent my student days. He could only go on his own experience. At the seminary, his fellow students – the serious ones – carried their files, books, papers in briefcases.

Yet again, he was probably disappointed I hadn't noticed he was trying. Trying to affirm my choices to be 'me.' To go to university and study what I wanted to study, even if it meant I didn't become a missionary or, at least, a minister. Here was a gift to help me on my way. I'll never know what he felt, because when I gave him back his gift, he seemed quite glad to give me the money so I could choose my own backpack. He used that brown leatherette case himself to carry his own books and papers for the rest of his Master's at seminary. He still has it. I've seen it, filled with sermon notes, Sunday School lessons, missionary correspondence.

I still have the backpack I traded mine for, but I don't use it for books and papers any more. When I moved to Edmonton to start the PhD, I got one of those soft leather briefcases, the old-fashioned kind with the flap that falls over the front and fastens with two little clips. Now I use the backpack for juice, extra sweaters, and trail mix when we go hiking in the mountains. I tell people my dad gave me this backpack.

To trouble the paternal law, however, is not to dispense with it. For we must remember that both novels were written with the broken tusk of an emigrant son's pain. In *Finding Our Fathers: The Unfinished Business of Manhood*, Harvard psychologist Samuel Osherson asserts that sons often internalize their complex relations with their fathers, creating a psychological scar. 'The internalized, wounded father is rooted in the son's experience of the father,' Osherson writes, 'a composite of fantasy and reality, not always corresponding to the reality of what the father was really like or exactly what went on within the family' (23). It is every man's task, Osherson continues, to heal this wounded father within (43). I read Mistry's and Begamudré's novels as emigrant sons' attempts to rewrite and heal that composite internalized father, to compose through fiction a new relationship with that old inner pain. In so doing, I ask whether such a recomposition constitutes a subvention or a subversion of the patriarchal law.

Each novel deploys multiple plot lines, but the one I will focus on in both is essentially the same. An Indian father, socialized in the romance of family progress, has made elaborate plans for his eldest son to become an engineer and so to realize for the family dreams of prestige and success. In both novels, the sons incline more to art than science, an inclination too idealistic and impractical for the fathers' comprehension. The sons, with varying degrees of nerve, reject their fathers' plans. The fathers and sons become estranged from each other. At the end of both novels, the fathers and sons come to some accommodation, though there is no certainty that they have reached any kind of full reconciliation.

It is important to recognize that the mothers in both Mistry's and Begamudré's novels play absolutely essential roles in their sons' development. We would do well to heed Jonathan Rutherford's reminder that the mother–son relationship is as fundamental to the son's development as the father–son dyad (24). In *Such a Long Journey*, the mother, Dilnavaz, intervenes repeatedly in the struggles between Gustad and Sohrab, trying desperately to mediate between them, and in *Van de Graaff Days*, Hari's mother, Rukmini, and grandmother Ajji raise him for the formative first six years of his life (and roughly the first half of the novel) while Krishna is out of the picture in far-off America. I do not intend to devalue the mothers' function in these novels, but instead to focus intensely upon the paternal anxiety that causes the fathers in both novels to invest themselves so completely in their plans for their sons' futures. For clearly, in both novels, the father's identity is at stake: the mother assents to the practical benefits of the father's plan, but she has not invested so much of her own hopes in it that she cannot consider alternatives. His investment, and the attendant risks, bedevil the father.

Such a Long Journey shows the romance of family progress at work in the country of origin long before any of the family members emigrates. Here, in a nutshell, are Gustad and Dilnavaz Noble's plans for their eldest son, Sohrab:

they had been discussing it endlessly, making plans and provisions. How he would live in the student hostel at Powai, and come home at the weekends, or they would visit him with a picnic lunch, the college was so close to the lake and the scene-scenery was so beautiful. And after he finished IIT [Indian Institute of Technology] he would go to an engineering college in America, maybe MIT. (27)

The emigrant path rises readily out of the educational one because the narrative of migrant progress leading from the colony to the imperial centre forms a sometimes silent but always essential feature of the curriculum of the colonial school whose teachers, language of instruction, materials, methods, and disciplines all assume the superiority of the imperial metropolitan ideal (see Ngugi, Lamming, Viswanathan, and Gooneratne). So the parents' plans for the son are shaped by the discourses and institutions of the kind of colonialist Orientalism I described in the previous chapter.

As I argued in that chapter, such public or social discourses gradually weave themselves into intimate family systems. In *Such a Long Journey*, they manifest themselves in the father's own disappointments and fears. Gustad wants for his son what he was unable to achieve himself, and he worries that his son will miss the chance to escape the dead end in which he feels himself trapped. So when Sohrab angrily rejects his father's plans and refuses to enrol in IIT, Gustad is devastated. 'In me,' the distraught father cries to Dada Ormuzd, the Parsi deity, 'when I was young, You put the desire to study, get ahead, be a success. Then You took away my father's money, left me rotting in the bank. And for my son? You let me arrange everything, put it within reach, but You take away his appetite for IIT' (55). 'What kind of life was Sohrab going to look forward to?' he frets. A member of the approximately 120,000 Parsis in Bombay, descendants of the seventh-century Zoroastrians who fled the Muslim invasion of Persia for the relative safety afforded by the Hindu Gujarat kings, Gustad sees the current tide of political and ethnic conflict turning against his community and narrowing his children's opportunities in 1970s Bombay. 'It was going to be like the black people in America,' he thinks, 'twice as good as the white man to get half as much. How could he make Sohrab understand this? How to make him realize what he was doing to his father, who had made the success of his son's life the purpose of his own?' (55).

The projection onto the son of the father's own ambitions becomes the major source of the son's irritation. As the psychologists Calvin Colarusso and Robert Nemiroff explain in 'The Father in Midlife: Crisis and the Growth of Paternal Identity,' the father's own lack of individuation constitutes the familiar solipsism by which 'fathers search for immortality through their children, particularly through their sons' (316). 'The duty and good works which a son performs,' affirms the *Shâyast lâ Shâyast*, the ancient Pahlavi book of Zoroastrian laws, 'are as much the father's as though they had been done by his own hand' (quoted in Modi 2). Evidently then, though Parsis do not share the Hindu belief in reincarnation, they do share the 'strong projective identification of fathers with their sons' that Indian psychologist Sudhir Kakar identifies in the surrounding Hindu traditions. In 'Fathers and Sons: An Indian Experience,' Kakar explains that, according to Hindu belief, 'the father himself is born as the son, and with the placing of his own seed in the womb he has placed his own self' (419; see also Tuli 98). Producing a son is not only a duty one performs for one's ancestors, whereby the father discharges his obligation to maintain his forefathers (Kakar 417–18), but also an act of emotional and sensual gratification. 'The touch of soft sandal paste, of women, of [cool] water is not so agreeable as the touch of one's own infant son locked in one's embrace,' declares Shakuntla in the *Mahabharata*. 'There is nothing in the world more agreeable to the touch than the embrace of one's son' (quoted in Kakar 418). However, such an embrace, as both Sohrab and Hari indicate in *Such a Long Journey* and *Van de Graaff Days*, can be stifling for the son; it expresses the anxious desires of the father without much consideration for what feelings the son might have, and produces a situation wherein, in Gerald Pearson's memorable phrase from *Adolescence and the Conflict of Generations*, 'two wounded narcissisms dislike each other' (44).

Dad's a real brick. He sometimes drives Mom crazy with the way he can trudge on and on with no apparent need for a change of pace, a break from the mundane. He's so much the definition of regularity that the rest of us have come to assume his homeostasis. He gets migraine headaches that put him under for a while, but, even when he's in their cranial vice, he just retires quietly to bed with a hot-water bottle and a bottle of aspirins until they untwist enough to let him get up again.

So I was surprised to come across Mom's matter-of-fact statement in one of the letters John filed away back in the seventies: 'You must remember Daddy in your prayers. He's been quite depressed and finds it hard to get out of bed in the mornings. He hates going to work.' The letter is dated 1974 and bears our Sheshemane address. It's a strange and revealing thing to read these old letters between our scattered family members from those traumatic years. They were tough times for all of us – John and Sharon in Canada worrying about what might be happening to the rest of us in the new Ethiopia – but I couldn't have known until I'd had my own brushes with depression as an adult the toll those years took from Mom and Dad.

In 1974 Dad was working as station manager at Sheshemane, where the mission had a big operation: there were two hospitals (one for leprosy and one general), a special ward for TB patients, a big farm which provided employment and food for the lepers who were literal outcasts from local society, a school, and two churches – again, one for lepers and their kids and one for the general public. Dad had given up the church-planting and Bible-school teaching he had loved at Woliso in response to mission council's need for his composure. His quiet courtesy, absolute loyalty to the mission, and fluency in Amharic made him good at mediating between mission council and both government agencies and the mission's Ethiopian employees. He'd worked for a couple of years at HQ in Addis before agreeing to serve as station manager at Sheshemane.

Nineteen seventy-four was the year Haile Selassie was deposed and the military junta began to form itself into the new government. For much of those first couple of years, nobody knew exactly who was in power. But one thing was clear. Haile Selassie's feudal style of government with its dependence on the NATO bloc was on the way out; the new leadership included an uneven mix of Marxist intellectuals who had witnessed Kent State and the Black Panthers during their overseas scholarships and personally ambitious army officers who supplied the necessary muscle to press through the growing demands for change. 'Ethiopia First' was the new motto. The fat kulaks who had sucked the blood of their rural fiefs became enemies of the state. They were imprisoned, their palatial homes in Addis seized, their rural lands subdivided into communal farms. Units of cadres dispersed throughout the country to educate the populace to their new rights, to raise their vigilance against any attempted return of the decadent landlords, and to explain why His Beloved Majesty must be replaced.

Missions such as ours had enjoyed fairly smooth working relations with Haile Selassie's government. We had offered educational and medical services that reflected well on his administration. This meant the new leaders saw missions as collaborators with the old regime. Hadn't the emperor granted the mission the huge tract of farmland at Sheshemane in exactly the same manner he granted fiefs to the blood-suckers from Addis? The cadres suspected that these whites who came from outside weren't as well meaning and disinterested as they appeared. Everyone could see the rich harvests gathered each year on the farm. There were hospital fees and school fees. Every four or five years the white station manager would be replaced by a new white manager. Did they not leave with suitcases bulging with money, the profits from this fat operation? Meanwhile the workers' wages remained pretty much the same, and the food got no better in the hospitals.

The lepers were reminded not to be so readily grateful. They were the backbone of this operation, but what did they get out of it? A few loaves of bread and an old house with a tin roof. A union was organized. They demanded higher wages, shorter working hours, better housing, free schooling for the kids. Dad became de facto Management in a battle with an angry union.

As Gustad's prayer of complaint to Dada Ormuzd indicates, the father's anxieties congeal in specific social and political conditions. Gustad's fears are multiple. He watches the development of ethnic fundamentalism among Hindu groups like Shiv Sena who proclaim that, since Bombay ceased being officially bilingual and became the capital of Maharashtra state, Gujarati-speaking people such as the Parsis should convert completely to Marathi, the language of Maharashtra (see Moraes 114–15; Malhotra 63). This would constitute one more step in the steady decline of Parsi influence in Bombay. Under the British, they had used their comprador position to become magnates of shipping, retail, and banking.

'Until about the 1950s,' writes Dom Moraes, 'the Parsis were probably the wealthiest community in India' (62). But independence undermined the Parsis' privilege, and, like Indira Gandhi's Parsi husband, Feroze, they have since been sidelined from the centre stage of power. As Dinshawji, Gustad's bank colleague, puts it, 'Parsis were the kings of banking in those days. Such respect we used to get. Now the whole atmosphere only has been spoiled. Ever since that Indira nationalized the banks' (38).[2]

The decline of the Parsi community is not just a general occurrence; Gustad has experienced it personally in his own family. His grandfather had been a builder of fine wood furniture who ran his own shop; his father had operated a successful bookstore. During a period of illness, however, Gustad's father had handed over the management of the store to a dissolute brother who drank and gambled away the family assets. When his father got out of hospital, he faced the bailiff and bankruptcy. The strain sent his mother to hospital, where she died not long after. The family could no longer afford Gustad's tuition, so he had to drop out in his second year of college and go to work as a junior clerk in the Parsi bank. The family's position continues to deteriorate during Gustad's own times: with the refugee tax resulting from the war in what will become neighbouring Bangladesh and the devaluation of the rupee, the Nobles are unable to afford any longer the creamery milk they used to buy and have to settle for the watery stuff sold by the local milk *bhaiya*. All of Gustad's ceremonial Parsi undershirts, his *sudras*, have tears in them, and he cannot afford to buy new ones. When Roshan, their daughter, falls ill, Dilnavaz pawns her wedding gold bangles to afford the medication.

So Gustad's fears for his son reach beyond the two of them. They are founded in a nostalgia for better times when his father afforded a horse-drawn carriage, threw parties, entertained well-dressed guests; when his grandfather operated the furniture store and commanded a labour force of carpenters. They rise out of a shame he still feels at his father's failure and a fear that he himself might be failing, stuck as he is in the bank. In his article 'Fathers and Adolescent Sons,' psychologist Aaron Esman observes that if the father 'is insecure about his occupational or educational achievements, he may drive his son to pursue unattainable goals, or set impossible standards and expectations' (272). Gustad's plans for Sohrab may not, strictly speaking, be unattainable or impossible, but they certainly do rise out of his own insecurities, his own sense that his life is disappointing. Rather than wanting his son to follow in his footsteps, he wants Sohrab to avoid the barriers that have blocked his path. When Sohrab proclaims that he does not want to go to IIT, but would rather remain among his friends at the arts college, Gustad shouts, 'Don't talk to me of friends!' The wounds of his best friend Jimmy Bilimoria's abandonment are fresh in his mind. 'If you have good reasons, I will listen. But don't say friends! You must be blind if you cannot see my own example and learn from it' (48–9). Gustad's plan for Sohrab – his romance of family progress – takes its shape from the increasingly besieged status of the Parsi minority in Bombay, from the downward mobility in social class he himself has experienced, and from his belief that Sohrab will be able to counteract the decline through education and eventual success overseas.

The parents' plans for their son in Begamudré's *Van de Graaff Days*, like Gustad and Dilnavaz's for Sohrab, reflect a particular set of social circumstances. Krishna and Rukmini are younger than Gustad and Dilnavaz, and their version of the romance of family progress puts them on the education–emigration path themselves, along with their son. Returning by train from their native South India to the northern Hindu University in Benares, where Krishna teaches as Senior Lecturer in Electrical Engineering, the parents talk over their plans for their new-born son:

'Perhaps I should go to America after all,' Krishna wondered aloud, 'and get my doctorate. But I am not sure now whether I want to return. Whether the boy should grow up here.' This was the India we freed, he thought; for our sons and our son's sons. 'What happened to the country we fought for?' he asked. 'Everyone now claims, "You Brahmins helped the British rule us. Now it is our turn to tell you what you can or cannot do." Brahmin quotas, Harijan quotas. Can we reverse five thousand years of history in less than a decade? The British had their faults, oh yes they had their faults. And yet they rewarded talent and hard work. I see this now. The Americans also have their faults, but they will not care what caste I am from ... It is true I shall begin at the bottom, but there may be no limit to how high I can rise. Not like here.'

'My brother has done well for himself [here in India],' Rukmini said.

Krishna nodded ... She understood little about careers, ambition – the things which mattered to a man. (58–9)

Again, the migrant narrative of progress takes the route of education – this time for the parents (Rukmini intends to study also) as well as, eventually, the child.

Like Gustad's Parsi heritage, Krishna's Hindu caste and regional affiliation have become liabilities in modern India. Having been an early student leader against the British during the Quit India campaign, he is dismayed to find his application for work in the nation he helped to liberate disregarded because he, a southerner, attended Delhi University. He explains that he had to go north because the quotas on brahmans at southern universities had disqualified him, but this brings no sympathy from the personnel officer. What does bring the officer onside is the name of his father, a famous engineer in the Bangalore area. The mention of Ajja, his father, is a particularly sore point for Krishna. Ajja's irritability with his boy's intellectual innocence, his upper-class rejection of Krishna's brother for marrying a British shopkeeper's daughter in England, and his ultimate abandonment of the family for a life of solitude in his elderly years cause Krishna to swear that he will never make the same mistakes with his own son (31). Furthermore, Krishna is disgusted that, despite the Independence movement and the huge sacrifices he and others made to bring about change, social and government bureaucracies still operate on systems of graft and patronage (57).

The words of the Sikh physician in Madras who signs Rukmini and Hari's emigration papers indicate how widely Krishna's disillusionment is shared. 'If I had a son,' Dr Singh tells Rukmini, 'I wouldn't want him to grow up in India either. Not the India we took back from the British and corrupted. There's no future for someone like you here. Your son deserves better' (150). The place is a dead-end. It is too corrupt, too backward, too hopelessly enmeshed in a belligerent past to offer the young any hope.

Different from Gustad, Krishna sees himself as a model for Hari to follow. For him, sportsmanship represents an avenue for masculine success. He himself won Rukmini's heart by vanquishing her previous fiancé in a tennis match (36). The tall stature and broad shoulders that made him a star on the cricket pitch or tennis court gave him a bearing and dignity that served him well in his early career at Benares. He believes Hari will need to develop athletic skills too. On a brief visit to Bangalore from his studies in New York, he envisions a grand athletic narrative for his pre-school son:

He looked at Hari and imagined him coming home from school. Hari would go straight to his room and finish his homework before going out to play. Baseball, basketball, American-style football – Hari would become an all-rounder. Team sports, not individual ones. Tennis was all very well, but it taught a boy nothing about working with others. (87)

The mention of these decidedly American sports indicates how Krishna's athletic plan for Hari ties into the narrative of immigrant assimilation. Sports are one way that a newcomer can compete, show his skills on a literal 'level playing field,' join into a cooperative venture with the locals. After the family has moved together to Ottawa after six years of separation, Krishna decides the best way to help Hari fit in at Woodbine, the private school in which he has enrolled the boy, is to give him cricket lessons on the lawn behind their apartment building. Small for his age and not particularly coordinated, Hari decides, after several near misses from Krishna's terrifying bowls, that he does not want to learn cricket.

Krishna approached to scoop up the ball. 'You will learn!' he snapped. He towered over Hari and blocked out the sun. Krishna shook his finger and said, 'You'll show Merlin and that pompous fool Hodgson you're just as good as them. If not better!'

What cricket had to do with either Merlin or Hodgson, Hari couldn't guess, but he picked up the bat and took his position while Krishna strode away. When Krishna turned and called, 'Are we ready?' Hari nodded. He decided to wait a little longer to call Krishna, 'Appa.' (180)

Living out his own conflicts through his son, Krishna imagines that Hari's athletic prowess will command respect from the two school administrators, Merlin and Hodgson, whose condescending attitude during the application interview had so embarrassed Krishna. Where Sohrab had responded to the suffocating paternal law with outright rebellion, Hari quietly resists the filial contract when he refrains from uttering the diminutive form of the name of the father.

So the father's plan is derailed by both sons. Each rejects the pragmatism of engineering for the idealism of arts – Sohrab the liberal arts and Hari the piano – and the father feels betrayed. The son's rejection of the father's plan poses a direct challenge to his authority. Sohrab humiliates Gustad by choosing to declare his refusal during the special dinner celebrating his sister Roshan's birthday and his qualifying for IIT. When Gustad and his guest Dinshawji sing 'For He's a Jolly Good Fellow,' Sohrab exclaims:

'I'm sick and tired of IIT, IIT, IIT all the time. I'm not interested in it, I'm not a jolly good fellow about it, and I'm not going there ... Why can't you accept it? IIT does not interest me. It was never my idea, you made all the plans. I told you I am

going to change to the arts programme, I like my college, and all my friends here.'
(48)

Such an outbreak against the father may be common enough in North
American families, and we might dismiss the incident as a familiar case
of teenage rebellion, but we need to recall that it is not the norm in Indian
families, where, as Mistry tells Dagmar Novak in an interview, 'children
have to respond to their parents in a certain way, in an open, almost
stylized show of respect' (260). Sohrab's refusal shocks Gustad to the
core. And, like Krishna in *Van de Graaff Days*, he resorts to violence.

That, in moments of confusion and fear, both fathers turn to violence
reveals much about the nature and motives of paternal violence. Certainly it is an assertion of power, but it also indicates powerlessness in so
far as the violent father attempts to compensate with physical strength
for a loss of moral or relational authority. And, in both cases, the mother
intercepts the violence directed at the son. When Gustad gets out the belt
to whip Sohrab after Dinshawji has left, Dilnavaz runs between them and
takes the lash on the back of her legs (51). The night Hari frightens
Krishna during their first year in Ottawa by staying out late on Hallowe'en
night, Krishna raises his hand to slap his son; Rukmini leaps into the fray,
and Krishna's slap knocks her glasses to the floor and breaks them (217).
In both incidents the father's violence reveals how pitiful his authority
has actually become. Gustad has been shamed by his son in front of his
friend; his wife will not let him dispense the paternal discipline to which
he feels entitled; and, in the end, he is cowed by the shouts from their
elderly neighbour, Miss Kutpitia, to quiet down and settle it in the
morning. Krishna's anger at Hari mixes his immigrant's fear that Canada,
in the form of friendly neighbours handing out apples and candy bars,
may take his son away from him with his fear that his sexual failure with
Rukmini since their reunion in Canada may be a sign of the demise of
their marriage. In both cases, the father's violence constitutes his visceral
reaction to the undermining of his authority, his sense of betrayal.

So my father became the workers' enemy. There was a day when Dad told a
group of seasonal workers there was no more work till next seeding. One of
them went after Dad with an axe. Somebody warned Dad in time and the guy
was disarmed.

Meanwhile, the grant with which the Ethiopian Department of Health
matched the mission's subsidy for Sheshemane was being withheld. For a

couple of weeks, they couldn't plough because there was no fuel for the tractors. They began to worry about maintaining enough diesel to keep the hospitals' emergency generators running. More workers had to be laid off while they waited for money and fuel. And the rumours about trunks full of money continued to spread like dry season stubble fire.

This was not why Dad and Mom had come to Ethiopia. They didn't want to be the enemy. They didn't want to be Management. They had come to help. They had come to bring Christ to the poor and the needy. They longed for the simple, old days at Woliso when they had visited neighbours and talked with young people in evening Bible-study groups. Their neighbours had loved and respected them, and they in turn had taken great pleasure in bringing school, medical care, and the gospel to these open country folk. We kids still chuckle at a few resonant images of Dad from those Woliso days: he whistled when he walked across the open area from the school to our house for lunch. And he rubbed his palms together, the warm friction speaking his delight. A lover of early mornings, he had the wood stove burning and the pot of porridge steaming by the time the rest of us emerged from our rooms, eye-rubbing in wrinkled pyjamas.

By 1974 when Dad woke to dread each day at Sheshemane, I was a teenager away at boarding-school in Addis. It's hard to picture him hating his beloved morning quiet, dreading the sunrise that betrayed the oblivion of sleep. What must his prayers have been like? Was this how God rewarded the life of service? How does a person communicate God's mercy and love while refusing people's desire for better pay and nicer houses? How does a person trained in biblical exegesis and homiletics become overnight a financial wizard who can produce wages and benefits out of thin air?

Twenty years have passed and he's still a brick. He's still got the quiet humour that'll surprise you. Like the belly-button lint removers he put in each of his sons' and sons-in-law's Christmas stockings this year. But it's been years since I heard him whistle and he seems to forget to rub his hands together, even on a cold winter day in Alberta.

The son's betrayal becomes the focal point of a whole series of betrayals that besiege the father in wider society. Gustad feels betrayed on multiple levels: he has been undermined by family misfortunes, by friends, by political corruption, and by his own ageing process, as well as by his son. 'If I could let the rotten world go by,' he says to himself with a sigh at one low point,

spend the rest of life in this chair. Grandpa's chair, that used to sit with the black desk in the furniture workshop. What a wonderful world, amid the din of hammering and sawing, the scent of sawdust and sweat and polish. And in Pappa's bookstore, with its own special sounds and smells, the seductive rustle of turning pages, the timeless fragrance of fine paper, the ancient leather-bound volumes in those six enormous book-filled rooms, where even the air had a special quality, as in a temple or mausoleum. Time and the world stretched endlessly then, before the bad days came and everything shrank. And this is how my father must have felt, in this very chair, after the profligate brother had destroyed all, after the bankruptcy, when there was nothing left. He, too, must have wanted not to move from this chair, just let what remained of time and the shrunken world go by. (141)

His betrayal in the present attaches to his nostalgia for the past. 'There is a specifically masculine form of nostalgia which addresses the problems of men's historicity,' writes Jonathan Rutherford. 'Problems which are products of a transitional loss of cultural authority and a psychological feeling of loss' (125). Certainly, Gustad's longing for the security and order symbolized by his grandfather's chair conveys his sense that whatever authoritative grip he may have had in his family or in society at large is waning quickly. 'I don't understand this world any more,' he confesses to Dilnavaz. 'First, your son destroys our hopes. Now this rascal. Like a brother I looked upon him. What a world of wickedness it has become' (142). Not only has he been betrayed by his father's bankruptcy and his son's rebellion, he is now also undermined by 'this rascal,' a long-time friend named Jimmy Bilimoria. Indeed, Bilimoria's treachery becomes a double betrayal because his apparent faithlessness turns out to be part of a political scandal that shakes Gustad's trust in the government of Indira Gandhi.

Once again we are reminded that the private and the public, the psychological and political, remain inseparable. As Arun Mukherjee points out, Mistry never lets us forget the larger forces that are the determining circumstances of the characters' lives ('Narrating India' 82–3). By setting Gustad's familial turmoil amid a fictionalized account of the notorious Nagarwala incident of 1971, a scandal in which a Parsi secret-service agent named Rustum Sohrab Nagarwala was said to have mimicked Prime Minister Gandhi's voice in a phone call to the State Bank of India demanding the immediate withdrawal of six million rupees, and by making Gustad's good friend Jimmy Bilimoria the novel's version of Nagarwala, Mistry links the personal betrayal with the larger atmosphere of political corruption.[3] Jimmy had prayed the *kusti* prayers with

Gustad every morning; he had been the familiar 'Major Uncle' to Gustad's children; he had been Gustad's closest confidante. Now, unaccountably, he places a great smear upon the Parsi community by playing dirty politics with a corrupt government. And he very nearly ruins Gustad by embroiling him in his money-laundering scheme.

Jimmy is not the only friend whose trustworthiness is compromised by politics. For Malcolm, the childhood friend who had helped Gustad rescue a few precious pieces of his grandfather's furniture (including the chair) from the bailiff during his father's bankruptcy, the Christian part-ner on trips to Crawford meat market who instructed the Parsi Gustad on the virtues of beef in a Hindu economy, the dear old friend who sympa-thetically took Gustad to Mount Mary Church to pray for his daughter's and friend's health, this good old friend commits the novel's final treach-ery as he turns out to be the municipal officer who oversees the destruc-tion of the wall of holy pictures that was Gustad's ingenious contribution to the health and redolence of Khodadad community. So the peculiarly masculine elements of Gustad's anxieties register not only in the classic struggle between father and son, or the male's negotiation of the political realm, but also in the troubled dynamics of male friendship.

A third friend betrays Gustad too – but this time unintentionally. This third treachery comes with the hospitalization and eventual death of Gustad's malodorous, secretary-harassing bank co-worker Dinshawji. In his rapid demise from stomach cancer, Gustad's dear friend represents in only too painful detail the process of ageing that presses upon Gustad as the ultimate betrayal. Not only does Dinshawji manifest the treachery of bodily decrepitude, but, as ribald poet laureate among the bank workers, he also articulates accurately Gustad's fears of change, the perfidy of time. 'Names are so important,' he tells Gustad during a debate about the changing of street names from English to Marathi:

I grew up on Lamington Road. But it has disappeared, in its place is Dadasaheb Bradkhamkar Marg. My school was on Carnac Road. Now suddenly it's on Lokmanya Tilak Marg. I live at Sleater Road. Soon that will also disappear. My whole life I have come to work at Flora Fountain. And one fine day the name changes. So what happens to the life I have lived? Was I living the wrong life, with all the wrong names? ... Tell me what happens to my life. Rubbed out, just like that? (74)

As it happens, his life is in fact rubbed out, leaving Gustad with the haunting fear that he, too, might be living the wrong life, out of place, out of time. And this fear of irrelevance connects to his conflict with Sohrab. For, as Colarusso and Nemiroff observe, around the time that a middle-aged father becomes aware of his own ageing process and the loss of his youthful body, he also lives in daily contact with his adolescent sons, and so his 'struggle is heightened by the painful contrast between their bodies and his own' (317). Gustad bears on his body the sign of the transfer of physical vitality from father to son in the aching hip that he broke years ago, saving Sohrab from being crushed by a speeding taxi. Now, with Sohrab's rejection, that sign, like the street signs of Dinshawji's youth, seems to point to a life and purposes bypassed in the onrush of time.

Wendy's guiding her shopping-cart among the fruit and vegetable islands in the produce section at Safeway. She reaches around a lady rummaging apples to tear off a plastic bag from the dispenser roll. The woman – sixties-ish, hunched in the shoulders, salt-and-pepper hair – turns to her, 'How's your brother John doing these days? Any better? We're praying for him, you know.'

Wendy doesn't know this woman from Adam. Complete blank. 'Excuse me?'

'Your brother-in-law, John. John Coleman. We've been praying for him, that the Lord will lift him up during this time of difficulty. How's he doing?'

None of this helps. Wendy can't piece together this absolute stranger with the references to my brother. John had gone through some emotional turmoil. Therapy, medication, the whole business. That was true enough, but how did complete strangers by the grocery store apples come to know about it?

And then the penny drops: the prayer chain. That's it. My missionary parents send out quarterly newsletters to their supporters to keep them posted on their lives, and on their emotional, spiritual, financial needs. This woman must be on the mailing list for the Coleman Communiqué. *My parents must have requested prayers for John, and now here was someone who obviously knew who Wendy was, checking in to see how her prayers were being answered.*

It was one of the many moments of Wendy's marital culture shock. When she married me, she married a whole system: not just a boy from a missionary family, but the whole missionary constellation altogether with its satellites of churches, prayer groups, and supporters. Her private act plugged her unwill-ingly into a system that drew no lines between private and public. It was like a huge extended family. Hundreds of people were praying earnestly for my brother. At my parents' request.

Some years after the encounter in the Safeway store, Wendy and I moved to Edmonton so I could start the PhD program. That year was hell for me. The combination of living in an unfamiliar city, leaving an intimate circle of

friends, desperately trying to keep up with a super-humanly demanding
course-work load, and teaching at the same time shattered me. Where I'd been
full of cheerful self-confidence, I suddenly fell into despair and self-doubt. I
began to lose my hair. I'd wake up to a pillowcase scattered with it after nights
of fitful sleep. Finally, we decided I should get some help – professional help. I
needed to see a counsellor.

Just before one of my folks' visits that year, Wendy asked, 'Are you going to
tell your parents what's going on? That you're going for counselling?'

'I guess so. Why?'

She told me about the woman in the grocery store.

Ah, the prayer chains of the extended missionary family. And the times
Mom and Dad's love for and trust in that extended family made them betray
confidences I felt belonged in our nuclear unit alone.

'No, I guess not,' I said.

Krishna, too, feels profoundly betrayed in *Van de Graaff Days*. Two
related circumstances undermine his paternal authority: migration and
marriage. In his plan to study abroad and then bring his wife and son
over to join him there, Krishna had not counted on the way in which the
circumstances of migration themselves sever the familial bonds that
would facilitate the success of that plan. The migrant version of the
romance of family progress envisions the father's triumph in the son's
success abroad, but it does not take into account the disruptions to family
continuities that cross-cultural refraction involves. First of all, Hari lives
the first six years of his life without any conception of Krishna as father.
When Krishna comes back from his studies in the United States to visit
Hari and Rukmini in Bangalore, Hari thinks of him as his 'holiday father'
and cannot distinguish him from any other visiting uncle. No sooner
does Hari begin to develop some feelings for Krishna than Krishna
departs, without farewell, back to New York. So Hari grows up in a
world of women – mother, aunts, grandmothers, female cousins, ayahs –
until he is suddenly thrown at age six into the very male world of his
father's small apartment and the Woodbine boys' school in Ottawa. The
physical absences and the resulting emotional distance between Krishna
and Hari, the jarring effects of dislocation and relocation on them both –
these are the elements of migrant experience which conspire to refract
Krishna's original plans for himself and his son.

In addition, the timing of the abrupt transfer from India to Canada
could not have been more traumatic for Hari, for it occurs just as the boy
passes through what Kakar calls the 'second birth' in his schema of

Indian male development. Taking the notion of the 'second birth' from the Hindu ceremony of initiation in which boys aged five or six from the upper three castes (Brahman, Kshatriya, and Vaishya) are invested with the sacred thread and apprenticed to a *guru* to begin their education (Converse 82), Kakar elaborates a critical moment in a Hindu boy's psychological development:

The second birth refers to the sudden widening of the world of Indian childhood from the intimate cocoon of maternal protection to the unfamiliar masculine network woven by the demands and tensions, the comings and goings, of the men of the family ... Even more than the suddenness of the transition, the *contrast* between an earlier, more or less unchecked benevolent indulgence and the now inflexible standards of absolute obedience and conformity to familial and social standards is the most striking feature of the second birth. (419)

For Hari, his 'second birth' becomes doubly overloaded by the fact that his transfer from the world of women to the world of men involves the added bewilderments and disorientations of migration to Canada. His mother has doubts about the wisdom of this migration: Rukmini 'wondered whether she should have brought him here, from a land of brightness and women to this land of darkness and men' (229). It cannot endear Krishna to his son that he is the reason Hari had to leave that bright, comfortable world and come to this dark, confusing one.

Migration places extra strains on the relation not only between father and son, but also between husband and wife. In her study of changing gender roles in rural India, sociologist Scarlett Epstein observes that male emigration often increases women's status in domestic and public spheres. 'To ensure survival,' she writes, 'the gap caused by male absence has been filled by the women. Changed circumstances compel these women to venture outside the narrow domestic domain ... There is undoubtedly a shift of importance in favor of the woman while her man is away' (21).[4] Although Rukmini's circumstances as a high-caste, upper-class, urban woman are markedly different from the rural women of Epstein's study, certainly her development from girl-wife afraid of childbirth to a PhD in Engineering traces a similar progression of growing independence during her husband's absence. When the family reunites in Ottawa, Krishna and Rukmini realize that they hardly know each other. Who could have predicted that Krishna would encounter difficulties with his thesis supervisor in New York and leave his studies for a job in Canada and that, ironically, Rukmini, who had stayed behind in India, would complete her

PhD there and thus qualify for better jobs than her husband in this new land? When Krishna meets his family at Dorval airport in Montreal, he encounters a son who does not know him and a wife who no longer needs him to make her a living.

About the marital and filial stresses in the family, Begamudré has said that 'the relationships would probably have been not that different if the characters had remained where they were, in the same place. It's just that they tend to be strained and perhaps exaggerated when people immigrate' ('Writing Dislocation' 9). This extra strain widens the cracks in the cement of the family structure, cracks that undermine Krishna's paternal authority. In the introduction to *Masculine Migrations*, I referred to Rivka Eisikovits and Martin Wolins's article entitled 'Cross-Cultural Uses of Research on Fathering' in which the two sociologists suggest that the father undergoes the greatest strain among family members during the process of migration. Since the father's status within the family is often based on his occupational and social positions in the wider community, the refractions of migration which displace him from these authorizing roles undermine his position in the family as well (239). Eisikovits and Wolins claim, however, that this stress upon the father need not produce family collapse. Instead, the change in social status can cause the father to find new roles for himself within the family. The two sociologists report studies of Indian and Pakistani immigrants in Canada and Italian immigrants in Australia (Siddique; Phillips) which show that the fathers often become more active parents, taking on greater responsibilities in the family. In the absence of the extended family network they left at home, the immigrant families become more self-reliant, requiring a more equal distribution of labour between the parents (241). The question in *Van de Graaff Days*, as Krishna himself realizes, is whether or not he can adapt to his new circumstances. Driving home from the airport with his newly arrived family, Krishna realizes that he will no longer have the car to himself. Suddenly a father and husband, he recognizes that he must exchange his solitary pleasures for shared ones. 'He wondered what other changes he would have to make, and he wondered whether he could make them after so many years on his own' (160).

As it turns out, he cannot retool himself enough to fashion a renewed relationship with Rukmini, and she moves to a teaching position at the University of Toronto. The plans he and Rukmini discussed so long ago on the train to Benares are no longer shared. So the family itself, whose romance of progress those original plans expressed, teeters, at the end of the novel, on the verge of dissolution. Migration may not have destroyed the marriage, but it certainly contributed to its deterioration. And, to Krishna's mind, migration may be destroying his hopes for his son. Rather than becoming a cricket all-rounder, in place of developing the skills of an electrical engineer, instead of taking after his father, Hari heads off into a foreign world and develops a passion for the piano. The plans of the father, to all appearances, have come to naught.

Neither *Such a Long Journey* nor *Van de Graaff Days*, however, is a father's story pure and simple. Both of them are, instead, stories written by emigrant sons focused largely on the previous generation, on their fathers' generation. So we must ask ourselves what it means when the son writes a fictional account of the times and circumstances of his parents' generation. Despite the fact that both son-characters are drawn to the arts, neither of these novels could be described as a *Künstlerroman*; the account of the previous generation does not serve simply to trace the emergence of the artistic son. Nor can we read either of these tender and somewhat nostalgic books as some kind of attack upon a fictionalized version of the father.

Craig Tapping's observation of a widespread autobiographical impulse in Indo-Canadian and Indo-American fiction points, I believe, in the right direction (35). In the writing of fiction, these immigrant writers find the opportunity to rethink, even reimagine, the traumas of their own disjointed history, to renegotiate the divide between here and there, present and past. And in this process of self reconstitution – carried out, as Boelhower observes, in a genealogical mode – they have the chance to address some of those disruptions in fictional form. 'I don't want to forget anything about Bombay. The life, the places, the people,' Mistry explains in an interview with Geoff Hancock. 'I think it's something I owe to the place where I grew up' (146–7). 'Writing is very much a matter of rediscovering my roots,' says Begamudré in one interview ('Process' 14). In another, he adds, 'I suppose writing about my family was a way of trying to come to terms with them and with what had happened to us' ('Writing Dislocation' 10).

In these two novels, I believe Mistry and Begamudré attempt to write their way towards a resolution of an old rupture with their fathers. One of the best ways for a son to heal the internalized wounded father, writes Osherson, is to plunge into the father's history (178). Learning about the father, he suggests, facilitates the son's process of individuation, so that the son learns that he 'is not chained to his father's attitudes and values. So the process of exploration may lead to an acceptance of the father, even if not a deep connection with him' (182). Mistry and Begamudré deploy this kind of exploratory process in their fiction. And the exploration involves struggle, for, as Ashok Mathur has written in his discussion of *Tales from Firozsha Baag*, 'Rohinton Mistry does battle within himself, within his selves, manipulating fact and subverting ordered systems to break free in fiction' (28–9). In *Such a Long Journey* and *Van de Graaff Days*, these two emigrant sons recast in fiction – in the stories of Gustad and Krishna – the circumstances of their parents' lives, sifting through the details to find a way to understand their fathers and hoping that, by doing so, they will find a way to individuate themselves from the 'wounded father within.'

But what could be the nature of the conflict these author-sons had with their fathers? That both fictional stories place the artistically oriented son's rejection of the pragmatic plans of the father at the centre of conflict provides a broad hint. Bharati Mukherjee supplies further indication. 'I know the immigrant world well enough,' she writes, 'to know that each young writer is a doctor, accountant, or engineer lost; a bright hope, a bitter disappointment' (400). The romance of family progress inculcated in children by their parents' calls for success in practical terms: financial wealth and social status. So that the son might launch a career which would enrich the family as a whole, an expensive education was bought by the family at considerable sacrifice. Using that education to become a writer looks very much like betrayal. Mistry studied Math and Economics at the University of Bombay before taking a job as a bank clerk in Toronto; Begamudré trained in Administration and worked as a civil servant. Both gave up these practical careers for the less certain life of the writer. Both have enjoyed varying degrees of success – financial and social[5] – but neither one has remained on the more conservative path familiar to his parents' generation. Neither has remained true to the original vision.

Both books are first novels and as such constitute the author-son's first opportunity to develop in fulsome detail his self-justifying story. These are not the works of writers long assured of their vocation; instead, they can be read as manifestos, declarations of a young author's intent. Both books are written into the future in so far as they attempt to forecast a conclusion to the narrative even while the conflict itself is still in the exposition phase. Amid the present irresolution they may feel in regard to their fathers, both authors rework the details of the past in fictional form to envision how a reconciliation with the father might be possible. Conscious of the need to resist the father's unpalatable script, his paternal law, each tries to write a version that could work. In both novels that projected resolution involves, first, the reduction of the father through an account of his limitations and betrayals. The author-son writes his way free of the father's authority. Second, it involves the discovery of a shared language through which one character moves towards the other. In *Such a Long Journey* this shared language takes the form of ritual prayer in the face of grief, and Sohrab moves. Sohrab, giving no indication of a change of mind about IIT, comes to the reduced Gustad when his father pours out his confusion and grief in prayers for yet another death – this time Tehmul's. The absurdity of a world that destroys even this mentally simple child-in-a-man's-body strikes Sohrab as forcefully as it does Gustad, and, for this brief moment at least, they understand each other. In that moment the son comprehends something of his father's sense of betrayal and despair.

In *Van de Graaff Days* this shared language is the language of music, and Krishna moves. Having resisted Hari's musical interests every step of the way, he grudgingly gives in, first to piano lessons, and later to allowing Hari to use the money Rukmini sent to buy a piano (instead of banking it for Hari's future education as he would have preferred to do). This compromise requires much humility from Krishna because that piano represents for him an extravagance that Rukmini's superior salary can afford, but which he himself cannot. On the night the delivery men place the second-hand piano in the apartment's living-room, Krishna hears Hari play for the first time. Hari plays from the Canadian Glenn Gould's interpretation of Bach's *Goldberg Variations*, which was one of the first records Krishna had bought when he arrived years ago in New York. Krishna 'sat down with the album on his knee,' we read in the novel's closing scene, 'and listened to Hari repeat the notes.' His son

was forcing Krishna to listen, forcing him to wait for the next note and the next ... Krishna had never felt so amazed. He seemed to be discovering something about himself, and he was discovering it in music which had been with him for years. He simply had not listened to it often enough. At last he understood. The best music, music like this, could take a man out of his everyday world and bring him back to a world which could never be the same. Hari, the boy, his son seemed to know this. He led, and Krishna followed. (292–3)

Here the son compels the father to listen to a new language, a language the father had previously ignored. He teaches the father to hear and the father is moved. For this brief moment, they share a common understanding. There is no indication that Krishna has given up his fatherly projections. Despite the fact that he slaps aside the soccer ball he had bought for Hari's birthday and reaches instead for the picture of Ganesha which he helps Hari hang above the piano, Krishna's enthusiasm for Hari's musical skill could easily be a translation of his eagerness for his son to prove his worth in sports. But, for this one moment at least, they share a common passion. Neither novel delineates a full and final resolution; both end with suggestions of where resolution might be found, where to go to heal the phantom limb.

I have a notebook. Nothing special to look at – mottled yellow Bristol-board covers, wire spiral binding, gold embossed lettering that says 'notebook' over a silhouette of a student writing at a desk. Inside the back cover, the silhouette appears again, this time in black ink, with the words 'Student, Shanghai, China' underneath. There are some Chinese ideographs and the numbers '406– 50.' The lined pages, once white, are now yellow-beige. Little stanzas of verse cover the pages in handwriting that gradually matures from awkward irregularity to letters much more deliberate and certain. At the top of each page, there appears a date and some kind of address. The dates begin with March 28, 1978, and go to November 1987. The addresses range from Ras Tessema Suffir, Addis Ababa, and Rift Valley Academy, Kijabe, Kenya, to RR #1, Wheatley, Ontario, and 4144 Castle Road, Regina, Saskatchewan.

This book is a collection of the songs I wrote on my guitar. And Dad gave it to me. I had been away from the family for a year, living in Calgary while they were in Addis, and, when I came back to live with them in 1978, I brought with me a penchant for composing songs that I sang accompanied by my twelve-string guitar. Dad bought this notebook – a deluxe one by Ethiopian standards – and suggested that I gather all my songs in it. Until then, I had left them floating around in the bottom of my guitar case on loose sheets of paper.

I don't even know the tunes or chords for some of these songs any more. But I still have the notebook.

In their catalogue of the characteristics of a minor or 'deterritorialized' literature, Gilles Deleuze and Felix Guattari insist that everything in these writings is political, including relations between fathers and sons (17). Certainly, we have seen how political and social forces shape the relations between fathers and sons in these two migrant – or 'deterritorialized' – novels, but what are the political implications for gender relations of the emigrant son's rewriting of the father's story? In so far as they reject and write alternatives to the paternal law, these novels could possibly read as subversive descriptions of the weakness and inadequacy of the father's law. But in so far as they rewrite the father's story, might they not also participate in the reinscription of the patriarchal text? Does the act of revising the story of the father and his troublesome son undermine or affirm the Name-of-the-Father?

The main problem I encounter in trying to address these questions is that the theory of patriarchy itself tends to short-circuit the possible answers. For, as Robert Connell has observed, 'patriarchy,' or the 'law of the father,' in the writings of Lacan and Juliet Mitchell, 'is less the structure of social relations than the structure of how the world is imagined' (202). As the structure of the imagined world, then, patriarchy operates transparently as normative ideology. Functioning as the medium of perception, it disappears as the object of perception; so we lose sight of it as a social operation. The chief effect of this invisibility is that, in much gender analysis of the past twenty years, patriarchy has been removed from history. It has been posited as a constant transhistorical – and often transcultural – structure that exists beyond the vagaries of history. And this ahistorical patriarchy exerts a passive kind of repression by disappearing beyond the ken of the liberatory imagination; by silently defining the field of social relations, it disqualifies alternative practices and arrangements. 'Patriarchy suddenly disappears beyond the reach of political challenge,' writes Peter Middleton, 'because of the circularity of this structure which allows no place for intervention ... For men trying to challenge patriarchy there is simply no position to occupy other than that of the upholder of the law' (97). The place to evaluate the political function of these son's stories of their fathers, then, is not in the abstract realm of theories of patriarchy and gender relations, but in the specific social relations and practices in which these novels are cast.

For these two novels reveal that fathers do wield special powers in their families, but these powers are always subject to the limitations of multiple social systems and practices as well as the vicissitudes of history. 'Masculinity,' writes Lynne Segal in *Slow Motion: Changing Masculinities, Changing Men*, 'is never the undivided, seamless construction it becomes in its symbolic manifestation' (102). Colonial history, ethnic identity, political intrigue, the inevitable process of ageing, the betrayal of friends, marital breakdown, the disruptions of emigration: all of these, along with the son's rebellion, constitute limitations upon Gustad's and Krishna's paternal and masculine authority. Patriarchy does not operate in a social vacuum.

These novels put into play the social forces that contest the father's law from within, and, in so doing, they demonstrate not only the practices that fathers employ to shore up their law, but also the social forces that constantly refract and destabilize that law.

Afterword:
Masculine Innovations and
Cross-Cultural Refraction

Masculine Migrations will not conclude. My purpose has been to write towards an opening of possibilities rather than towards closure or settlement. I have been concerned to trace masculinities *in process*, in transition, in movement. To impose certitudes, claims of arrival, solutions at this point would be to commit the Great Male Disappointment of premature ejaculation. This, then, is an afterword, an ending *in medias res*, a rhetorical way of stepping back from an ongoing process to meditate on its implications even while they continue to unfold.

Masculine Migrations is about men's negotiations of social constraints and their innovations within those constraints. Its chapters examine narratives of men's migration to see how masculine codes and practices are reassessed and challenged in the process that I have called cross-cultural refraction. Just as a wave of light or sound changes velocities and directions when it passes from one medium into another, so also a cultural form such as masculine practice will change or 'bend' when it enters into a new cultural environment or medium. The closer the two cultural media are to one another, the more minimal the change in cultural forms; the greater the difference between cultures, the more dramatic the change. As in physical refraction, the change from one side of the refractor to the other is both real and illusory.

Since, as Robert Connell claims, 'the naturalization of gender is the basic mechanism of sexual ideology' (290), my attempt has been to intervene in the self-perpetuating assumptions of conventional ideologies of masculinity by showing how the disruptions of cross-cultural refraction *denaturalize* the notion of a coherent, authoritative, biologically based masculine gender. This book shows that socio-economic marginalization; the discursive histories of slavery, colonialism, and

indenture; mutual inflection between diverse traditions of male performativity; inherited patterns of family narration; political intrigues
in postcolonial nations; the natural process of ageing; and the physical
and cultural dislocations of migration all shape and determine a whole
variety of masculine practices and performances. Furthermore, by focusing on the etiology or historicity of these shaping factors, I have emphasized a kinetic, rather than static, conception of gender. I have tried to
show how the displacements and distortions of cross-cultural refraction
cause migrant males to innovate or improvise new masculine practices:
as they move from one cultural medium to another, these men must
adapt to their new situations. The narrative of migration intensifies the
pressure for adaptation since one culture's requirements of its male subjects will be somewhat different from another's. Thus, *Masculine Migrations* is about men dealing with change, change in their perceptions of
their own gender identifications, change in their relation to various authorizing masculine codes.

   As we have seen, however, the narrative of migration is never free of
social constraints. Indeed, since migration involves the negotiation of the
continuities and disjunctures between at least two cultural communities,
the migrant often experiences an intensification of struggle with social
limits. Clarke's Joshua, for instance, is very aware that the codes of
metropolitan capitalism in Toronto require him to prove his masculine
worth through socio-economic success. He is also aware, though, that the
subtle codes of metropolitan racism conspire to exclude him as a non-
white immigrant from the means to achieve that financial success.
Laferrière's text addresses the discursive history behind the kind of
racism Joshua confronts and shows how that discourse continues to
reproduce harmful stereotypes of super-phallic masculinity that plague
men of African ancestry. Raj, the protagonist of Bissoondath's novel, feels
great discomfort under masculine heroic ideals which constrain him to
exhibit an aggressivity and decisiveness from which he is debarred by the
traumas of his own family's migrant history. In his autobiographical
narrative, Michael Ondaatje finds his desire for reconnection with *pater*
and *patria* thwarted by the alienating, upper-class narratives he has
inherited from his extended family in Sri Lanka. Finally, both Mistry's
and Begamudré's novels demonstrate that, even though the father's
authority is undermined by social decline and personal disappointment,
the son's own narrative emerges from the need to come to terms with the
father's continuing story.

   In each case, the conservative nature of established cultural patterns and social structures threaten to contain whatever potential there may be for masculine change or innovation. Each one of these narratives can be read in such a way as to confirm the inevitability of the *status quo*: Joshua needs to assimilate himself to the law of capitalist success in Toronto; Vieux's parody of black men's sexualization can be easily recommodified in an economy of racist images; Raj's growing self-awareness accompanies a heightening of conventional masculine isolationism, and his passionless disidentification with his West Indian homeland reinforces the patronizing attitudes that are used to justify North American neo-imperialism in the islands; the Orientalist discourse, woven deep into the Ondaatje family's narrative, continues to alienate Michael Ondaatje from his past; and Mistry's and Begamudré's novels place the father and his authority at the centre of attention. Further, more sobering considerations arise when we observe that, in the first three cases – in Joshua's improvisation, Vieux's parody, and Raj's self-awakening – the men's innovative responses to their social circumstances come at the expense of women. These considerations remind us that we should assume no simple correlation between masculine innovation and social justice in gender relations.

The advantage of working with a model of cross-cultural refraction, however, is that it destabilizes the conservative, constraining, perhaps even reactionary elements of these narratives. Always, in refraction, one remains aware both of (conservative) continuity and of (unsettling) distortion. In each of the chapters of *Masculine Migrations*, I have focused on how the disruptions of migration require adaptive behaviour from male subjects. Sometimes, these disruptions are caused by the inflections that occur when a male character tries to adapt the masculine practices of a familiar culture to an unfamiliar one. Other times this adaptive behaviour reveals itself in discomfort under, or sometimes conflict between, inherited or imposed codes of masculinity. Whatever the case, the restlessness, the confrontation, or the adaptation testify to the diverse and contradictory forms of practice that are often homogenized under the rubric of a monolithic 'masculinity.' This instability makes possible what I have called 'masculine innovations' in so far as it causes the male subject to improvise new masculine practices within the dynamic tensions between cross-cultural refraction's continuities and distortions. By tracing the tensions between masculine constraints and innovations, limited as the latter may be, I have hoped to show how masculinities do in fact change, that social gender structures are in fact altered over time by human practices.

The struggles and conflicts I have enumerated in this book will not be easily contained in conventional ideologies of masculine dominance. Clarke's Joshua will continue to question Canadian assumptions about what constitutes success in masculinist corporate culture. Laferrière's troubling metaparody will continue to confront white Canadian readers with the mirror image of our own racist stereotypes and those stereotypes' connections to psychosocial structures of fantasy and fear. Bissoondath's novel will continue to raise discomforting questions about the ethics of the 'gentle' man who does not want to perpetuate social evils, but whose passivity too readily complies with them. Ondaatje's fictionalized memoir will continue to seduce readers with its exotic discourse of the lost home and the lost father, but it will also present them with a masculinity which increasingly understands itself in interdependent rather than individualistic terms. Mistry's and Begamudré's novels will never let the notion of secure, intergenerational patrilineage rest at ease, and will call our attention to the ways in which the law of the father must compete with a whole constellation of social forces for its authority. In other words, the tensions between social constraints and innovative practices elaborated in these narratives of cross-cultural refraction show masculinities which are definitely not settled, unified, and self-assured. Indeed, these masculinities are troubled and confused, self–re-creating and inventive, frustrated and lost. Anything but stable. They are masculinities in process, masculinities in migration.

One indication of the instability produced by these masculinities can be observed in the way in which each chapter of *Masculine Migrations* tends to call into question certain values that are assumed in the preceding chapter. The first chapter, on Clarke, argues that mutual inflections between diverse traditions of male performativity produce a parodic performance that critiques and exposes Canadian metropolitan masculinity. The second chapter, on Laferrière, takes up the topic of performative parody and shows how it brilliantly exposes the discursive history of a dominant discourse's demeaning stereotypes, but it also observes the ways in which hyperbolic parody can be recommodified by the very discursive system it seeks to subvert. The third chapter then turns to an analysis of a kind of masculinity that shuns hyperbolic performance and observes how Raj's disidentification (rather than parodic engagement) with masculine performative codes can point towards the possibility of masculine innovation. But the fourth chapter, on *Running in the Family*, calls into question the kind of severed individualism that Raj espouses. Instead, it argues that Ondaatje's memoir tries to bridge masculine severance from the lost father and lost homeland by weaving the male subject's self-constituting narrative into the warp and woof of his extended family's narratives. The fifth chapter, on Mistry's and Begamudré's novels, however, points out that, for some sons, the father is definitely not lost but is suffocatingly present. These two narratives are fuelled by the need to break the father's grip by pointing out the array of social forces that undermine the authority of his narratives. But if we then think back to the first two chapters, we cannot help but notice that fathers are not presented as a significant concern at all in Clarke's and Laferrière's texts.

Thus, each chapter of *Masculine Migrations* unsettles certain assumptions or values in other chapters. The particular social circumstances of each migrant narrative gives us a new lens to look through and, by so doing, refracts the perspectives we held moments ago. This series of mutually distorting refractions serves as a useful reminder of the indeterminacy inherent in reading across cultures. It reminds us of the importance of minding our p's and q's, of keeping ourselves mindful of the provisos and qualifications inherent in the cultural medium that shapes our own interpretations.

Furthermore, we should remind ourselves that migration destabilizes the assumptions of masculinity on both sides of the refracting cultural divide; it is not simply a matter of the migrant bringing new perspectives to the culture of destination. Whereas Joshua's adaptations of masculine traditions from the Caribbean and from African-American urban culture inflect his performance of metropolitan masculinity in Toronto, Montgomery's illustrative story with which I began the introduction to *Masculine Migrations* shows that the migrant's own perspective of the Guyana he left behind becomes distorted when he looks back from his new residence in Toronto. As I pointed out in that passage, his present unhappiness produces a nostalgia that makes him represent a more certain masculinity in Guyana than the realities of that country's cultural history will verify.

Sometimes the migrant's projections back onto the culture of origin, now inflected by his new cultural medium, can produce liberating images of masculinity in that original culture. H. Nigel Thomas's 1993 novel, *Spirits in the Dark*, provides an example of how such a projection backward through the refracting lens of migration can provide the possibility of masculine innovation. The *Bildungsroman* traces the life of Jerome Quashee, a closet homosexual and descendant of black and mulatto parents, from boyhood to young manhood on a fictional island in the West Indies. Jerome's shame and self-hatred over his sexual orientation alienate him from friends, family, and community, and land him a couple of times in an asylum for the mentally insane. Eventually, Jerome finds a community to belong to among the Esosusus, a secret spiritualist society, whose syncretic blend of African rituals and the sayings of Jesus offers him a path towards not only social inclusion, but also self-acceptance. Despite the somewhat nostalgic and idealized ending, Thomas's novel intervenes in and complicates the kind of nationalist homogenizations and pressurized solidarities that often characterize anti-colonial politics by showing that same-sex preference, mental instability, and racial hybridity can be as virulently despised within 'oppressed' or 'marginalized' communities as elsewhere.

But Thomas has written this exploration of latent male homosexuality in the ethos of gay, lesbian, and queer politics in Canadian and American metropolitan culture.[1] This kind of activism had not yet emerged openly in the Caribbean, where Heinemann, the publisher, baulked at including Thomas's novel in its prestigious Caribbean Writers Series because of its homosexual content. Despite the fact that the homosexual content is rather timid compared with most metropolitan gay literature, the publisher feared adverse reaction from West Indian readers.[2] What we have, then, is a novel written 'back' towards the migrant author's culture of origin from the perspectives of the culture of destination, so that, on one level, the novel distorts and brings trouble to ideologies of the heterosexual imperative in the Caribbean.

Before we Canadian readers begin to congratulate ourselves on the wonderful way in which our culture continues to bring 'enlightenment' to the rest of the world, however, we need to notice that, on another level, Jerome's multiple 'eccentricities' – gay, mentally deranged at certain times, and mulatto – destabilize the various categories of identification based on sexuality, rationality, status as victim/victimizer, race, or class that we in metropolitan societies use to understand ourselves and others. By taking some of our most commonly assumed categories of human definition and showing how they only inhibit understanding of the complexities of Jerome's particular situation, Thomas's novel calls attention to the refractions that occur when they are applied across cultures. The novel reminds metropolitan readers and critics of the partiality and provisionality of our own ways of knowing.

In this way, the cross-cultural refraction of masculine codes and practices contributes to the slow process of social change. Throughout the past twenty years, the conundrum of men's participation in and response to feminist politics has plagued male and female gender reformers alike. Why would the powerful wish to give up their advantages? How do you motivate men to change if they perceive themselves to enjoy unlimited privileges under the status quo? One place to start – and I admit it is a slow and unprepossessing beginning – is to try to make men aware of the constraints attendant upon those privileges. Another related entry point is to describe the many kinds of masculinity that for reasons of race, ethnicity, sexual orientation, class, physical disability, or cultural displacement do not enjoy unlimited social privileges. In other words, we need to call attention to the many masculinities that belie complacent masculine myths of self-sustaining coherence and power. Cross-cultural refraction provides one useful model for doing so.

As the wise and disillusioned King Solomon once said, there is nothing new under the sun. But there are new combinations of old things. From these new combinations, from the ways in which elements from diverse media and different traditions inflect and reshape one another, innovations emerge. As the sociologist H.G. Barnett observed in *Innovation: The Basis of Cultural Change* (1953), innovations, even important ones, are everyday commonplaces (3). A given innovation's significance can be gauged only after the fact, once subsequent influences and effects from that innovation can be appraised. Furthermore, the combinations that produce innovation are always constrained in two realms: in the social realm of the combination's antecedents and the personal realm of the individual innovator's potentialities and liabilities. Writing in a period before poststructuralist theories of the human subject undermined confidence in human genius and agency, Barnett tends to claim more autonomy for the individual mind than current theorizing would allow. It seems to me, however, that moments of cross-cultural refraction create volatile instability, cause confrontation and mutual distortion between different cultural codes that force people between cultures to have to improvise a social practice that necessarily combines old antecedents in new ways. If it is true that innovations take place every day, and that their significance depends upon how and if they are 'taken up' later on, then criticism can be one way we can contribute to the social effectivity of a given innovation. By calling attention to the distortions, inflections, disidentifications, confrontations, dissatisfactions, recombinations of a diverse range of masculine codes in cross-cultural migrant narratives, this book attempts to contribute to the wider circulation of their innovative potential.

Billy Cole and I have gone out hunting for birds while my parents visit his folks on their mission station at Adaba, Bale province. It's rainy season and our rubber boots have grown great gumbo hooves, the mud clinging fierce as barnacles. We've clumped along all morning with our heads tipped crazily back, scanning the branches of acacias, eucalyptus, fig trees for the elusive turrocco whose cackling laugh has toyed with us along the muddy creek banks. We are thirteen-year-old taxidermists eager for a chance to try our skills on this most exotic member of the parrot family, with its emerald crest, white cheeks, and scarlet wings. My neck's beginning to ache, my stomach wants lunch, and the pellet gun's getting heavy. 'Over on the other side,' whispers Billy. We slide down the slope to the creek and are about to slop through to the other side, when a great fart erupts from my gumbo hoof. A huge toad, longer than the mud-club of my boot, belly-flops into a backwater pool.

'Ho-lee!' I fumble a pellet into the barrel.

For the next half-hour, Billy and I empty our guns into that puddle. You can see the fat fella right there in the water, clear as a bell. Place the sight bead right between his marble eyes. Pull the trigger. He just sits there laughing at us. Frustration mounts. We try every angle we can think of: aim above him, below him, to this side, to that. We never even make him budge – that is, until we've plugged very single last pellet into the puddle and finally Billy wades in. With one kick of the powerful hind legs, the old boy vanishes into the creek water rushing by.

'I'm tired of hunting,' I rub at the blurry feeling in my eyes.

'Me too,' Billy says. 'Let's go see if it's time for lunch. And I wanna show ya our pet baboon. It's mother got smunched on the road, so we brought it home. I feed it with a baby bottle Mom gave me.'

'We had a pet monkey once,' I say, scratching doubtfully at the scars on my chin. But I don't feel like telling the story.

After fifteen years on the Canadian prairies, I have learned that there is no prescribed way to find a gopher in its home. You simply start with the hole nearest you, and from there gradually trace the rhizome-like maze of tunnels that make the animal's residence. Similarly, there are any number of ways a person could approach the endlessly suggestive topic of migrant masculinities in Canadian literature. From the first European explorer's narratives to the present day, Canadian writings have borne testimony to migrant men's cultural, geographical, political, and emotional disruptions. I simply started with the hole nearest me: contemporary narratives of migration by writers who moved to Canada, like I did, from non-European places. Now, having entered the tunnel-works, I have become aware of how many entrances and passages are connected to this network. Useful correlations, for example, could be traced in representations of masculinity as they appear in writings by Canadian women authors who are also members of the group of recent postcolonial immigrants – writers such as Dionne Brand, Bharati Mukherjee, M. Nourbese Philip, Suniti Namjoshi, Olive Senior, Rachna Mara, Claire Harris, Yeshim Yashar Ternar, and Makeda Silvera. In addition, the recent publications of the Thomas novel I mentioned above and of the Selvadurai novel I discussed in my introduction make possible an examination of the practices and performances of gay masculinities in postcolonial migrant narratives. In both novels, the young protagonist's growing recognition and acceptance of his own homosexuality displaces his gender, race, class, ethnicity, and even nationality in ways that question the prior claims of each of these categories of identification. Furthermore, important work needs to be done on masculinities and migration in earlier phases of Canadian literary history. Significant insights into early European relations with First Nations peoples and with Canadian landscapes, for example, could be gained through analysis of masculinity, cultural displacement, and the male gaze in exploration literature. Or, research in European immigration to Canada during the early decades of the twentieth century could elucidate the ways in which the plurality of ethnic groups, and their many and various masculine practices, fragmented and fractured the fledgling ideology of a singular Canadian 'race' that circulated in public discourse at that time.

There are also many theoretical questions that would reward further consideration. I have tried to show in *Masculine Migrations* how cultural difference and disjuncture between the migrant's place of origin and destination challenge and sometimes even disorient mainstream assumptions about masculinities in Canada, but how do we turn the recognitions of analysis into social change? How can the social mainstream be made to respond creatively to challenges from some of Canadian society's newest members? Can the recognition of masculine constraints be paralleled by discussions of promising innovations in such a way as to attract Canadian men to new ways of social interaction and behaviour? How can critics read literary depictions of limited male innovations in such a way as to maximize the potential for an articulation of masculine ideologies that are liberatory for men and women alike? Though it is not a new question, still we must ask ourselves: what is the relation between scholarly analysis and social justice? My exploratory and tentative answer to this question has been an attempt to trace the desires that motivate and the investments that determine my own scholarly analysis. 'Reason needs some motive for its attentions,' writes Peter Middleton in his discussion of the ways in which the masculine discourse of scholarly objectivity severs men from consciousness of their own feelings (187). Perhaps an attention to the emotions or desires that motivate our analysis of a whole range of masculinities can reveal some of the connections between analysis and social change.

My own motivation to write and research *Masculine Migrations*, for example, rises out of several needs, including the need to find an appropriate way as a straight male academic to contribute to progressive sexual politics, the need to participate from within the constraints of the particular form of WASP ethnicity that shaped me in contemporary discussions of Canadian multiculturalism, and the need to make some kind of connection between my past life in Ethiopia and my present life in Canada. These needs interconnect in the conflicted feelings I have about my distance from my past – in my embarrassment over my ignorance of the culture into which I was born, my filial need to justify the decision not to follow in my father's footsteps and become a missionary, my misplaced but persistent guilt over remaining ex-patriate to Ethiopian culture in experience and sensibility, my discomfort about growing up in a missionary culture which willingly or not participated in the continuance of neo-imperialist relations. And I am aware, even as I try to articulate these emotions, of the ways in which they are the products of retrospective cross-cultural refraction. They are the interpretations and perspectives (both real and imaginary) that my present cultural medium in the Canadian academic milieu imposes upon the cultural milieu of my past.

These troubling feelings seem to concentrate themselves most powerfully around my memories of Negusee. I have no idea how to make sense of his death, or of the terrible timing that raised and dashed my hopes of resolution during that brief visit in the clinic where he died in 1993. It comes down to this: I have lost Negusee's friendship, the opportunity to learn from him, hear his story, hear his version of my family's story. My family and I are not to blame for what happened to him; none the less, we were unknowingly implicated in his suffering. And I wish I could hear him say it is all right. I know, even as I say this, that the wish is naïve, that it proceeds from the 'white man's burden' which assumes 'we' can right the world, that it projects onto Negusee's memory my own guilts and confused loyalties; but I still feel that silence as a profound loss. It is a loss with which I live, and it is a loss that drives me.

Loss, as *Masculine Migrations* shows, returns again and again as a masculine theme. As an indication of crisis, loss represents a moment of instability that can be tipped towards either constraint or innovation. As the emotional manifestation of a consciousness of lack, loss can be a very positive sign of a man learning to live without the illusions of autonomy and completeness that sustain traditional modes of masculinity. But the discomforts of loss have caused many men to retreat to the false security of anachronistic images of male certitude. This is how I understand the immense popularity of the mythopoetic archetypes such as 'king,' 'warrior,' 'magician,' and so on purveyed by Jungian-influenced, pop-psychology solutions to contemporary men's sense of displacement. Such images play on the nostalgic myth that there was a 'time before' – before industrialism, before Vietnam, before alienation – when everything was stable and secure; if we could just return to that time, we could heal our troubled selves. The nostalgia is the product of the kind of retrospective refraction that causes Montgomery to construct his pre-migration birthplace as a zone of masculine certainty.

In many ways, the fragments of autobiographical reflection I have included above partake in the nostalgic wish that longs to discover healing or resolution in the artefacts of the past. But, as Michael Ondaatje's family memoir demonstrates, the past is irrecoverable, even as we endlessly proliferate its myths. There is a sense, then, in which the purpose of such retracings becomes the delineation of a genealogy of loss, of the ways in which one's own social formation is a product and reproductive of the distortions and refractions of social history. In other words, they become ways by which, especially in a multicultural context, we can try to become aware of the subjunctive mode of our perceptions of ourselves and of others. They become means by which we can do the difficult work of realizing the contingencies and limits of our own archives, our own discursive histories. They become ways by which we ourselves can become aware, not just of the distortions, but also of the possible innovations afforded by the displacements and defamiliarizations of cross-cultural refraction.

Notes

Introduction: Reading Masculine Migrations

1 De Lauretis's appropriation of postcoloniality for American feminism is troubling because it bypasses the charges of racism levelled by women of colour against the white feminist mainstream and strips the postcolonial of its historical referent by misapplying it to another marginalized group, American lesbians.

2 Every one of the writers in this study acknowledges publication subventions from the Canada Council, the Ontario Arts Council, and/or Multiculturalism and Citizenship Canada for one or more of his books.

3 The essays in James Olney, ed., *Autobiography: Essays Theoretical and Critical*; Paul John Eakin's *Fictions of Autobiography*; and Shirley Neuman's review essay 'Inventing the Self' provide useful surveys of the theoretical debates over the fictionalizing element in autobiographical writing.

1: 'Playin' 'Mas,' Hustling Respect

An earlier version of this chapter was published in *Masculinities* 3.1 (Spring 1995): 74–88.

1 In *El Dorado and Paradise*, Lloyd Brown organizes his study of Clarke's oeuvre around two myths that impinge upon the lives of Clarke's Barbadian characters: Caribbean as Paradise and Canada as El Dorado.

2 The scenario is identical in both stories, and so is the name – at least the 'J.M.G.M.-C.' of 'A Man' matches the 'Joshua Miller-Corbaine' of 'How He Does It' – but other details do not match exactly. In the first story, Joshua is from Barbados, and, in the second, he's rumoured to be from Trinidad. And, in the first, Trudeau was the Canadian prime minister, while, in the second,

the present date is 1986, during the term of Prime Minister Brian Mulroney. Perhaps the time difference is an indication of how long Joshua manages to maintain his performance. And one could also speculate that the different places of origin indicate the indeterminacy of the gossip that surrounds Joshua, particularly in the second story.

3 For a comparison to Abraham's study of performance folklore, see Graham Dann's sociological research on masculine behaviour in *The Barbadian Male: Sexual Attitudes and Practice*.

4 bell hooks distinguishes between 'patriarchy' and 'phallocentrism' by suggesting that the former refers to the system which assumes a man's masculinity resides in his ability to provide for and protect his family, while the latter refers to the system that believes his masculinity resides in the phallus, a belief that she argues was produced by a capitalism that needed workmen who could be separated easily from family relationships. (*Black Looks* 89ff.)

5 Many commentators on the hustler express an ambivalence about his relation to the mainstream Protestant ethic. Richard Majors and Janet Mancini Billson put the following words in the hustler's mouth: 'I hustle, white man, because it is something you hate, and it therefore defies the principles you are most proud of ... the Protestant work ethic' (88). But they also acknowledge Hudson's suggestion that 'although the hustling ethic appears to be diametrically opposed to the Protestant ethic, it is really an outgrowth of it ... [I]n the final analysis this behavior could be appropriately classified as adaptive behavior' (Hudson 424). Valentine, in her brilliantly titled *Hustling and Other Hard Work*, sees hustling as a black alternative route towards the American success dream (120). West Indian British critics Kobena Mercer and Isaac Julien maintain no such ambivalence: 'The figure of the "hustler" is often romantically depicted as a social outsider, whereas in fact this life-style involves an essential investment in the idea that a "real" man must be an active and independent economic agent, an idea which forms the cornerstone of patriarchal capitalism and its ethic of "success"' (114).

2: How to Make Love to a Discursive Genealogy

1 Any translation involves approximations between linguistic incommensurabilities. The narrator of the French original is regularly referred to as 'Vieux' (the colloquial for 'man,' as in 'Cool, man!'). Although this is not a name and is not used in Homel's translation, I use 'Vieux' as a convenient way to refer to the narrator. The nickname will also serve as a reminder that this chapter deals with a text in translation. Homel's translation uses

various approximations such as the overpowered 'fuck' for *baiser* and the underpowered 'negro' for *nègre*. See Homel's 'How to Make Love with the Reader ... Slyly' and 'Tin-Fluting It' for discussions of his decisions. I am grateful to Richard Banville for discussing with me these nuances in the translation and in the francophone criticism of Laferrière's works. Also, Monique Tschofen's paper 'Race and Gender in Dany Laferrière's *Comment faire l'amour avec un Nègre sans se fatiguer*' challenged my thinking on this chapter.

2 Although this chapter does not focus on issues of translation, a reader equally fluent in English, French, and Laferrière's Haitian Creole could make much of the complexities translation adds to the interpretive instability I trace in the following pages. Translation involves the layering of voices, much like parody, and the necessary slippages between layers destabilizes a secure and single meaning (see Godard, 'Theorizing ...' 49–50). Furthermore, although Laferrière's comment to Homel downplays the issue, translation involves a change in implied audiences, which in turn shifts the parody's field of reference. For example, an English-speaking audience is not likely to register the targets of Laferrière's parody in the same way anglophobic Quebecers might – particularly when English-speaking women are among the primary targets of the parody.

3 Laferrière's cosmopolitan scope is even more clearly emphasized in his later novels, *Eroshima* and *Why Must a Black Writer Write About Sex?*, which are set in the United States.

4 In her article 'The Unspeakable Limits of Rape' and book *Allegories of Empire*, Jenny Sharpe traces the genealogy of the rape metaphor in Indian colonial history to the British need to explain their own violence against the sepoys of the 1857 Mutiny. In other words, the metaphor started out as a justification for rather than a protest against colonial aggression.

5 Both Pamela Banting and Anne Vassal have raised this possibility in their very different readings of Laferrière's novel.

6 Several francophone reviewers admire Laferrière's jazzy, staccato style and read his sexual mischief as light-hearted social satire (Marcotte; Jonassaint and Racette). Marie-Roger Biloa's interview with Laferrière in *Jeune Afrique* engages with the elements of racial protest in his novel to the exclusion of sexual issues. Réginald Martel asserts that the pretext of the novel is sex, but the true subject is racism. Ivanhoe Beaulieu reads the novel as a banal, melodramatic story of black victims and white racists. English reviewers, likewise, found themselves attracted by Laferrière's audacity. 'Laferrière brilliantly and hilariously sifts through the tired, frigid beliefs that Western culture lays on African-derived males,' wrote Joe Wood in *The Village Voice*.

James Adams of *The Edmonton Journal* admired the ribald energy and go-for-broke chutzpah that makes other Canadian writing seem anemic by comparison.

7 This is not to say that the text has no implications for Canadian and Québécois situations. George Elliott Clarke reads the novel in relation to individualist versus nationalist impulses in Québécois literature, and Anne Vassal interprets the novel as a *péquiste* allegory.

3: Resisting Heroics

1 Research on homophobia shows that phallocentric heterosexual norms are structured by a pathological fear of sexual passivity. Just as the straight male sexual imaginary identifies itself as active penetrator and female as passive and penetrated, so also that imaginary fears homosexual penetration as a threat to the male body's boundaries. Leo Bersani and Antony Easthope both trace this fear of passivity/penetration to the heart of phallocentric and homophobic culture. In a revealing study of homosexuality in Chicano culture, sociologist Tomàs Almaguer points out that it is passive receptivity rather than homosexual practice per se that is most stigmatized. He reports that the active penetrator who (occasionally) engages in homosexual practices can retain macho status; the passive/penetrated partner, however, is virulently despised and rejected.

2 See 'The Post Always Rings Twice: The Postmodern and the Postcolonial' for the published version of Hutcheon's talk.

3 Diana Brydon registers concern over Bissoondath's upper-class dismissal of revolution as the confused action of an uneducated peasant class ('Cultural Alternatives').

4 The exceptions here are Kaja Silverman's analysis of male masochism in *Male Subjectivity at the Margins*; Jonathan Rutherford's evaluation of the limitations of the 1970s British movement, 'Men Against Sexism,' in his *Men's Silences*; and mythopoetic, self-help discussions of the 'soft male' such as Robert Bly's in *Iron John*.

5 Further discussions of Indian indenture in the Caribbean include Dabydeen and Samaroo, Brereton and Dookeran, Ramchand, Poynting, and Selvon's 'Three Into One.'

6 I'm thinking here particularly of V.S. Naipaul's *Guerrillas*, in which a similarly impotent man not only remains passive while his female partner is murdered, but even colludes in covering up her murder. The difference between Naipaul's and Bissoondath's approach to the situation lies in the

way Naipaul submits Jane to horrific rape and murder in the interests of playing out the allegory of Britain's degeneration and violent collapse in the colonies, whereas Bissoondath treats his characters more tenderly, presenting Jan and Rohan's deaths as personal rather than allegorical tragedies, tragedies which can, nevertheless, be traced to the ongoing progression of colonially initiated violence.

4: Michael Ondaatje's Family Romance

A version of this chapter was published as 'Masculinity's Severed Self: Gender and Orientalism in *Out of Egypt* and *Running in the Family*,' in *Studies in Canadian Literature* 18.2 (1993): 62–80.

1 The interrelational mode of female self-representation is important for the way it points out the partiality and specificity of the individualistic-masculinist mode. However, it is not necessarily a more or less successful way of constituting a self. Linda Warley points out that, while Mason's and Friedman's 'argument has been a persuasive one for Western feminist critics and has produced insightful readings of women's autobiographies, it is problematized by Suleri's *Meatless Days*. Although the narrator does investigate the nature of her relatedness to those who figure prominently in her life ... the textual construction and positioning of the "I" in relation to an "other" does not necessarily produce a more coherent portrait of the self' (115). Warley's article examines how the multiplicity of relationships and identifications that compose Suleri's 'I' blur and destabilize any totalized or complete delineation of the subject in Suleri's autobiography.

5: The Law of the Father under the Pen of the Son

1 Both authors have previously published collections of short stories: Mistry, *Tales from Firozsha Baag* (1987), and Begamudré, *A Planet of Eccentrics* (1990). Begamudré's novella, *Sacrifices* (1986), reads like an early draft of the first half of *Van de Graaff Days*, consisting as it does of a sketchy version of the story of Hari's youthful years in Mauritius and India before coming to Canada.
2 For Parsi historical and cultural background, see Karaka, Modi, and Boyce.
3 Brief accounts of the Nagarwala scandal appear in Arun Mukherjee's 'Narrating India,' 82–4; Inder Malhotra 146–7; and Dom Moraes 195–6.
4 Meena Acharya qualifies Epstein's liberatory enthusiasm when she writes

that 'male migration to urban areas or foreign countries ... increases women's responsibilities and power within the households but male out-migration may have contradictory effects on women's emancipation from domestic seclusion' (128–9).

5 *Such a Long Journey* was the winner of the Governor General's Award for fiction in 1991 as well as runner-up for the Booker Prize the same year. Mistry's second novel, *A Fine Balance*, won the Giller Prize in 1995. Begamudré's *A Planet of Eccentrics* won the F.G. Bressani literary prize for prose; he has also won the City of Regina Writing Award and the Okanagan Short Story Award.

Afterword: Masculine Innovations and Cross-Cultural Refraction

1 In 'Capitalism and Gay Identity,' John D'Emilio surveys the historical emergence of homosexual communities in the United States to show that the metropolitan capitalist systems of free labour and wage incomes contributed to the liberation of homosexuals from the family-unit economies of earlier times. These socio-economic developments enabled homosexuals to live outside of heterosexual arrangements and develop independent and sustainable subcultures.

2 Heinemann's main concern was that the homosexual content would disqualify the novel from school curricula and, therefore, a major market in the islands, but the publisher did eventually include the book, despite this concern, in the Caribbean series in 1994. I'm relying here on information Nigel Thomas sent me in a couple of letters about the publication arrangements for the novel.

Works Cited

Abrahams, Roger. *The Man-of-Words in the West Indies: Performance and the Emergence of Creole Culture.* Baltimore: Johns Hopkins UP, 1983.

Acharya, Meena. 'Changing Division of Labor and Participation.' *The Changing Division of Labor in South Asia: Women and Men in India's Society, Economy, and Politics.* Ed. James Warner Björkman. New Delhi: Manohar, 1987. 128–40.

Adams, James. Review of *How to Make Love to a Negro. Edmonton Journal.* Quoted on page 126 in *How to Make Love to a Negro.*

Algoo-Baksh, Stella. *Austin C. Clarke: A Biography.* Toronto: ECW; Press of the U of the West Indies, 1994.

Almaguer, Tomás. 'Chicano Men: A Cartography of Homosexual Identity and Behavior.' *The Lesbian and Gay Studies Reader.* Ed. Henry Abelove, Michèle Aina Barale, and David H. Halperin. New York and London: Routledge, 1993. 255–73.

Althusser, Louis. 'Ideology and Ideological State Apparatuses (Notes Towards an Investigation).' *Lenin and Philosophy and Other Essays.* Trans. Ben Brewster. London: New Left, 1971. 123–73.

Ang, Ien. 'On Not Speaking Chinese: Postmodern Ethnicity and the Politics of Diaspora.' *New Formations* 24 (1994): 1–18.

Ashcroft, Bill, Gareth Griffiths, and Helen Tiffin, eds. *The Post-Colonial Studies Reader.* London and New York: Routledge, 1995.

Awkward, Michael. *Negotiating Difference: Race, Gender, and the Politics of Positionality.* Chicago and London: U of Chicago P, 1995.

Bakhtin, Mikhail. 'Author and Hero in Aesthetic Activity.' *Art and Answerability: Early Philosophical Essays by M.M. Bakhtin.* Ed. Michael Holquist and Vadim Liapunov. Trans. Vadim Liapunov. Austin: U of Texas P, 1990. 4–256.

– *The Dialogic Imagination: Four Essays by M.M. Bakhtin.* Ed. Michael Holquist. Trans. Caryl Emerson and Michael Holquist. Austin: U of Texas P, 1981.

– *Problems of Dostoevsky's Poetics*. Ed. and trans. Caryl Emerson. Minneapolis: U of Minnesota P, 1984.

Bailey, Cameron. 'How to Make Love to a Nation *sans disparaître.' Territories of Difference*. Ed. Renee Baert. Banff, AB: Walter Phillips Gallery, 1993. 73–88.

Ball, John C. 'Postcolonialism and the Discourse of Satire.' Paper delivered at the Canadian Association for Commonwealth Literature and Language Studies Conference. Carlton University, Ottawa, 31 May 1993.

Banting, Pamela. 'Reading in Bed: Postcolonial Sex in Dany Laferrière's *How to Make Love to a Negro*.' Paper presented at the Edmonton Conference on Post-Colonialism: Audiences and Constituencies. University of Alberta, Edmonton, 3 October 1993.

Barbour, Douglas. *Michael Ondaatje*. New York: Twayne, 1993.

Barnett, H.G. *Innovation: The Basis of Cultural Change*. New York: McGraw-Hill, 1953.

Beaulieu, Ivanhoe. 'Comment lire un roman sans se fatiguer.' *Le Devoir* 23 November 1985: 27.

Begamudré, Ven. *A Planet of Eccentrics*. Lantzville, BC: Oolichan, 1990.

– 'Process, Politics, and Plurality': Interview with Zool Suleiman. *Rungh* 2.3 (Spring 1994): 14–18.

– *Sacrifices*. Erin, ON: Porcupine's Quill, 1986.

– *Van de Graaff Days*. Lantzville, BC: Oolichan, 1993.

– 'Writing Dislocation: Transculturalism, Gender, Immigrant Families': Interview with Daniel Coleman. *Canadian Literature* 149 (1996): 36–51.

Bennett, Donna. 'English Canada's Postcolonial Complexities.' *Essays on Canadian Writing* 51–2 (1993–4): 164–210.

Bersani, Leo. 'Is the Rectum a Grave?' *AIDS: Cultural Analysis/Cultural Activism*. Ed. Douglas Crimp. Cambridge, MA: MIT Press, 1987. 197–222.

Bhabha, Homi. K. 'Of Mimicry and Man: The Ambivalence of Colonial Discourse.' *October* 28 (Spring 1984): 125–33.

– 'Postcolonial Criticism.' *Redrawing the Boundaries: The Transformation of English and American Literary Studies*. Ed. Stephen Greenblatt and Giles Gunn. New York: Modern Language Assoc., 1992. 437–65.

Birbalsingh, Frank. 'West Indians in Canada: The Toronto Novels of Austin Clarke.' *Journal of Caribbean Studies* 5.1&2 (Fall 1985/Spring 1986): 71–7. Rptd in Birbalsingh's *Passion and Exile: Essays in Caribbean Literature*. London: Hansib, 1988. 137–41.

Bissoondath, Neil. *A Casual Brutality*. Toronto: Macmillan, 1988.

– *The Innocence of Age*. Toronto: Knopf, 1992.

– 'The Possibility of Possibilities': Interview with Bruce Meyer and Brian O'Riordan. *Lives and Works*. Windsor, ON: Black Moss, 1992. 16–25.

- *Selling Illusions: The Cult of Multiculturalism in Canada*. Toronto: Penguin, 1994.

Blodgett, E.D. 'Ethnic Writing in Canadian Literature as Paratext.' *Signature* 3 (Summer 1990): 13–27.

Bly, Robert. *Iron John: A Book about Men*. Reading, MA: Addison-Wesley, 1990.

Boelhower, William. 'Italo-Canadian Poetry and Ethnic Semiosis in the Postmodern Context.' *Canadian Literature* 119 (Winter 1988): 171–8.

Bonnefoy, Yves. *Mythologies*. Restructured trans. of his *Dictionaire des mythologies et des religions des sociétés traditionelles et du monde antique*. Ed. Wendy Doniger. Trans. Gerald Honigsblum et al. Chicago: U of Chicago P, 1991.

Booth, Wayne. *A Rhetoric of Irony*. Chicago: U of Chicago P, 1974.

Boxill, Anthony. 'Austin C. Clarke.' *Dictionary of Literary Biography*. Vol. 53. *Canadian Writers since 1960*. 1st ser. Ed. W.H. New. Detroit: Gale, 1986. 124–9.

Boyce, Mary. *Zoroastrians: Their Religious Beliefs and Practices*. London: Routledge, 1979.

Brenkman, John. *Straight Male Modern: A Cultural Critique of Psychoanalysis*. New York and London: Routledge, 1993.

Brereton, Bridget, and Winston Dookeran, eds. *East Indians in the Caribbean: Colonialism and the Struggle for Identity*. Millwood, NY; London; and Nendeln, Liechtenstein: Kraus International, 1982.

Brown, Lloyd W. 'Austin Clarke in Canadian Reviews.' *Canadian Literature* 38 (Autumn 1968): 101–4.

- *El Dorado and Paradise: Canada and the Caribbean in Austin Clarke's Fiction*. London, ON: Centre for Social and Humanistic Studies, U of Western Ontario; Parkersburg, IA: Caribbean Books, 1989.

Brydon, Diana. 'Cultural Alternatives?' *Canadian Literature* 108 (Spring 1986): 160–3.

Butler, Judith. *Bodies That Matter: On the Discursive Limits of 'Sex.'* New York and London: Routledge, 1993.

- *Gender Trouble: Feminism and the Subversion of Identity*. New York and London: Routledge, 1990.

Chambers, Iain. *Migrancy, Culture, Identity*. London and New York: Routledge, 1994.

Chow, Rey. *Writing Diaspora: Tactics of Intervention in Contemporary Cultural Studies*. Bloomington and Indianapolis: Indiana UP, 1993.

Clarke, Austin. *Nine Men Who Laughed*. Toronto: Penguin, 1986.

Clarke, George Elliott. 'Liberalism and Its Discontents: Reading Black and White in Contemporary Québécoise Texts.' *Journal of Canadian Studies* 31.3 (Fall 1996): 59–77.

Cleaver, Eldridge. *Soul on Ice*. New York: McGraw-Hill, 1968.

Colarusso, Calvin A., and Robert A. Nemiroff. 'The Father in Midlife: Crisis and the Growth of Paternal Identity.' *Father and Child: Developmental and Clinical Perspectives.* Ed. Stanley H. Cath, Alan R. Gurwitt, and John Munder Ross. Boston: Little, Brown, 1982. 315–27.

Coleman, Daniel. 'Hustling Status, Scamming Manhood: Race, Performance, and Masculinity in Austin Clarke's Fiction.' *masculinities* 3.1 (Spring 1995): 74–88.

– 'Masculinity's Severed Self: Gender and Orientalism in *Out of Egypt* and *Running in the Family.' Studies in Canadian Literature* 18.2 (1993): 62–80.

Connell, Robert W. *Gender and Power: Society, the Person and Sexual Politics.* Stanford: Stanford UP, 1987.

Converse, Hyla S. 'Hinduism.' *The Religious World: Communities of Faith,* 3d ed. Ed. Richard C. Bush. New York: Macmillan 1993. 61–125.

Corneau, Guy. *Absent Fathers, Lost Sons: The Search for Masculine Identity.* Trans. Larry Shouldice. Boston and London: Shambhala, 1991.

Dabydeen, Cyril. 'The Bowl to Apollo: The Indo-Caribbean Imagination in Canada.' *Canadian Ethnic Studies* 21.1 (1989): 106–14.

Dabydeen, David, and Brinsley Samaroo, eds. *India in the Caribbean.* London: Hansib, 1987.

Dann, Graham. *The Barbadian Male: Sexual Attitudes and Practice.* London and Basingstoke: Macmillan Caribbean, 1987.

Dash, Michael. 'In Search of the Lost Body: Redefining the Subject in Caribbean Literature.' *After Europe.* Ed. Stephen Slemon and Helen Tiffin. Sydney: Dangaroo, 1989. 17–26.

De Lauretis, Teresa. *Alice Doesn't: Feminism, Semiotics, Cinema.* Bloomington: Indiana UP, 1984.

– 'Eccentric Subjects: Feminist Theory and Historical Consciousness.' *Feminist Studies* 16.1 (Spring 1990): 115–50.

– *Technologies of Gender: Essays on Theory, Film, and Fiction.* Bloomington and Indianapolis: Indiana UP, 1987.

Deleuze, Gilles, and Félix Guattari. *Kafka: Toward a Minor Literature.* Trans. Dana Polan. Minneapolis: U of Minnesota P, 1986.

D'Emilio, John. 'Capitalism and Gay Identity.' *The Lesbian and Gay Studies Reader.* Ed. Henry Abelove, Michèle Aina Barale, and David H. Halperin. New York and London: Routledge, 1993. 467–76.

Demers, Dominique. 'Un Haïtien errant.' *L'Actualité,* 1 September 1991: 44–51.

Dollimore, Jonathan. 'Introduction: Shakespeare, Cultural Materialism, and the New Historicism.' *Political Shakespeare: New Essays in Cultural Materialism.* Ed. Jonathan Dollimore and Alan Sinfield. Manchester: Manchester UP, 1985. 2–17.

Dyson, Michael Eric. *Reflecting Black: African-American Cultural Criticism.* Minneapolis and London: U of Minnesota P, 1993.

Eakin, Paul John. *Fictions of Autobiography: Studies in the Art of Self-Invention.* Princeton: Princeton UP, 1985.

Easthope, Antony. *What a Man's Gotta Do: The Masculine Myth in Popular Culture.* Rev. ed. Boston: Unwin Hyman, 1990.

Eisikovits, Rivka, and Martin Wolins. 'Cross-Cultural Uses of Research on Fathering.' *Fatherhood and Family Policy.* Ed. Michael C. Lamb and Abraham Sagi. Hillsdale, NJ: Erlbaum, 1983. 235–46.

Epstein, Scarlett T. 'Cracks in the Wall: Changing Gender Roles in Rural South Asia.' *The Changing Division of Labor in South Asia: Women and Men in India's Society, Economy, and Politics.* Ed. James Warner Björkman. New Delhi: Manohar, 1987. 17–32.

Esman, Aaron H. 'Fathers and Adolescent Sons.' *Father and Child: Developmental and Clinical Perspectives.* Ed. Stanley H. Cath, Alan R. Gurwitt, and John Munder Ross. Boston: Little, Brown, 1982. 265–73.

Fanon, Frantz. *Black Skin, White Masks.* Trans. Charles Lam Markmann. 1967. London: Pluto P, 1986. Translation of *Peau Noire, Masques Blancs.* Paris: Editions de Seuil, 1952.

Felman, Shoshana. 'Turning the Screw of Interpretation.' *Literature and Psychoanalysis: The Question of Reading: Otherwise.* Ed. Shoshana Felman. Baltimore and London: Johns Hopkins UP, 1977, 1980. 94–207.

Fine, Gary Alan. 'Obscene Joking across Cultures.' *Journal of Communications.* Special Issue 'Laughing Matter' 26 (Summer 1976): 134–40.

Freud, Sigmund. 'Family Romances.' *The Standard Edition of the Complete Psychological Works of Sigmund Freud,* vol. 9. Trans. James Strachey. London: Hogarth, 1959. 235–241.

– *Jokes and Their Relation to the Unconscious.* Trans. James Strachey. New York: Norton, 1960.

Friedman, Susan Stanford. 'Women's Autobiographical Selves: Theory and Practice.' *The Private Self: Theory and Practice of Women's Autobiographical Writings.* Ed. Shari Benstock. Chapel Hill: U of North Carolina P, 1988. 34–62.

Frye, Northrop. 'Conclusion.' *The Literary History of Canada: Canadian Literature in English.* Ed. Carl F. Klinck, Alfred G. Bailey, Claude Bissell, Roy Daniells, Northrop Frye, and Desmond Pacey. 2d ed. Vol. 2. Toronto: U of Toronto P, 1976. 333–61.

Garber, Marjorie. *Vested Interests: Cross-Dressing and Cultural Anxiety.* New York: HarperPerennial, 1993.

Godard, Barbara. 'The Discourse of the Other: Canadian Literature and the

Question of Ethnicity.' *The Massachusetts Review* 31.1–2 (Spring–Summer 1990): 153–84.

– 'Theorizing Feminist Discourse/Translation.' *Tessera* 6 (Spring 1989): 42–53.

Goddard, Horace. 'The Immigrants' Pain: The Socio-Literary Context of Austin Clarke's Trilogy.' *ACLALS Bulletin* 8 (1989): 39–57.

Gooneratne, Yasmine. *Diverse Inheritance: A Personal Perspective on Commonwealth Literature.* Adelaide: Centre for Research in the New Literatures in English, 1980.

Gusdorf, Georges. 'Conditions and Limits of Autobiography.' Trans. James Olney. *Autobiography: Essays Theoretical and Critical.* Ed. James Olney. Princeton: Princeton UP, 1980. 28–48.

Hassan, Ihab. *Out of Egypt: Scenes and Arguments of an Autobiography.* Carbondale and Edwardsville: Southern Illinois UP, 1986.

– 'Parabiography: The Varieties of Critical Experience.' *Georgia Review* 34.3 (Fall 1980): 593–612.

Hassan, Marwan. *The Memory Garden of Miguel Carranza.* Dunvegan, ON: Cormorant, 1991.

Hemphill, Essex. *Ceremonies: Prose and Poetry.* New York: Plume, 1992.

Henry, Keith S. 'An Assessment of Austin Clarke, West Indian-Canadian Novelist.' *College Language Association Journal* 29.1 (September 1985): 9–32.

Hernton, Calvin C. *Sex and Racism in America.* New York: Anchor, 1965, 1988.

Hickey, Bernard. 'Michael Ondaatje's Return: *Running in the Family.' Cross-Cultural Studies: American, Canadian and European Literatures: 1945–1985.* Ed. Mirko Jurak. Ljubljana, Slovenia: Filozofska fakulteta 1988. 37–40.

Hoch, Paul. *White Hero Black Beast: Racism, Sexism and the Mask of Masculinity.* London: Pluto, 1979.

Homel, David. 'How to Make Love with the Reader ... Slyly': Translator's preface to *How to Make Love to a Negro* by Dany Laferrière. Toronto: Coach House, 1987. 7–10.

– 'Tin-Fluting It: On Translating Dany Laferrière.' *Culture in Transit: Translating the Literature of Quebec.* Ed. Sherry Simon. Montreal: Véhicule, 1995. 47–54.

hooks, bell. *Black Looks: Race and Representation.* Toronto: Between the Lines, 1992.

– *Yearning: Race, Gender, and Cultural Politics.* Toronto: Between the Lines, 1990.

Hudson, Julius. 'The Hustling Ethic.' *Rappin' and Stylin' Out.* Ed. T. Kochman. Urbana: U of Illinois P, 1972. 410–24.

Hutcheon, Linda. *The Canadian Postmodern: A Study of Contemporary English-Canadian Fiction.* Toronto: Oxford UP, 1988.

– Introduction. *Other Solitudes: Canadian Multicultural Fictions.* Ed. Linda Hutcheon and Marion Richmond. Toronto: Oxford UP, 1990. 1–16.

- 'Modern Parody and Bakhtin.' *Rethinking Bakhtin: Extensions and Challenges.* Ed. Gary Saul Morson and Caryl Emerson. Evanston, IL: Northwestern UP, 1989. 87–103.
- 'The Post Always Rings Twice: The Postmodern and the Postcolonial.' *Textual Practice* 8 (1994): 205–38.
- *Splitting Images: Contemporary Canadian Ironies.* Toronto: Oxford UP, 1991.

JanMohammed, Abdul. 'Sexuality on/of the Racial Border: Foucault, Wright, and the Articulation of Racialized Sexuality.' *Discourses of Sexuality: From Aristotle to AIDS.* Ed. Domna C. Stanton. Ann Arbor: U of Michigan P, 1992. 94–116.

Jonassaint, Jean, and Anne Racette. 'L'Avenir du roman québécois serait-il métis?' *Lettres québécoises* 41 (Spring 1986): 79–80.

Kakar, Sudhir. 'Fathers and Sons: An Indian Experience.' *Father and Child: Developmental and Clinical Perspectives.* Ed. Stanley H. Cath, Alan R. Gurwitt, and John Munder Ross. Boston: Little, Brown, 1982. 417–23.

Kamboureli, Smaro. 'The Alphabet of the Self: Generic and Other Slippages in Michael Ondaatje's *Running in the Family.*' *Reflections: Autobiography and Canadian Literature.* Ed. K.P. Stich. Ottawa: U of Ottawa P, 1988. 79–91.

Kanaganayakam, Chelva. 'A Trick with a Glass: Michael Ondaatje's South Asian Connection.' *Canadian Literature* 132 (Spring 1992): 33–42.

Karaka, Dosabhai Framji. *The History of the Parsis.* 2 vols. London: Macmillan, 1884.

Kareda, Urjo. 'An Immigrant's Song.' *Saturday Night* no. 98 (December 1983): 44–51.

Kearns, Emily. 'Indian Myth.' *The Feminist Companion to Mythology.* Ed. Carolyn Larrington. London: Pandora, 1992. 189–226.

Keith, A. Berriedale. 'The Mythology of the Puranas.' *The Mythology of All Races.* Vol. 6: *Indian and Iranian.* Ed. Louis Herbert Gray. New York: Cooper Square, 1964. 1–250.

King, Thomas. 'Godzilla vs. Post-Colonial.' *World Literature Written in English* 30.2 (1990): 10–16.

Kroetsch, Robert. 'The Grammar of Silence: Narrative Pattern in Ethnic Writing.' *Canadian Literature* 106 (Fall 1985): 65–74.

Laferrière, Dany. *How to Make Love to a Negro.* Trans. David Homel. Toronto: Coach House, 1987. Translation of *Comment faire l'amour avec un Nègre sans se fatiguer.* Montreal: VLB, 1985.
- Interview with David Homel. *Books in Canada* 17.1 (January-February 1988): 37–8.
- 'Problème: La Sexualité comme miroir de l'identité': Interview with Marie-Roger Biloa. *Jeune Afrique* 1481 (24 May 1989): 66–8.

– *Why Must a Black Writer Write about Sex?* Trans. David Homel. Toronto: Coach House, 1994. Translation of *Cette granade dans la main du jeune Nègre est-elle une arme ou un fruit?* Montreal: VLB, 1993.

– 'Why Must a Negro Writer Always Be Political?' *Voices: Canadian Writers of African Descent.* Ed. Ayanna Black. Toronto: HarperPerennial, 1992. 127–33.

Lamming, George. *In the Castle of My Skin.* New York: Schocken, 1953, 1983.

Lawson, Alan. 'A Cultural Paradigm for the Second World.' *Australian Canadian Studies* 9.1–2 (1991): 67–78.

Lawson, William. *The Western Scar: The Theme of the Been-to in West African Fiction.* Athens: Ohio UP, 1982.

Lim, Shirley Geok-Lin. 'Immigration and Diaspora.' *An Interethnic Companion to Asian American Literature.* Ed. King-Kok Cheung. Cambridge: Cambridge UP, 1997. 289–311.

Loriggio, Francesco. 'The Question of the Corpus: Ethnicity and Canadian Literature.' *Future Indicative: Literary Theory and Canadian Literature.* Ed. John Moss. Ottawa: Ottawa UP, 1987. 53–69.

MacIntyre, Ernest. 'Outside of Time: *Running in the Family.' Spider Blues: Essays on Michael Ondaatje.* Ed. Sam Solecki. Montreal: Véhicule, 1985. 315–19.

Majors, Richard, and Janet Mancini Billson. *Cool Pose: The Dilemmas of Black Manhood in America.* New York: Lexington, 1992.

Malhotra, Inder. *Indira Gandhi: A Personal and Political Biography.* London: Hodder, 1989.

Marcotte, Gilles. 'Comment faire l'amour avec le lecteur sans se fatiguer.' *L'Actualité* February 1986: 126.

Martel, Réginald. 'Dany Laferrière: Montréal en noir sur rose.' *La Presse* 30 November 1985, E3.

Mason, Mary G. 'The Other Voice: Autobiographies of Women Writers.' *Autobiography: Essays Theoretical and Critical.* Ed. James Olney. Princeton: Princeton UP, 1980. 207–35.

Mathur, Ashok. 'The Margin Is the Message: On Mistry, Mukherjee and In Between.' *Critical Mass* 1 (Spring 1990): 19–29.

Mercatante, Anthony S. 'Ganesha.' *Facts on File Encyclopedia of World Mythology and Legend.* New York: Facts on File, 1988.

Mercer, Kobena, and Isaac Julien. 'Race, Sexual Politics and Black Masculinity: A Dossier.' *Male Order: Unwrapping Masculinity.* Ed. Rowena Chapman and Jonathan Rutherford. London: Lawrence and Wishart, 1988. 97–164.

Middleton, Peter. *The Inward Gaze: Masculinity and Subjectivity in Modern Culture.* London and New York: Routledge, 1992.

Mishra, Vijay, and Bob Hodge. 'What Is Post(-)Colonialism?' *Colonial Discourse and Post-Colonial Theory: A Reader.* Ed. Patrick Williams and Laura Chrisman.

New York: Columbia UP, 1994. 276–90. Originally published in *Textual Practice* 5.3 (1991): 399–414.

Mistry, Rohinton. Interview with Geoff Hancock. *Canadian Fiction Magazine* 65 (1989): 143–50.

– Interview with Dagmar Novak. *Other Solitudes: Canadian Multicultural Fictions*. Ed. Linda Hutcheon and Marion Richmond. Toronto: Oxford UP, 1990. 255–62.

– *Such a Long Journey*. Toronto: McClelland and Stewart, 1991.

– *Tales from Firozsha Baag*. Markham: Penguin, 1987.

Modi, Jivanji Jamshedji. *The Religious Ceremonies and Customs of the Parsees*. Bombay: British India Press, 1922.

Moraes, Dom. *Mrs Gandhi*. London: Cape, 1980.

Mordecai, Pamela C. 'The West Indian Male Sensibility in Search of Itself: Some Comments on *Nor Any Country, The Mimic Men* and *The Secret Ladder*.' *WLWE* 21.3 (Autumn 1982): 629–44.

Morson, Gary Saul. 'Parody, History, and Metaparody.' *Rethinking Bakhtin: Extensions and Challenges*. Ed. Gary Saul Morson and Caryl Emerson. Evanston, IL: Northwestern UP, 1989. 63–86.

Mukherjee, Arun. 'The Exclusions of Postcolonial Theory and Mulk Raj Anand's "Untouchable": A Case Study.' *Ariel* 22.3 (July 1991): 27–48.

– 'Narrating India.' *TSAR: Toronto South Asian Review* 10.2 (Winter 1992): 82–91.

– 'The Poetry of Michael Ondaatje and Cyril Dabydeen: Two Responses to Otherness.' *Journal of Commonwealth Literature* 20.1 (1985): 49–67.

Mukherjee, Bharati. 'Writers of the Indian Commonwealth.' *Literary Review*. Special Issue 'Writers of the Indian Commonwealth.' Ed. Bharati Mukherjee and Ranu Vanikar, 29.4 (1986): 400–1.

Mundwiler, Leslie. *Michael Ondaatje: Word, Image, Imagination*. Vancouver: Talon, 1984.

Naipaul, V.S. *Guerillas*. Harmondsworth: Penguin, 1975.

– Introduction. *East Indians in the Caribbean: Colonialism and the Struggle for Identity*. Ed. Bridget Brereton and Winston Dookerman. Millwood, NY; London; and Nendeln, Liechtenstein: Kraus International, 1982. 1–9.

Neuman, Shirley. 'Inventing the Self.' *The Southern Review* 22.2 (Spring 1986): 407–15.

Ngugi wa Thiong'o. *Decolonizing the Mind: The Politics of Language in African Literature*. London: Currey, 1986.

Olney, James, ed. *Autobiography: Essays Theoretical and Critical*. Princeton: Princeton UP, 1980.

Ondaatje, Christopher. *The Man-Eater of Punanai: A Journey of Discovery to the Jungles of Old Ceylon*. Toronto: HarperPerennial, 1992.

Ondaatje, Michael. *Running in the Family*. Toronto: McClelland and Stewart, 1982.
– *There's a Trick with a Knife I'm Learning to Do: Selected Poems, 1963–1978*.
    Toronto: McClelland, 1979.
Osherson, Samuel. *Finding Our Fathers: The Unfinished Business of Manhood*. New
    York: Free P, 1986.
Pankhurst, Richard. *A Social History of Ethiopia: The Northern and Central
    Highlands from Early Medieval Times to the Rise of Emperor Téwodros II*. Trenton,
    NJ: Red Sea, 1990, 1992.
Pearson, Gerald. *Adolescence and the Conflict of Generations*. New York: Norton,
    1958.
Pêcheux, Michel. *Language, Semantics and Ideology*. Trans. Harbans Nagpal.
    London: Macmillan, 1982.
Philip, M. Nourbese. *Frontiers: Selected Essays and Writings on Racism and
    Culture, 1984–1992*. Stratford, ON: Mercury, 1992.
Phillips, D. 'The Effects of Immigration on the Family: The Case of Italians in
    Rural Australia.' *The British Journal of Sociology* 26 (1975): 218–26.
Poynting, Jeremy. '"The African and the Asian Will Not Mix" (A. Froude):
    African-Indian Relations in Caribbean Fiction: A Reply.' *Wasafiri* 5 (Autumn
    1986): 15–22.
Ramchand, Kenneth. 'Indian African Relations in Caribbean Fiction: Reflected in
    Earl Lovelace's *The Dragon Can't Dance*.' *Wasafiri* 1.2 (Spring 1985): 18–23. Rptd
    in longer form in *The Journal of West Indian Studies* 2.2 (October 1988): 1–14.
Ramraj, Victor. 'Still Arriving: The Assimilationist Indo-Caribbean Experience
    of Marginality.' *Reworlding: The Literature of the Indian Diaspora*. Ed.
    Emmanuel S. Nelson. Westport, CT: Greenwood, 1992. 77–85.
– 'Temporizing Laughter: The Later Stories of Austin Clarke.' *Short Fiction in
    the New Literatures in English*. Ed. Jacqueline Bardolph. Nice: Faculté des
    Lettres et Sciences Humaines de Nice, 1989. 127–31.
Richards, David. 'Burning Down the House: Neil Bissoondath's Fiction.'
    Narrative Strategies in Canadian Literature: Feminism and Postcolonialism. Ed.
    Coral A. Howells and Lynette Hunter. Buckingham: Open UP; Philadelphia:
    Milton Keynes, 1991. 49–60.
Robert, Marthe. *Origins of the Novel*. Trans. Sacha Rabinovitch. Bloomington:
    Indiana UP, 1980. Translation of *Roman des origines et origines du roman*. Paris:
    Grasset, 1972.
Rosen, David. *The Changing Fictions of Masculinity*. Urbana and Chicago: U of
    Illinois P, 1993.
Ross, John Munder. 'In Search of Fathering: A Review.' *Father and Child:
    Developmental and Clinical Perspectives*. Ed. Stanley H. Cath, Alan R. Gurwitt,
    and John Munder Ross. Boston: Little, Brown, 1982. 21–32.

Rutherford, Jonathan. *Men's Silences: Predicaments in Masculinity*. London and
New York: Routledge, 1992.

Said, Edward W. *Orientalism*. New York: Vintage, 1979.

Sanders, Leslie. 'Austin Clarke.' *Profiles in Canadian Literature*. 4th ed. Ed.
Jeffrey M. Heath. Toronto and Charlottetown: Dundurn, 1982. 93–100.

Scott, Joan W. 'Experience.' *Feminists Theorize the Political*. Ed. Judith Butler and
Joan W. Scott. New York and London: Routledge, 1992. 22–40.

Sedgwick, Eve Kosofsky. *Between Men: English Literature and Male Homosocial
Desire*. New York: Columbia UP, 1985.

Segal, Lynne. *Slow Motion: Changing Masculinities, Changing Men*. New Bruns-
wick, NJ: Rutgers UP, 1990.

Seidler, Victor. *Rediscovering Masculinity: Reason, Language and Sexuality*.
London and New York: Routledge, 1989.

Selvadurai, Shyam. *Funny Boy*. Toronto: McClelland, 1994.

Selvon, Sam. *Moses Ascending*. Caribbean Writers Series. London: Heinemann,
1975, 1984.

– 'Three Into One Can't Go – East Indian, Trinidadian or West Indian?' *Wasafiri*
5 (Autumn 1986): 8–11.

Sharpe, Jenny. *Allegories of Empire: The Figure of Woman in the Colonial Text*.
Minneapolis and London: U of Minnesota P, 1993.

– 'The Unspeakable Limits of Rape: Colonial Violence and Counter-Insur-
gency.' *Colonial Discourse and Post-Colonial Theory: A Reader*. Ed. Patrick
Williams and Laura Chrisman. New York: Columbia UP, 1994. 221–43.
Originally published in *Genders* 10 (Spring 1991): 25–46.

Siddique, C.M. 'On Migrating to Canada: The First Generation Indian and
Pakistani Families in the Process of Change.' *Sociological Bulletin* 26 (1977):
203–26.

Silverman, Kaja. *Male Subjectivity at the Margins*. New York and London:
Routledge, 1992.

Slemon, Stephen. 'Post-Colonial Writing: A Critique of Pure Reading.' *Mediating Cultures: Problème des kultures transfers*. Ed. Norbert H. Platz. Essen: Die
Blaue Eule, 1991. 51–63.

– 'Unsettling the Empire: Resistance Theory for the Second World.' *World
Literature Written in English* 30.2 (1990): 30–41.

Smith, Sidonie, and Julia Watson. 'De/Colonization and the Politics of Discourse in Women's Autobiographical Practices.' Introduction to *De/Colonizing
the Subject: The Politics of Gender in Women's Autobiography*. Ed. Smith and
Watson. Minneapolis: U of Minnesota P, 1992. xiii–xxxi.

Stallybrass, Peter, and Allon White. *The Politics and Poetics of Transgression*.
Ithaca, NY: Cornell UP, 1986.

Staples, Robert. *Black Masculinity: The Black Male's Role in American Society*. San Francisco: Black Scholar, 1982.

Sugunasiri, Suwanda H.J. '"Sri Lankan" Canadian Poets: The Bourgeoisie that Fled the Revolution.' *Canadian Literature* 132 (Spring 1992): 60–79.

Suleri, Sara. *Meatless Days*. Chicago and London: U of Chicago P, 1989.

– *The Rhetoric of English India*. Chicago and London: U of Chicago P, 1992.

Tapping, Craig. 'South Asia/North America: New Dwellings and the Past.' *Reworlding: The Literature of the Indian Diaspora*. Ed. Emmanuel S. Nelson. Westport, CT: Greenwood, 1992. 35–49.

Thieme, John A. '"Historical Relations": Modes of Discourse in Michael Ondaatje's *Running in the Family*.' *Narrative Strategies in Canadian Literature: Feminism and Postcolonialism*. Ed. Coral A. Howells and Lynette Hunter. Buckingham: Open UP; Philadelphia: Milton Keynes, 1991. 40–8.

Thomas, H. Nigel. *Spirits in the Dark*. Concord, ON: Anansi, 1993.

Tiffin, Helen. 'History and Community Involvement in Indo-Fijian and Indo-Trinidadian Writing.' *Reworlding: The Literature of the Indian Diaspora*. Ed. Emmanuel S. Nelson. Westport, CT: Greenwood, 1992. 87–98.

– 'Post-Colonial Literatures and Counter-Discourse.' *Kunapipi* 9.3 (1987): 17–34.

Tschofen, Monique. 'Race and Gender in Dany Laferrière's *Comment faire l'amour avec un nègre sans se fatiguer*.' Comparative Literature Lecture Series. University of Alberta, Edmonton, February 1993.

Tuli, Jitendra. *The Indian Male: Attitude Towards Sex*. New Delhi: Chetana, 1976.

Valentine, Bettylou. *Hustling and Other Hard Work: Life Styles in the Ghetto*. New York: Free P, 1978.

Vallières, Pierre. *White Niggers of America*. Trans. Joan Pinkham. Toronto: McClelland and Stewart, 1971.

Vassal, Anne. 'Lecture savante ou populaire: Comment faire l'amour avec un nègre sans se fatiguer, de Dany Laferrière.' *Discours-social/Social Discourse* 2.4 (Winter 1989): 185–202.

Viswanathan, Gauri. 'The Beginnings of English Literary Study in British India.' *Oxford Literary Review* 9.1–2 (1987): 2–26.

Wallace, Michele. *Black Macho and the Myth of the Superwoman*. New York: Dial, 1978, 1979.

Warley, Linda. 'Assembling Ingredients: Subjectivity in *Meatless Days*.' *a/b: Auto/Biography Studies* 7.1 (Spring 1992): 107–23.

Williams, Patrick, and Laura Chrisman, eds. *Colonial Discourse and Post-Colonial Theory: A Reader*. New York: Columbia UP, 1994.

Williams, Raymond. *The Country and the City*. New York: Oxford UP, 1973.

Wood, Joe. Review of *How to Make Love to a Negro*. *Village Voice*. 28 February 1989: 47.

Index